The Dyadic Developmental Psychotherapy Casebook

The Dyadic Developmental Psychotherapy Casebook

Edited by Arthur Becker-Weidman, PhD

JASON ARONSON
Lanham • Boulder • New York • Toronto • Plymouth, UK

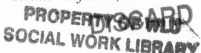
PROPERTY OF
SOCIAL WORK LIBRARY
DISCARD

Published by Jason Aronson
A wholly owned subsidiary of The Rowman & Littlefield Publishing Group, Inc.
4501 Forbes Boulevard, Suite 200, Lanham, Maryland 20706
http://www.rowmanlittlefield.com

Estover Road, Plymouth PL6 7PY, United Kingdom

Copyright © 2011 by Jason Aronson

All rights reserved. No part of this book may be reproduced in any form or by any
electronic or mechanical means, including information storage and retrieval systems,
without written permission from the publisher, except by a reviewer who may quote
passages in a review.

British Library Cataloguing in Publication Information Available

Library of Congress Cataloging-in-Publication Data
The dyadic developmental psychotherapy casebook / Edited by Arthur Becker-Weidman,
PhD.
     p. ; cm.
   Includes bibliographical references and index.
   ISBN 978-0-7657-0815-1 (cloth : alk. paper) — ISBN 978-0-7657-0817-5 (electronic)
1. Family psychotherapy. I. Becker-Weidman, Arthur, 1953– editor.
   [DNLM: 1. Family Therapy—methods. 2. Adolescent. 3. Child. 4. Mental
Disorders—therapy. 5. Object Attachment. 6. Psychotherapy—methods. WM
430.5.F2]
   RC488.5.D945 2011
   616.89'156—dc22   2010052545

∞™ The paper used in this publication meets the minimum requirements of American
National Standard for Information Sciences—Permanence of Paper for Printed Library
Materials, ANSI/NISO Z39.48-1992.

Printed in the United States of America

Contents

Acknowledgments

I would like to acknowledge the many families that have contributed to this volume. The parents and children who have agreed to have their stories told so that others may learn have my deepest appreciation. This book could not have been written without them. My editor at Jason Aronson, Julie Kirsch, has been a support through this, our third book together. I also want to thank the many participants in my master classes in Dyadic Developmental Psycho-therapy and workshops that I have provided in the United States and around the world. Teaching them and their questions and concerns have helped me clarify my thinking about the application of the components of treatment and phases of treatment.

Finally, the support of Susan, my spouse of more than thirty years, and of my three children, Emily, David, and Samantha, has allowed me to engage in this project and complete it. Their understanding and encouragement sus-tained me. We live and grow in families.

Chapter One

Introduction

Arthur Becker-Weidman, PhD

This casebook was written so that those interested in the practice of Dyadic Developmental Psychotherapy, an evidence-based, effective, and empirically validated treatment, can gain a better appreciation for its practice. As the reader will see, each therapist has his or her own unique style, while at the same time, each therapist uses the core components of Dyadic Developmental Psychotherapy differentially, depending on the phase of treatment. I prepared this book so that therapists will see that Dyadic Developmental Psychotherapy is an experientially based treatment in which the therapist's use of self is paramount. That being said, there is a framework for practice within which the therapist practices. This framework is provided by the phases concept and the components of Dyadic Developmental Psychotherapy, which are used differentially, depending on the phase of treatment. These components are used by each therapist in a manner reflecting the therapist's unique personality and use of self.

There are many excellent texts and DVDs that describe the phases and components of Dyadic Developmental Psychotherapy (Becker-Weidman, 2008a; Becker-Weidman, 2008b; Becker-Weidman, 2010a; Becker-Weidman, 2010b; Becker-Weidman and Hughes, 2008; Becker-Weidman and Shell, 2008; Becker-Weidman and Shell, 2010; Hughes 2004; Hughes, 2007; Hughes, in press, Hughes and Becker-Weidman, 2010). This casebook is a collection of session transcripts with analysis that will provide the reader with a detailed understanding of how the components of Dyadic Developmental Psychotherapy are used in a differential manner in the various phases of treatment. Furthermore, this casebook will provide readers with a detailed analysis of what the therapist was experiencing and how this is reflected in the therapist's work.

The seven contributors to this book are each skilled practitioners of Dyadic Developmental Psychotherapy and represent a broad range of styles. There are contributors from across the globe with representatives from Canada, Finland, Singapore, the United Kingdom, and the United States. The broad range of styles and nationalities will serve to demonstrate the broad applicability of Dyadic Developmental Psychotherapy.

Dyadic Developmental Psychotherapy is an effective, empirically validated, and evidence-based approach to treatment. It was developed by Dr. Daniel Hughes, to whom I owe a debt of gratitude for his friendship and his counsel. Each of the cases in this book illustrates the application of Dyadic Developmental Psychotherapy principles and components within the phase that the therapeutic process is occurring. This next section outlines the strong evidence base for this treatment.

Two empirical studies have provided evidence of the effectiveness of Dyadic Developmental Psychotherapy for the treatment of children with complex trauma and reactive attachment disorder (Becker-Weidman, 2006a; Becker-Weidman, 2006b). In each study, the pre-test data was collected from sixty-four families as part of their assessment screening, before the study was formulated. The children in the study had an average of three treatment episodes (three separate episodes of treatment with a licensed mental health provider at other clinics) before beginning treatment in the studies. The children in the treatment group were aged six to fifteen years, averaging 9.4 years. They received an average of twenty-three sessions of Dyadic Developmental Psychotherapy over eleven months. The primary measures were the scales of the Child Behavior Checklist, also called the Ackenbach (Ackenbach, 1991). There were thirty-four children in the treatment group, who received Dyadic Developmental Psychotherapy, and thirty children in the "usual care" group. The two groups did not differ in any significant way on a variety of demographic and social data, and their pre-test scores on the Ackenbach were not clinically or statistically different. The "control" group was actually a "usual care" group because the children in that group received other treatments, such as play therapy, cognitive-behavioral therapy, and family therapy, from other licensed mental health providers at other clinics. One year after treatment ended, in one study, and four years after treatment ended in the second study, an intern, who was blinded to the study, collected Child Behavior Checklist tests on each child.

The first study (Becker-Weidman, 2006a) found that one year after treatment ended the Ackenbach scores for the children in the treatment group were clinically and statistically lower, having moved from the "clinical" range into the "normal" range. The Ackenbach scores for children in the usual care group were not clinically or statistically different one year after treatment ended, remaining in the clinical range.

The second study (Becker-Weidman, 2006b) found that four years after treatment ended the Ackenbach scores for the children in the treatment group remained clinically and statistically lower than their pre-test scores. All the scores for the children in the treatment group were in the normal range. The Ackenbach scores for the children in the usual care group, four years later, remained in the clinical range and actually became statistically significantly worse on four of the seven scales. The scores were statistically significantly worse for the usual care group four years after treatment ended on the anxious/depressed, attention problems, rule-breaking behavior, and aggressive behavior scales. It should also be noted that the children in the usual care group continued to receive various forms of treatment in the intervening four years, but not Dyadic Developmental Psychotherapy, averaging fifty sessions during that time period. Tables 1.1 and 1.2 present the findings from these two studies.

Craven and Lee (2006) determined that Dyadic Developmental Psychotherapy is a supported and acceptable treatment (category 3 in a six-level system). However, their review was only based on results from a partial and preliminary presentation of an ongoing follow-up study, subsequently completed and published in 2006. This study compared the results of Dyadic Developmental Psychotherapy with other forms of treatment, "usual care," one year after treatment ended. A second study extended these results to four years after treatment ended. Based on the Craven and Lee classifications (Saunders et al., 2004), inclusion of those studies would have resulted in Dyadic Developmental Psychotherapy being classified as an evidence-based category 2, "Supported and probably efficacious."

The transcripts you will be reading represent a cross-section of therapists from around the world who are using Dyadic Developmental Psychotherapy components and principles in their own unique way. This illustrates that Dyadic Developmental Psychotherapy can be taught as a treatment method, and that it requires the therapist to integrate the principles and use these components in an emotionally authentic way, staying with experience.

The next chapter will describe the components and phases of Dyadic Developmental Psychotherapy. While all components are used throughout treatment, different components take on greater salience in different phases of treatment. I use the term *phase* and not *stage* because phase connotes an ever-shifting emphasis. Just like the phases of the moon, the whole is always present, but different aspects of the whole are highlighted. These phases occur in a cyclical and repetitive manner. An alliance is necessary to create the secure base. Exploration requires a secure base. As the alliance is developed, maintained, and deepened, then exploration can occur at ever deeper levels. As exploration proceeds, integration occurs, and that leads to healing. Higher

Table 1.1.   Statistical Analysis of Treatment Group

CBCL Syndrome scale scores	Pre-test		Post-test				Second Post-test		
	Mean	SD	Mean	SD	t-value	p-value	Mean	SD	t-test probability
Withdrawn	65	11.8	54	6.0	4.897	<.0001	56	6	.008
Anxious/depressed	62	10.5	58	8.1	2.665	.006	58	5	.006
Social problems	67	9.7	59	5.5	4.376	<.0001	56	5	.001
Thought problems	68	9.5	65	3.9	6.133	<.0001	60	8	.02
Attention problems	72	12.5	57	6.1	5.836	<.0001	57	6	<.0002
Rule-breaking behavior	69	6.9	53	3.8	12.181	<.0001	52	3	<.0001
Aggressive behavior	71	9.1	55	4.5	10.576	<.0001	54	4	<.0001

Table 1.2. Statistical Analysis of Control Group

CBCL Syndrome scale scores	Pre-test		Post-test				Second Post-test		
	Mean	SD	Mean	SD	t-value	p-value	Mean	SD	t-test probability
Withdrawn	65	10.5	63	9.45	1.427	.16	71	49	.18
Anxious/depressed	62	10.6	60	10.3	1.060	.30	70	10	.03*
Social problems	64	11.1	65	11.25	-0.854	.40	65	2	.5
Thought problems	63	8.6	62	8.1	0.984	.33	67	8	.8
Attention problems	68	11.9	55	10.8	0.927	.36	77	9	.02*
Rule-breaking behavior	67	7.4	66	9.6	1.8691	.07	81	4	.02*
Aggressive behavior	70	10.2	68	9.4	0.919	.37	81	4	.02*

* Statistically Significant

levels of integration and healing allow for a stronger secure base and alliance, which enables further exploration, integration, and healing. As you will see in the chapter "Assessment Session—Exploration Begins," exploration and integration can occur even within a session whose purpose is evaluation rather than treatment.

"ASSESSMENT SESSION: EXPLORATION BEGINS"—ARTHUR BECKER-WEIDMAN, PHD

In this chapter I am meeting a young teenager for the first time. She is in secure detention and the purpose of our meeting is for an assessment. Within the first few minutes, by using the principles of Dyadic Developmental Psychotherapy and the components of PACE (playful, accepting, curious, and empathic), particularly acceptance and curiosity, we move quickly into the exploration phase. This transcript clearly illustrates the iterative and rapidly shifting quality of the phases of Dyadic Developmental Psychotherapy.

In this chapter I illustrate the important principle that the phases of Dyadic Developmental Psychotherapy occur in an overlapping manner and that the exploration phase, for example, can occur within the very first session, or, in this instance, even before formal treatment has begun. In this transcript the reader will observe how unconditional acceptance and the use of PACE very quickly creates enough of an alliance and secure base so that exploration begins.

"BEGINNINGS"—SIAN PHILLIPS, PHD, C.PSYCH.

The chapter titled "Beginnings," by Sian Phillips, PhD, C.Psych., a Canadian therapist, is a delightful presentation of early treatment and the imaginative implementation of Dyadic Developmental Psychotherapy components to develop and maintain the alliance with Sarah, a five-year-old foster child with some very difficult and disturbing behaviors. In this first session, Sian illustrates a variety of approaches to keeping Sarah engaged. In particular, Sian's use of follow-lead-follow demonstrates the differential use of this component in an early phase of treatment; an emphasis on the follow element. In addition, PACE (especially the playful element) is illustrated in numerous instances. As in other sessions that are beginning, this chapter clearly demonstrates how building and maintaining the alliance can quickly lead into initial exploration. This cyclical and iterative shifting of phases is one of the hallmarks of Dyadic Developmental Psychotherapy. By focusing so directly on the intersubjective experience, the therapist can move quickly into initial exploration which serves to strengthen the alliance and lead to deeper exploration and integration.

"DEVELOPING THE ALLIANCE (AND MUCH MORE): A SURPRISING FIRST SESSION"—MARY-JO LAND, CPT

"Developing the Alliance," by Mary-Jo Land, CPT, a Canadian therapist, illustrates the first phase of treatment, developing the alliance, and as her title suggests, much more as well. Five-year-old Sally has been in her family for three years. The session is the first one with the child and parents; the therapist had met with the parents on two previous occasions. This case highlights the importance of the parents. Dyadic Developmental Psychotherapy is a family-therapy model of treatment in which parents are the lynch-pin of treatment success. For this reason many therapists begin treatment with several sessions with the parents to assess and help develop the parent's sensitivity, reflective capacity, insightfulness, state of mind with respect to attachment, and commitment. In these sessions, the basic approach of Dyadic Developmental Psychotherapy is demonstrated by the therapist's interactions with the family, following the principle of "whatever you want the parents to be able to do with the child, you have to do with the parents." In this transcript the reader will observe a very skilled therapist developing an alliance with a young child. The reader will observe the use of many of the components of Dyadic Developmental Psychotherapy such as PACE, reflection, affective/reflective dialogue, nonverbal-verbal dialogue and the use of touch, co-creation of meaning, co-regulation of affect, and the use of self. The reader can also observe how in this first session the therapist creates an alliance and, by maintaining the alliance, begins exploration that leads into the integration phase. This case also illustrates the creative use of playfulness to develop and maintain the alliance. While therapy is serious business, the creation of a safe base can be accomplished in a delightful and playful manner, mirroring the early healthy parent-child relationship.

"HELLO, NORMA JEAN!"—CRAIG CLARK, MFT

"Hello, Norma Jean!" by Craig Clark, MFT, a U.S. therapist, clearly illustrates the importance of two phases of treatment: developing the alliance and maintaining the alliance. By carefully maintaining the alliance, Craig is able to move this highly disorganized child into brief forays into exploration and we can see the beginnings of integration. This chapter highlights the necessity of maintaining the alliance and the various components of Dyadic Developmental Psychotherapy that are used to keep the child regulated within the session. In particular, Craig's skillful use of touch, tone of voice, and playfulness all keep Norma Jean engaged and allow her mother to engage the child. The parallel process between Craig and the mother allows for the mother and Norma Jean to explore the meaning of her adoption and begin to co-create a more coherent autobiographical narrative. Craig's sensitivity to the mother's experiences as an adoptee are a powerful example of the healing power of affect and reflection.

"PEKKA: THE SILENT BOY WHO HAS ADHD"—PIRJO TUOVILA, M.SOC.SC., LIC.A.(PSYCH.)

The chapter by Pirjo Tuovila, M.Soc.Sc., Lic.A.(Psych.), a Finnish therapist, illustrates the practice of Dyadic Developmental Psychotherapy in what we may consider an institutional setting; in a group home–type setting with "professional" foster parents, staff, and a number of other children. Pekka is twelve and has been in treatment for about a year and the transcript is from their twenty-fifth session. In this transcript we see how Dyadic Developmental Psychotherapy can be practiced with a "professional" caregiver and child in a residential group care facility. Various components of Dyadic Developmental Psychotherapy are illustrated within, primarily, the maintaining the alliance and exploration phases. In particular, the components of follow-lead-follow, PACE, interactive repair, "talking for," and the affective/reflective dialogue are amply illustrated in this transcript.

"EXPLORATION AND INTEGRATION: WHEN PAST AND PRESENT MEET"—KIM S. GOLDING, B.SC., M.SC., D.CLINPSY.

"Exploration and Integration: When Past and Present Meet," by Kim S. Golding, B.Sc., M.Sc., D.ClinPsy., a UK therapist, is a delightful chapter that illustrates the ebb and flow among maintaining the alliance, exploration, and integration and how this leads into healing. In this session transcript we find a boy who has a very difficult time trusting any adult opening up and engaging in some very powerful exploration and integration. Kim's exposition of her thinking and experience during the session will help readers appreciate the emotional engagement and use of self required by this sort of work. The chapter is a clear illustration of how intersubjectivity is a core element of the therapeutic process that leads to healing and growth.

"ERIKA'S SHAME: MIDDLE TREATMENT"—ARTHUR BECKER-WEIDMAN, PHD

Erika is nearly seventeen years old with a long history of multiple placements, residential treatment, a disrupted adoption, and a substantial history of physical and sexual abuse. In this transcript from the middle of treatment after six months I would like the reader to observe how shame can be managed within the context of the strong alliance I have with Erika while engaged in the exploration and integration phases of Dyadic Developmental Psychotherapy. The transcript also illustrates how even when the therapist may have a misconceived notion of "what is going on," a deep alliance will allow the child and therapist to correct this misunderstanding and co-create meaning.

"THE CASE OF THE MURDERED SWIMMING TOWEL!"—GERALDINE CASSWELL, B.SC. HONS., M.SC. CLINPSY., M. PSYCHOTHERAPY

"The Case of the Murdered Swimming Towel!" by Geraldine Casswell, B.Sc. Hons., M.Sc. ClinPsy, M. Psychotherapy, a UK therapist, illustrates a number of important concepts in the application of Dyadic Developmental Psychotherapy. The family had previously been in treatment with Geraldine and returned to treatment after the placement of a new child in the home. This is a common occurrence. Families often return to treatment at important developmental junctures and when significant changes are occurring. In this transcript the reader will note how quickly Geraldine moves into exploration, integration, and healing. The family already has a good working alliance and so Geraldine does not need to focus as much on developing and maintaining the alliance and secure base. The previous positive experiences in therapy allow the family to readily enter into the work. The child is quite able and willing to work with Geraldine without any shame or significant difficulty.

This transcript also illustrates how whatever we wish the parents to be doing with their child, the therapist has to be able to do with the parents. By modeling and creating experiences with the parents that the therapist wants the parents to create with the child, the therapist enables the parents to act therapeutically.

In this transcript the reader will see many components of Dyadic Developmental Psychotherapy illustrated. These include the following:

- PACE
- Follow-lead-follow
- Insightfulness
- Reflective function
- Commitment
- Therapist use of self
- Talking for and talking about
- Co-creation of meaning
- Co-regulation of emotion
- Affective/reflective dialogue
- Interactive repair
- Verbal/nonverbal dialogue

Several phases of treatment are illustrated in this transcript, including maintaining the alliance, exploration, integration and healing. As this transcript and the others clearly illustrate, the phases are not rigidly defined, but occur in a fluid ebb and flow directed by the therapist and grounded in the immediate experience of the session and the intersubjective sharing of experience.

"INTEGRATION IN DYADIC DEVELOPMENTAL PSYCHOTHERAPY: AMRAN'S STORY" —KAREN SIK, MCLINPSY

Karen Sik, MClinPsy, senior psychologist with the Singapore Ministry of Community Development, Youth, and Sports, has written a chapter that demonstrates how Dyadic Developmental Psychotherapy can be used in different cultures and across cultural lines. The chapter involves a Malay and Muslim child and family working with Karen through a translator. This rich chapter illustrates the powerful integrative effect of Dyadic Developmental Psychotherapy. Amran had an extensive history of physical abuse and severe neglect. He is in foster care and presented with many very difficult and challenging behaviors. By working closely with the foster mother, Karen was able to increase the foster mother's commitment and involve her quite effectively in treatment. The session you will read is the ninth session and involves the birth mother, Amran, and his godmother. The transcript illustrates how the therapist moves quickly through the phases into integration and healing by the creative use of self and the various components of Dyadic Developmental Psychotherapy.

"ENDINGS"—SIAN PHILLIPS, PHD, C.PSYCH.

Sian Phillips's "Endings" chapter illustrates the use of components near the end of treatment when the predominant phases are integration and healing. In this chapter we meet Zach—age twelve when he was adopted and with a significant and extensive history of abuse, neglect, and multiple placements—and his family. In this session a crisis has brought the family back into treatment. As a result of the deep and strong alliance that Sian has with the family and Zach, they quickly move into the exploration and integration phases of treatment and the reader will see healing occurring in this session. The transcript also demonstrates that in these phases of treatment various components of Dyadic Developmental Psychotherapy are used somewhat differently at times than in early phases. For example, the lead element of follow-lead-follow can be emphasized now because Zach and the family have experienced Sian as being helpful and as trying to help them, so that they are more able and willing to follow her lead. In this transcript, the components of insightfulness, affective/reflective dialogue, co-regulation of affect, use of self by the therapist, and co-creation of meaning are particularly well illustrated. The chapter also shows the importance of getting the parents ready for treatment so that they can be reasonably supportive, insightful, sensitive, committed, and reflective. A lovely part of this session occurs when Sian is clearly emotionally affected by the intersubjective experience and shares this with the family.

"THE GIRL WHO BECOMES AGGRESSIVE" —ARTHUR BECKER-WEIDMAN, PHD

"The Girl Who Becomes Aggressive" illustrates my work in the integration and healing phases. It also highlights how important it is to remain regulated to co-regulate another's affect. The transcript begins with Mary hitting her mom and her mom acting to calm Mary. The session then moves on to Mary being much more reflective and insightful regarding her inner experience. This case also demonstrates how Dyadic Developmental Psychotherapy can be used with children who have significant developmental disabilities. Mary has an IQ of 76 and is developmentally many years younger than her chronological age. In this transcript the reader will observe my use of a variety of components of Dyadic Developmental Psychotherapy, including the co-regulation of affect, interactive repair, PACE, the affective/reflective dialogue, co-creation of meaning, and work on creating a coherent autobiographical narrative.

The book ends with a concluding chapter that summarizes material on the differential uses of the components of Dyadic Developmental Psychotherapy in different phases of treatment. Readers will be provided with many examples of the richness of experience of Dyadic Developmental Psychotherapy. Each practitioner has his or her unique style of implementing the components of treatment. All are guided by an appreciation of the differential use of the components of treatment in different phases of treatment and of the importance of use of self and immersion in intersubjectivity to be effective.

Chapter Two

Components and Phases of Dyadic Developmental Psychotherapy

Arthur Becker-Weidman, PhD

In this chapter the reader will be presented with a very brief description of the major principles, components, and phases of treatment of Dyadic Developmental Psychotherapy. A more thorough presentation of this material can be found in *Dyadic Developmental Psychotherapy: Essential Practices and Methods* (Becker-Weidman, 2010b). This chapter sets forth the framework within which the various transcripts the reader will encounter in the book are discussed and analyzed. Each of the following chapters presents a detailed transcript of a session and describes how the principles, components, and phases of treatment are illustrated within that transcript.

Dyadic Developmental Psychotherapy is an amalgam of a variety of evidence-based empirically validated principles (Becker-Weidman and Hughes, 2008). Dyadic Developmental Psychotherapy has been found to be an evidence-based, effective, and empirically validated treatment. Craven and Lee (2006) determined that Dyadic Developmental Psychotherapy is a supported and accepted treatment (category 3 in a six-level system). However, their review of this treatment was based on only a partial preliminary presentation of research. Based on the classification system used by Craven and Lee (Saunders et al., 2004) the current published empirical findings regarding the efficacy of Dyadic Developmental Psychotherapy result in the treatment being classified as an evidence-based category 2, "supported and probably efficacious" treatment. The principles of Dyadic Developmental Psychotherapy include the following principles.

First, the maintenance of a contingent, collaborative, sensitive, reflective, and emotionally empathic relationship between the therapist and client is a primary principle of treatment. The therapist is responsible for creating and maintaining positive concordant intersubjective experiences (Stern, 1985;

Trevarthen, 2001) with the client and for helping caregivers create these experiences with their children. Intersubjectivity is a comprehensive emotional, reflective, and behavioral experience of the other. It is the discovery within the relationship of the other. It emerges from shared emotions (attunement), joint attention and awareness, and shared complimentary intentions. Creating and maintaining an alliance is the vital first phase of treatment. The creation and maintenance of an alliance is necessary for the creation of a secure base, which allows for exploration, which is necessary for integration and, ultimately, healing.

Second, the caregiver's and therapist's state of mind with respect to attachment should be organized and largely resolved before beginning treatment with the child. The therapist's and the caregiver's state of mind with respect to attachment has been found to be very important for treatment success (Tyrell et al., 1999; Dozier et al., 2001).

Third, PACE and PLACE describe the basic stance of the therapist and caregiver. PACE describes the therapist's responsibility for creating a healing pace of treatment by being playful, accepting, curious, and empathic. PACE allows the therapist to generate and regulate the emerging emotional experiences that are explored in treatment. PLACE refers to the caregiver's responsibility for creating a healing place or environment by being playful, loving, accepting, curious, and empathic.

Fourth, interactive repair is another important principle of treatment. Inevitable conflicts, misunderstandings, and mistakes that occur in all relationships are directly addressed and repaired. This process facilitates emotional regulation. It is the responsibility of the adult to initiate and model this process.

Fifth, "resistance" is treated with PACE. Resistance is viewed as reflecting fear, shame, and the child's past negative experiences with caregivers. "Resistance" is not a pejorative and should not be interpreted as negative. Resistance is viewed as an expression of fear and may reflect that the therapist has gone too far, or too fast, for the client. Resistance may be viewed as an adaptive strategy for managing upsetting and disturbing affect. The response to resistance will then be interactive repair or more follow and less lead of the follow-lead-follow component, which is described below.

Sixth, the therapist continually assesses (Becker-Weidman, 2010a) the caregiver's readiness to be a sensitive, responsive, insightful, reflective, and committed attachment figure for the child. If the therapist has concerns about the child's emotional and psychological safety, the therapist will continue to work with the caregiver without the child to help the caregiver resolve whatever barriers exist for the caregiver's creating this secure base and sense of safety for the child. Parents and other caregivers are central to Dyadic Developmental Psychotherapy. Caregivers are the keystone for how treatment proceeds and its outcome. In many respects the best predictor of outcome is not "how disturbed" is the child, but rather the caregivers (Becker-Weidman, 2010a; Becker-Weidman, 2010b):

• State of mind with respect to attachment
• Reflective function and reflective abilities
• Commitment
• Insightfulness
• Sensitivity

Other elements of Dyadic Developmental Psychotherapy that have been found to have a strong evidence base in the psychotherapy outcome research literature include the following elements.

First, the principles and practice of Dyadic Developmental Psychotherapy are consistent with the basic principles of effective treatment for complex trauma (Cook et al., 2003, 2005). Cook and colleagues (2003, 2005) identify six core components of complex trauma treatment that are also elements of Dyadic Developmental Psychotherapy. The six core components that they identified are safety, self-regulation, self-reflective information processing, traumatic experience integration, relational engagement, and positive affect enhancement. These core components also make up central processes in the practice of Dyadic Developmental Psychotherapy.

Second, affect arousal has been found to be important for positive outcomes in psychotherapy (Beutler et al., 2004). Affect arousal (achieved by the components of follow-lead-follow, affective/reflective dialogue, and PACE, among others, and managed within the context of the co-regulation of affect and interactive repair) is a significant theme in Dyadic Developmental Psychotherapy.

Third, explaining how the past may be continuing to affect present behavior, emotions, and meanings has been found to be an effective mode of treatment in 63 percent of studies reported (Orlinsky et al., 2004).

Fourth, forming and maintaining a therapeutic alliance is a core principle of Dyadic Developmental Psychotherapy. The therapeutic alliance has been shown to be vital to successful treatment outcome (Norcross, 2001; Lambert and Ogles, 2004). The use of PACE is expected to help facilitate this. There is a significant positive association between outcome and the therapeutic bond (66 percent of the studies with an effect size of at least 0.25 in one quarter of the studies [Lambert and Ogles, 2004, p. 308]). In looking at the therapist's contribution to the therapeutic alliance, a significant positive association with outcome was also found: "The therapist's contribution was positively associated with outcome 67% of the time and never negatively implicated" (Lambert and Ogles, p. 321). "The strongest evidence linking process to outcome concerns the therapeutic bond or alliance" (Lambert and Ogles, p. 360).

Fifth, acceptance is a significant component of Dyadic Developmental Psychotherapy. Affirmation (acceptance, nonpossessive warmth, or unconditional positive regard) was found to be a significant factor in positive therapeutic outcome. Acceptance involves an entirely nonjudgmental stance directed toward the thoughts, feelings, intentions, and so on that characterize the child's "inner life." Described differently, the creation of concordant intersubjective experiences or the level of empathic understanding and personal rapport has a substantial history of having been shown to be important factors in positive outcome. There is now "general acceptance of empathy as a factor in outcome, which has been clearly confirmed again in a current meta-analysis" (Orlinsky et al., 2004, p. 350).

Sixth, Dyadic Developmental Psychotherapy has both cognitive and experiential dimensions. For both these dimensions there is a large body of empirical support. "The existing research is now more than sufficient to warrant a possible valuation of experiential therapy in four important areas: depression, anxiety disorders, trauma, and marital problems" (Elliott et al., 2004, p. 527).

Seventh, relationship factors loom large as important for successful treatment outcome (Lambert and Ogles, 2004). The development of a secure base from which exploration can occur requires the development and maintenance of an alliance. It is these common factors across therapies that account for a significant portion of treatment outcome: "A therapeutic relationship that is characterized by trust, warmth, understanding, acceptance, kindness, and human wisdom" (Lambert and Ogles, 2004, p. 180) is described as a broad set of factors that are common across therapies and associated with patient improvement. These are the very same factors that form the core attitude of Dyadic Developmental Psychotherapy: PACE.

COMPONENTS OF TREATMENT

This section briefly describes fourteen components of Dyadic Developmental Psychotherapy. These components are not discrete entities. There is substantial overlap and interrelationships among several of these components. For example, the affective/reflective dialogue includes insightfulness and reflective capacity. Intersubjectivity includes elements of empathy from PACE. The co-creation of new meanings requires reflection and insightfulness. The components are described as discrete components so that the reader will develop a deeper understanding of how these components are used in treatment. A much more detailed description of each component can be found in "Main Elements of Dyadic Developmental Psychotherapy Explained" (Becker-Weidman, 2010b). The reader will find all of these components fully illustrated in the transcripts to follow.

Components of Dyadic Developmental Psychotherapy

- Therapist use of self
- Process-focused: it's about connections not compliance
- PACE
- Intersubjectivity
- Reflective capacity
- Affective/reflective dialogue
- Commitment
- Insightfulness
- Coherent narrative
- Co-creation of meanings
- Co-regulation of emotions
- Follow-lead-follow
- Interactive repair
- Nonverbal-verbal dialogue

Therapist Use of Self

Dyadic Developmental Psychotherapy is primarily an experientially based treatment that uses the immediate intersubjective experience to effect change in family relationships and family members. As such, it requires that the therapist be emotionally present, engaged, involved, and active in the therapy. This use of self involves the creation and use of concordant intersubjective experiences. The therapist's use of self is always focused on helping the family and client achieve deeper self-knowledge, more flexible and functional modes of relating, and more authentic affective experiences that reflect the nature and quality of the current relationships. How the therapist uses the various components of Dyadic Developmental Psychotherapy is a function of the therapist's unique personality. For example, the use of PACE is strongly colored by the therapist's personality, history, and experiences.

Process-Focused

The therapist practicing Dyadic Developmental Psychotherapy focuses on process and relationships. The therapist also helps caregivers focus on connections and relationships. A useful catchphrase is "it's about connections, not compliance." What this phrase captures is that the way to secure compliance is through connections and relationships. We focus on connections rather than compliance. Focusing on compliance alone can lead to the use of punitive responses, excessive force, and shaming/blaming interactions. The way to secure genuine acceptance and adherence is by developing a relationship with emotional depth and valance. This leads to the child wanting to please the parent and valuing parental praise and approval. The therapist practicing Dyadic Developmental Psychotherapy continually moves away from a focus on surface symptoms or behaviors to a deeper exploration of what is driving or motivating the behavior or symptoms, the meaning and emotions underlying the behaviors.

PACE

It is the therapist's responsibility to maintain a healing PACE of treatment. PACE is the basic stance of the therapist and at the core of Dyadic Developmental Psychotherapy, as figure 2.1 illustrates.

The figure shows that the therapist begins with some behavior that occurred immediately in the room or in the past and, using acceptance and curiosity, uncovers the meaning for the client. Empathy is then used to normalize the client's experience and reduce shame. Finally, the clients communicate their new meanings and understandings and a new meaning for them emerges;

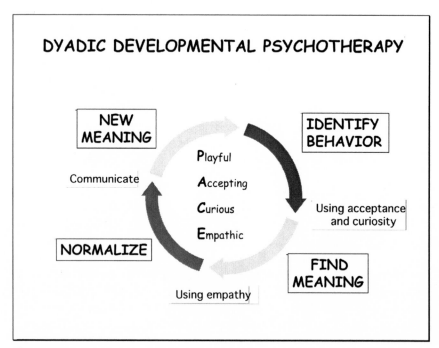

Figure 2.1.

they co-create a new and healthier meaning. The new meaning integrates past experience and enables the clients to develop a healthier and more positive understanding of the other's intentions, motivations, and underlying experiences.

Intersubjectivity

Intersubjectivity is shared emotion, intention, and attention. When all three elements are in accord, the intersubjective experience is rich and healing. Concordant intersubjective experiences (in which all three elements are in sync) form the central process through which therapeutic interventions are therapeutic. By considering an interaction that is not going well, the therapist can usually identify which of the three elements of intersubjectivity are not in accord. The therapist can then use that knowledge to engage in interactive repair to remedy the discord.

Reflective Capacity

The reflective function is described as the capacity to have a mental representation of self, other, and the relationship (Fonagy et al., 2002). This mental representation allows the person to anticipate the other's potential actions, feelings, thoughts, and perceptions. This is the basis for empathy. The reflective function is closely connected with mirror neurons and these may be the basis, in part, for our capacity for empathy and for our capacity to anticipate the actions of others (Psychology Wiki, 2010a). An important element of treatment is to develop and enhance the caregiver's reflective capacity so that the parent is better able to respond in an attuned manner. In addition, the therapist focuses on developing this capacity in the child. The reflective function is necessary for impulse control and for empathy.

Affective/Reflective Dialogue

The affective/reflective dialogue is a conversation that contains affective, cognitive, and reflective elements. It can be viewed as a relaxed and meandering dialogue that has a storytelling quality to it. The participants are co-creating meanings by collaborating in the evolving narrative. This is an interactive dialogue, not a lecture or psycho-educational presentation. The intention is to explore all aspects of the client's life and experience. The affective/reflective dialogue is necessary for the creation of the secure base that allows for exploration in treatment and that ultimately leads to integration and healing. The affective/reflective dialogue is one of the ways in which the therapist demonstrates that the therapist finds the client interesting, valuable, and fun to be with.

Commitment

Commitment is necessary for treatment and parenting to be effective. The therapist's commitment to the primary caregivers is essential since they are the keystone of treatment success. The therapist uses PACE and the affective/ reflective dialogue to create a secure base for the caregivers to explore themselves and their relationships. By creating this deeply felt connection with the caregiver the therapist is modeling what the therapist would like to see the caregiver be able to do with the child.

Caregiver commitment is the best predictor of placement stability (Dozier and Lindheim, 2006). Therefore an important dimension of treatment is monitoring the caregiver's level of commitment and exploring this with the caregiver. When necessary the therapist will work with the caregiver to determine if the level of commitment can be strengthened and enhanced and if it is sufficient for treatment to begin or continue. Experiences in treatment cannot deepen unless there is a sense of safety and security. Caregivers create this for the child primarily through their commitment to the child, which is communicated largely in a nonverbal manner. Commitment is an emotional connection. It is an experience of deep emotional connection to the child and that one's life as a parent would be substantially diminished if the child were not part of the parent's life. Before treatment begins and at the beginning of each session, the therapist must assess the caregiver's readiness to be an attachment figure for the child. When there are obstacles preventing the caregiver from being in this role, then the therapist must explore this with the caregiver.

Insightfulness

Insightfulness and the reflective function are closely related. Insightfulness requires reflection. To be insightful means to look at one's emotions and motivations, to look within, "in" "sight." Insight allows the therapist to understand what affect is being activated by the therapist's own past and to separate that from affect being activated in the immediate experience.

The therapist's ability to develop insightfulness among family members is one of the therapist's most important functions. The therapist's use of the affective/reflective dialogue, PACE, co-creation of meanings, nonverbal dialogue, and follow-lead-follow is how insightfulness is developed.

Coherent Narrative and Co-Regulation of Meanings

Trauma can lead to a disconnected, disjointed, and dissociated sense of self. One of the goals of therapy is to achieve integration and a coherent autobiographical narrative. A person with a secure state of mind with respect to attachment has a sense of self that is coherent, cohesive, integrated, and includes both positive and negative experiences. A person with a secure pattern of attachment is able to create a coherent meaning out of these varied experiences. Children who have experienced complex trauma frequently have disjointed, split-off, and dissociated autobiographical narratives. The episodic and emotional elements of the trauma are split off and disconnected from each other. While the emotional sequelae of the trauma are clearly evident in the child's behavior, the child is not aware of this. Revisiting the trauma in detail and in a titrated manner so that the emotions are experienced in the safe and secure setting of the therapy session and in the home allows for the integration of emotional and episodic memories and the conscious awareness of how these events and feelings are operating in the present.

The Dyadic Developmental Psychotherapist helps clients develop new meanings that lead to the creation of a coherent and integrated autobiographical narrative. The use of storytelling, psychodramas and role plays, and other methods serve this purpose. Many of the other components of Dyadic Developmental Psychotherapy aid in this process. PACE, the reflective function, affective/reflective dialogues, and insightfulness, for example, all aid in the integration of experiences into a coherent autobiographical narrative.

Co-Regulation of Emotions

Affect regulation develops within a responsive and sensitive relationship; it requires the safety of a secure base. The parent of an infant regulates the infant's physical and emotional states. Over time, the parent helps the child regulate emotions, and eventually the child's affect regulation capacity expands and becomes independent of the parent. Early trauma impairs this normal developmental process and the person's capacity to regulate emotions will be weakened. The therapist uses the model of the "good enough" parent. The sequence is, first the parent regulates the child, then the child is able to achieve emotional regulation with the parent's help, and then the child can self-regulate. The therapist co-regulates the person's level of arousal and emotions. Co-creating meanings can be one way that emotions are regulated. Touch, the affective/reflective dialogue, verbal-nonverbal dialogues, and PACE are all means that the therapist can use to co-regulate the client's emotional states.

Follow-Lead-Follow

This component of Dyadic Developmental Psychotherapy refers to the therapist's direction of the dialogue within treatment; sometimes following the client, then leading, and then following. The function of this component is to engage the client and to increase safety, security, and personal control. Initially the therapist follows the client's lead, accepting the client, what the client is saying, and the client's view. This facilitates the development and maintenance of the alliance. The therapist is creating a concordant intersubjective experience by sharing affect, attention, and having conjoint and complimentary intentions. At this point the therapist can deepen the experience or begin to lead the client in a slightly different direction, such as noting how a current experience is similar to one that occurred in the past. Once on this new path, the therapist then begins to follow the client and the process begins anew. This component of Dyadic Developmental Psychotherapy is used throughout treatment.

Interactive Repair

Tronick (1989, 2005) describes this process as one in which the parent or therapist responds to the inevitable breaks that occur in any interaction or relationship. What the therapist is to do is repair the relationship breach. It is the therapist's responsibility to manage the pacing of treatment. It is the therapist's responsibility to repair the break. Interactive repair involves the therapist's emotional reconnection with the client and achievement of concordant intersubjectivity. When the therapist is able to achieve interactive repair this helps the client recover from negative affective states, reduce shame, and have the positive experience that relationships can be repaired. Relationship repair is often a new experience for those with chronic histories of early maltreatment within a caregiving relationship. The healing dimension of interactive repair is that it reduces shame. Interactive repair can help a child progress developmentally from a shame-based identity to the experience of healthy and appropriate guilt. For many caregivers, this can also be a new experience. Modeling for the caregiver how to do this and the powerful positive effects of interactive repair can help enable a caregiver to be better able to do this with the child. Interactive repair is achieved using several other components of Dyadic Developmental Psychotherapy, PACE being the most prominent.

Nonverbal-Verbal Dialogue

A significant component of communication is nonverbal. The therapist must attend to the nonverbal and the verbal dimensions of communication, paying particular attention to disparities and incongruities between the verbal and nonverbal dimensions. Since many traumas have occurred at a pre-verbal level and may be dissociated from explicit memory, the therapist must make efforts to create experiences that allow for the exploration of these dissociated nonverbal memories and experiences. Nonverbal communication, involving eye contact, tone of voice, cadence, volume, touch, gestures, and movement, helps create affective attunement, which is therapeutic. The Dyadic Developmental Psychotherapist pays particular attention to the nonverbal cues occurring within the family during treatment and will often comment on these nonverbal statements to deepen the experience and to further develop insightfulness, new meanings, and reflective functions.

Phases of Treatment

This section briefly summarizes the phases of Dyadic Developmental Psychotherapy. These phases occur in a recursive and repetitive manner, much like the phases of the moon. The phases overlap and occur in a cyclical manner and so should not be considered discrete or rigidly defined. The value of considering these phases is that the various components of Dyadic Developmental Psychotherapy are used differently in the different phases of treatment (Becker-Weidman, 2010b). Like a continual spiral, development and treatment continue ever deeper with the phases represented by lines running up and down the spiral. As treatment proceeds, the therapist must continually work to maintain the alliance, explore to achieve integration and healing, and then ensure that the alliance remains strong enough to proceed.

A colleague described it this way: Dyadic Developmental Psychotherapy is "a coherent whole, with all parts equally important and always there. Sometimes though one part is seen (or focused on, or is visible to others) and is lit up, or in the foreground. That stays around a while before another part becomes visible. What you see depends on the relationship" (Hudson, 2010). The phases occur in a repetitive manner, much like a spiral. Exploration and integration can lead to a more secure alliance, which will allow for deeper exploration and further integration and healing. Healing often allows for a stronger alliance to develop, which will facilitate further integration.

At the center of this iterative repetitive process is healing, as shown in figure 2.2.

The transcripts that follow illustrate how the various components of Dyadic Developmental Psychotherapy are used differently in the phases of treatment. While the general principles remain constant, each phase requires a different mix of elements with a shifting emphasis on the various components. It is the application of the various components of Dyadic Developmental

Figure 2.2.

Psychotherapy in a differential manner that is the art of this treatment. It is most useful to think of the phases as occurring in a cyclical iterative manner. One phase may last several sessions, and many phases may be present in one session. Healing may begin in the very first session, for example. The phases described here are defined in terms of attachment theory: developing and maintaining the alliance (secure base), exploration, integration, and healing. An alliance is necessary to create and maintain a secure base. A secure base is necessary to begin exploration. Exploration leads to integration. Integration is the basis for healing. The transcript of Jessica, from an assessment session, illustrates how exploration and even beginning integration can occur within the first meeting.

- Developing the alliance
- Maintaining the alliance (developing a secure base)
- Exploration
- Integration
- Healing

Developing the Alliance

Developing the alliance is a most critical phase of treatment. Without an alliance, there can be no exploration, integration, and healing. Children and parents or caregivers with unresolved traumas and hurts will have a more difficult time forming an alliance with the therapist. In these instances, the therapist will have to pay particular attention to developing the alliance and relationship.

Creating a secure base in treatment becomes the therapist's primary task. There are four primary tasks in this phase:

- Forming a therapeutic alliance
- Developing a "treatment contract": Why are we here? Why are we meeting? What are we doing here?
- Forming initial theories of behavior: the meanings to be explored
- Creating a secure base

While all components of Dyadic Developmental Psychotherapy may be used, a few stand out as more salient in this phase: PACE, the "follow" dimension of follow-lead-follow, intersubjectivity, and the co-regulation of affect. Creating a secure base is a necessary and essential precursor to beginning the exploration phase. The therapist's use of self is also an important component in creating a secure base in treatment. The therapist must be emotionally engaged in the intersubjective experiences within treatment and this requires good self-awareness, reflective abilities, and insightfulness on the part of the therapist. In working with parents and caregivers, it is also important to help them appreciate the importance of the construct, "it's about connections, not compliance" (Becker-Weidman, 2010b; Hughes and Becker-Weidman, 2010).

Maintaining the Alliance

Maintaining the alliance is a phase that the therapist must attend to throughout treatment. At times it is in the forefront of the work, and at other times it recedes into the background. Focusing on this phase becomes particularly important when there has been some breach in the alliance or relationship and interactive repair becomes a prominent component used by the therapist. The therapist's use of self also is an important component in this phase. When the therapist has made a mistake it is vital to treatment that the therapist not allow the therapist's shame to preclude the therapist's acknowledging the mistake the therapist has made and the breach that results. One of the therapist's primary responsibilities is to maintain a healing and therapeutic pace of treatment. As described elsewhere (Becker-Weidman, 2010b), it is not mistakes that cause problems in treatment. It is the lack of acknowledgement and repair of those mistakes that creates problems in treatment.

Once the alliance has been formed, the therapist acts to deepen, strengthen, and maintain the alliance. As with the other phases, this phase overlaps the other phases and the other phases cycle back to this phase. For example, exploration that leads to integration and healing helps maintain and strengthen the alliance.

The primary tasks of maintaining the alliance are as follows:

• Deepening and strengthening the therapeutic alliance
• Managing emotional proximity
• Exploring initial theories of behavior: the meanings to be explored
• Repairing relationship breaches

Five components of Dyadic Developmental Psychotherapy are particularly salient during this phase of treatment: PACE, intersubjectivity, follow-lead-follow, interactive repair, and the co-regulation of affect. In this second phase of treatment the therapist will want to pay particular attention to using follow-lead-follow as the beginning approach into the exploration phase. How the client responds to the "lead" step of follow-lead-follow is a measure of how quickly and deeply the therapist can move into exploration and a measure of the strength and depth of the alliance.

This phase of treatment takes on less importance as treatment progresses. The reason for this is that later in treatment the client has experienced the therapist's intentions to be helpful and exploration, integration, and healing have led to a more flexible and present-reality-grounded internal working model. Later in treatment the therapist does not have to focus as much on maintaining the alliance because the alliance has greater emotional depth and strength. The client will have experienced the therapist's intentions to be helpful and the client will have experienced the positive results of difficult explorations.

Exploration

Exploration requires a secure base (an alliance) and, as demonstrated in a few of the transcripts in this book, can occur within the very first meeting. Exploration requires some sense of safety (physical, emotional, and psychological) and security.

There are four primary tasks during the exploration phase. The goal is to explore history, memories, events, and experiences that continue to shape the client's relationships and that continue to affect behavior and functioning. Primary tasks in this phase are as follows:

• Exploring how the past is alive in the present
• Exploration of internal working models

- Exploring the meanings of events and behavior
- Developing the reflective function

The primary components of Dyadic Developmental Psychotherapy that are especially important in this phase are PACE, creating and maintaining intersubjectivity, developing the reflective function, insightfulness, follow-lead-follow, interactive repair, commitment, co-creation of meaning, and the co-regulation of affect. Of these, the co-creation of meaning and the co-regulation of affect are particularly important. PACE leads to concordant intersubjectivity. Concordant intersubjectivity, interactive repair, and the reflective function help co-regulate emotions. The affective/reflective dialogue and insightfulness, along with PACE, facilitate the co-creation of meaning.

Integration

Integration occurs in a cyclic manner. Exploration leads to integration, which allows for deeper exploration and further integration and healing. Integration includes neurological integration, emotional integration, and psychological integration. Its hallmark is the capacity to see shades of gray instead of absolutes. Integration is seen when a client is able to hold disparate feelings at the same time. Integration occurs repeatedly in treatment and over time. In many regards it is a developmental process in which experiences, memories, events, relationships, emotions, and one's autobiographical narrative are reworked in a flexible manner. Many mental health difficulties can be viewed as representing a lack of integration. For example, the flashbacks associated with post-traumatic stress disorder and complex trauma are a function of the lack of integration of episodic and implicit memories. Many of the cognitive difficulties associated with complex trauma are a function of problematic neurological integration.

Integration requires that past events, situations, and experiences be reviewed and revisited (exploration) so that the internal working models can be made explicit, subject to exploration, and new meanings thereby created. It is the new meanings that represent a new integration of emotions and cognitions. It is most useful to think of integration as a process or spiral. In this view, developmental tasks run vertically, and integration is an ascending spiral that returns to each element in a deeper and deeper fashion. In this way the person achieves greater levels of integration over time (Becker-Weidman, 2010b).

The primary task of integration is the development of a coherent autobiographical narrative. Creating a coherent autobiographical narrative involves two elements: the integration of trauma and reduction of splitting off implicit in episodic memories, and an enhanced reflective function. Within this phase the Dyadic Developmental Psychotherapy components that are most relevant are PACE, the affective/reflective dialogue, and co-creation of meaning. During this phase, which may constitute the bulk of treatment toward the middle and end of treatment, a review of the client's life story and a reflection on the client's current state and how the past may still be active in the present make up a large proportion of treatment. Exploration and integration occur in tandem and reinforce each other. Exploration leads to integration and integration allows for deeper exploration.

Healing

Healing occurs throughout treatment. Healing is not so much a separate phase as it is, in part, an outgrowth of integration. Integration is a healing process. However, it is important to note that the development and maintenance of an alliance can be healing in and of itself. The development of an emotionally meaningful relationship and alliance is healing and can remedy some of the effects of early, chronic maltreatment that has occurred within a caregiving relationship. The outcomes of healing include the development of a more complex, nuanced, and integrated autobiographical narrative, and a better developed reflective function. A few of the components of Dyadic Developmental Psychotherapy that may be more salient during healing include the following: co-creation of new meanings, insightfulness and reflection, affective/reflective dialogue, and PACE.

As the reader will see in the transcripts that are from the close of treatment, there is increased time spent reflecting on the treatment experience, a celebration of how life is now different, and reflecting on what good has occurred. This reflection on positive changes and a celebration of the long and difficult journey is an important element of beginning to end treatment and the integration of the experience into the individual and family narratives. This process helps frame the treatment experience and find its place in the family narrative (Becker-Weidman, 2010b).

SUMMARY

This chapter has provided the reader with a brief summary of the major components of Dyadic Developmental Psychotherapy and the phases of treatment. The chapters and transcripts that follow illustrate these components and phases. While each transcript presents several phases occurring in a cyclical and iterative manner, each transcript can be viewed as presenting work that primarily illustrates one or more phase.

Beginning Alliance

- "Developing the Alliance (And Much More): A Surprising First Session," by Mary-Jo Land
- "Beginnings," by Sian Phillips
- "Assessment Session—Exploration Begins," by Arthur Becker-Weidman

Maintaining the Alliance

- "Developing the Alliance (And Much More): A Surprising First Session," by Mary-Jo Land
- "Beginnings," by Sian Phillips
- "Pekka: The Silent Boy Who Has ADHD," by Pirjo Tuovila
- "Hello, Norma Jean!" by Craig Clark

Exploration

- "The Case of the Murdered Swimming Towel!" by Geraldine Casswell
- "Pekka: The Silent Boy Who Has ADHD," by Pirjo Tuovila
- "Erika's Shame," by Arthur Becker-Weidman
- "Assessment Session—Exploration Begins," by Arthur Becker-Weidman
- "Exploration and Integration: When the Present and Past Meet," by Kim S. Golding

Integration

- "The Case of the Murdered Swimming Towel!" by Geraldine Casswell
- "Endings," by Sian Phillips
- "Erika's Shame," by Arthur Becker-Weidman
- "The Girl Who Becomes Aggressive," by Arthur Becker-Weidman
- "Exploration and Integration: When the Present and Past Meet," by Kim S. Golding
- "Integration in Dyadic Developmental Psychotherapy: Amran's Story," by Karen Sik

Healing

Chapter Three

Assessment Session—Exploration Begins

Arthur Becker-Weidman, PhD

This transcript is from a part of an initial assessment and demonstrates how the exploration phase can be entered into during the very first few minutes of meeting the client (the session can be viewed on the DVD *An Introduction to Dyadic Developmental Psychotherapy*, Hughes and Becker-Weidman, 2010). This construct is also illustrated in "A Dyadic Developmental Psychotherapy Session" (Becker-Weidman and Shell, 2005/2008, pp. 57–68). The section transcribed occurs about ten minutes into our very first meeting as part of an assessment. Jessica is thirteen years old and is in secure detention because she had been aggressive toward her mother, hitting and shoving her, and repeatedly running away from home. The girl spent ten years in an Eastern European orphanage before being adopted by a couple. A year after the adoption, the father died as the result of a chronic illness. The girl had rarely been outside of the orphanage, didn't attend school on a regular basis, and was largely left to fend for herself in this orphanage. She'd been abandoned at birth. Jessica was brought to my office from secure detention in a jumpsuit and handcuffs that the officer would not remove for security reasons.

Jessica's experience of profound neglect in the orphanage left her without the ability to describe her internal experiences and emotions. This deficit was the primary cause of her impulsivity and her inability to regulate her behavior and emotions. If you don't know what you are experiencing, then you will not have the ability to reflect on your experience and choose a course of action that is to your advantage in the longer run.

We are sitting at a table across from each other. Jessica has on an orange jumpsuit and sits with her hands clasped in front of her on the table, linked by handcuffs.

Art: What was it like living in the orphanage? How would you describe it?

Jessica: I don't know. I was there in school sometimes, but I was kind of stupid.

Art: Hmm. What do you mean? [PACE: Rather than "correct" her or dispute her view, I become curious to try to understand what this means to her.]

Jessica: I don't know. I didn't know lots of stuff because, it's not really 'cause I'm stupid, but, um, I went outside there, but not really like in the world, the real world. Like I never went to church there or anything, I stayed in the building all the time.

Art: Hmm. That must have been quite a shock when you came here and were living in a real family, with a mom and a dad. . . . [I accept what she says and then wonder about how she may have felt and experienced, trying to go deeper into her experience.]

Jessica: No, I just went with it. . . .

Art: Hmm. Must have been different though . . . I mean different than the orphanage . . . was it?

Jessica: Yeah.

Art: So how was it in the beginning, living in a real family? How was that different for you than living in an orphanage? [I continue to be curious. I am very interested in how Jessica views her world, how she experiences her world and relationships, and what and how she thinks. It is my impression that my real interest in her allows her to become more revealing and comfortable in this first meeting.]

Jessica: I don't know because I, um, was kind of confused because the one that I had before, I thought the same things would happen with these ones. [What Jessica is referring to is that a few months before her prospective adoptive parents came to get her, she was moved from the orphanage to a family in the country to "teach her about living in a family."]

Art: Oh, you thought. . . .

Jessica: I left out of there and I thought I would leave out of here, too.

Art: Oh, I see.

Jessica: So I didn't know.

Art: So you've been kind of wondering all these years if your mom now would get rid of you like that other family? [I begin to try to co-create with Jessica some meaning about her experience.]

Jessica: No, it was like the first like day that I got there, but then after a while I kind of knew. . . .

Art: Oh.

Jessica: I definitely know now, but when I first came here that's why I thought it was another family just, you know, like . . .

Art: Hmm.

Jessica: But then I knew it. Like I was getting adopted and all that, like my cousin.

Art: Hmm. And your father died about a year ago, right?

Jessica: Yup. [Jessica says this is such a "matter-of-fact" way and with nearly no demonstrated affect that I become curious about that.]

Art: What was that like? [I find what she says and the way she says it unusual, and so I understand that to mean that I don't understand her and so I have to delve more deeply into her experience.]

Jessica: I don't know. It never happened before and my reaction to it was, I mean, when I went to the funeral thing, I didn't cry, but it was kind of new to me because I never really had no one die before. I didn't really know him or anything. . . .

Art: I see.

Jessica: . . . because he was sick and everything, tired all the time, so I didn't really get to know him.

Art: I see.

Jessica: I don't think it was *my* fault or my dad's because he was sick, so . . .

Art: Mmm.

Jessica: He was always tired and everything . . .

Art: And your mom's sick, too, right?

Jessica: Yeah. They both had MS but my dad's was really bad, so . . .

Art: And now you're not living with her?

Jessica: No.

Art: What's that like for you?

Jessica: Good. [I am surprised that she likes not living with her mother and being in secure detention, and so I want to understand this and her experience more deeply. As in many of my previous interventions I am relying on the follow dimension of follow-lead-follow to deepen the experience, develop intersubjectivity, and create and maintain an alliance.]

Art: Good? Do you like living in secure detention better than living with her?

Jessica: I don't know. I feel better than at home because I . . . if I do go home, I just know I'm going to end up in one of these places again and doing the same thing.

Art: You think so? How come? [We now appear to have a beginning alliance and in the next few exchanges we enter into the exploration phase.]

Jessica: I just know I will.

Art: But how do you know that? What makes you say that? I'm not disagreeing with you, Jessica. I just want to understand what makes you think that way. [In this remark I am sharing with Jessica my experience and my thinking as part of the affective/reflective dialogue we are having. I want her to understand that my question doesn't mean I disagree with her; it means that I am deeply interested in her experience. I am modeling for her the reflective function.]

Jessica: I don't know. My sister and my mom annoy me a lot. They don't take anger real well, but the weird thing is, I don't know when I'm getting angry. I just keep going until like something happens.

Art: What? You mean you're surprised when you get that angry? [Now I am beginning to understand her experience. Jessica is unaware of her internal world and emotional states and that leads to her being reactive and aggressive, I surmise.]

Jessica: Yeah, because I mean, I don't have any feelings or anything. When I just get angry, I just get angry.

Art: So you're kind of moving along and then all of a sudden you are angry. Oh, I see. [This remark reflects the empathy element of PACE as well as our beginning to co-create a new meaning for Jessica regarding her behavior.]

Jessica: Yeah, but I just keep going on; I don't always realize I'm angry. I never really do; I just fight. [This reflective comment by Jessica, part of our affective/reflective dialogue within the intersubjectivity of the exploration phase, could happen because of our building an alliance in our first few minutes together and reflect, I believe, her experience of me as someone deeply interested and concerned about her in a nonjudgmental manner.]

Art: Hm. Mmhm.

Jessica: . . . unless I'm doing it to someone I really like. [Here we see another very interesting reflective remark by Jessica that I decide to explore further by focusing on the relationship dimension of this experience. My next comment illustrates the lead part of follow-lead-follow.]

Art: So do you have anybody who you really like?

Jessica: Yeah.

Art: Who do you feel closest to?

Jessica: In the world?

Art: Yeah.

Jessica: My aunt.

Art: Your aunt . . .

Jessica: My mom's mom, uh, sister.

Art: Your mother's sister, oh.

Jessica: Yeah. Her name is Samantha. [It is important to note that Jessica would see Samantha very infrequently, perhaps five or six times a year. While Jessica has been in secure detention for a few weeks, Samantha has not visited once, while Jessica's mom has visited her every day.]

Art: Mm hmm. And anybody else or is that it?

Jessica: (shakes head no) That's it.

Art: OK. What about your mom or your sister? [Her cousin was adopted with Jessica and is now her sister.]

Jessica: No, not really. I'm not close to them.

[While I would have liked to continue this further, I also know we have some time constraints and I do have to complete the evaluation within the time allotted to me, so I reluctantly move on to the next step, which is to administer the Attachment Story Completion Test (Bretherton, Ridgeway, and Cassidy, 1990; Psychology Wiki, 2010b).]

Art: . . . and that's it. Um, what I'd like to do is . . . I'm going to tell you the beginning of a story and then I would like you to make up the rest of the story. Okay? Do you know what I mean?

Jessica: I'm not really good at that.

Art: That's okay. You do your best. I'm going to tell you the beginning of it and then you just finish the story. You tell me what happens and . . .

Jessica: Is it from the book?

Art: Is it . . . ? No, I'm going to give you the beginning of a story. You don't know these stories. You just make up the story and the ending.

Jessica: (surprised) Oh!

Art: You don't have to remember them. You have to make it up.

Jessica: The end?

Art: Yeah. I'm going to tell you the beginning and you tell me what happens and what are they doing and how they feel and you tell me what happens next. Okay?

Jessica: Okay.

Art: So here's the first one. Ready?

Jessica: Umhum.

Art: Ready?

Jessica: Uhhuh.

Art: Okay. While the family is seated at the dinner table, the younger child accidentally spills juice on the floor and the mother goes "OH!" about it. Finish the story.

Jessica: Uh, maybe the mom was shocked? And the kid . . . well I think the mom would take it really defensive because it's an accident and . . .

Art: But tell me what happens. Make up a story about it.

Jessica: (hesitantly) Oh. His mom probably expects him to wipe it up, wipe the juice off the table, then sit down or just go and get another cup of juice and be careful.

Art: And then what happens?

Jessica: Maybe they just keep eating.

Art: Okay. Ready for the next one?

Jessica: Sure.

Art: While the family is taking a walk in the park, the younger child climbs a rock, falls off, hurts their knee and cries. Tell me the rest of the story.

Jessica: Um. (ten-second pause) The mom tells the kid it's okay and next time don't do it if you know it's going to hurt you and just be careful what you do. [In this story we see three unusual features. The mom is critical in the story, the mom does not fix or help fix the injury, and they do not continue on; the problem is not resolved.]

Art: Mm hmm. That it?

Jessica: Mm hmm.

Art: Okay. Ready for the next one?

Jessica: Sure.

Art: After the child is sent upstairs to go to bed, the child cries out after hearing a strange sound.

Jessica: Um, the mom comes upstairs with her and maybe talks to the kid to see what's wrong and then the kid tells her what's wrong and then the mom tells her, "It's okay, it happens, and go to sleep 'cause it's late," and that's it. [In this story the parent seems to discount the child's feelings and there is no soothing or comforting of the child as one might expect.]

Art: Mm hmm. Ready for the next one?

Jessica: Yup.

Art: The parents leave for a weekend trip with grandmother staying behind to look after the two children.

Jessica: I think the grandmother would call the parents, um, to tell them how the kids are and the mom and dad would probably just enjoy themselves and talk to the kids and say "Hi" and "Be good." [In this story we don't observe any affect regarding the separation or the children's experience; only that the parents enjoy themselves and direct the children's behavior.]

Art: And then what, then what happens?

Jessica: Maybe they come back from the trip and they hear they were good and their mom might give them something good.

Art: OK, ready for the next one?

Jessica: OK.

Art: Grandmother looks out of the window on Monday morning and tells the children the parents are coming back.

Jessica: Hmm. Well . . . the morning, right? Did you say Sunday?

Art: Monday morning.

Jessica: Oh, Monday. Now the grandmother will get them ready for school, then the kids will come back from school and act really surprised when they see their parents.

Art: And then what?

Jessica: And they would . . . then they would just, I don't know, they would just act happy that they're home; tell them how they did at school and all. [In this story there is an unusual word choice. The children "act happy" rather than "are" happy. The other notable feature of this story is that there is no real greeting upon reunion.]

Art: Mm hmm. Okay. Mm hmm. Great. Ah, do you have a *best* friend, Jessica?

Jessica: Mm . . . No.

Art: No? Do you have *any* friends, anyone you think of as a friend, someone you can confide in or . . .

Jessica: No.

Art: No? No friends? Did you ever as . . .

Jessica: I don't really want any friends because I don't want, really, lots of people in my life.

Art: Hmm. And why's that? [Using PACE, acceptance of what she says and curiosity, I want to explore this further since it seems unusual to me that a teenager doesn't want friends and I want to understand what she means by this. As we will see, this unconditional acceptance of her responses creates the safe base necessary for exploration.]

Jessica: Because I mean, sometimes, they'll try to help you and you'll take it the wrong way and I don't want to hurt other people any more.

Art: Oh, you think, you think you always hurt people? [Here I accept her response and then, using follow-lead-follow, encourage her to go deeper in the exploration phase.]

Jessica: Well, when they try to help me I don't recognize that and then it's too late. Happens all the time.

Art: Why do you think that is?

Jessica: I don't know. Because I think they're like, being in my business, but they're not . . . really . . . they're just trying to look out for me. (Raises tone) But also, though, I don't know because if they're doing drugs and stuff and I would say no definitely, but I don't really . . . they would probably not want to be friends anymore because I don't want to do something bad that they were doing.

Art: So what about other people who don't do that? Why wouldn't you want to be friends with them?

Jessica: Well, if they had other friends that were doing it, well anything bad like that and they want me to do it, like joints, something bad . . .

Art: So what about being friends with other kids who don't do that?

Jessica: Nah.

Art: No? How come?

Jessica: 'Cause I don't really have time for them 'cause I go to school and then I come home . . . time goes too fast. . . .

Art: Oh.

Jessica: . . . to me.

Jessica was subsequently placed in a residential treatment center that used an attachment model of treatment with her and her family. I worked with Jessica, her mom, and her primary youth worker weekly for about nine months. On discharge, Jessica moved back home and attended school without any further problems. She has recently graduated high school and is attending college near her home so that she can come home on weekends.

Chapter Four

Beginnings

Sian Phillips, PhD, C.Psych.

I love the confluence of ideas and experiences. A few months ago I attended my daughter's violin performance in our local music festival. Although I loved the music she and the other children were playing, I was mesmerized by the strings adjudicator. She was an energetic, captivating woman who was equally as excited by the perfection as she was by the mistakes. As she gave feedback she used her cello, her voice, and her body to capture the message of the music that she wanted the children to understand. The competitive aspect of the festival melted away and about a dozen ten- to fourteen-year-old violinists were infected by her enthusiasm and picked up their violins, experiencing music in a different way. Their fear of making mistakes vanished and they began to take risks in their playing that half an hour before might have seemed impossible. I myself was captivated by her energy and confidence and passion and was intrigued by her quick ability to create a sense of safety for these children in an environment that had been about being evaluated. As she parted, she urged the children to go home and look up Benjamin Zander's educational seminar titled "Shining Eyes."

No matter what your musical tastes and abilities, I would recommend looking for "Shining Eyes" on the Ted.org series. Benjamin Zander also captivates his audiences through his passion, conviction, and absolute delight in what he is experiencing so that you too are transported into experiencing and understanding music differently.

A month later, a friend dropped off a book she thought I might enjoy: *The Art of Possibility* (2002). The authors were Rosamund Stone-Zander and her husband Benjamin Zander. In the first chapter, the authors distinguish between the world of measurement and the world of possibility. They posit that the world of measurement is one where we "struggle to survive in a world of scarcity and peril" (p. 15). In this world individuals compare themselves to others and determine how they measure up. It is a world where safety is paramount and taking risks in thinking or being is hampered by the need for safety. In contrast, the world of possibility is one where the concern for survival is gone and then, the authors argue, can the individual have unlimited imagination, invention, creativity, and generativity. They write, "The relationship *between* people and environment is highlighted, not the people and things themselves. Emotions that are often relegated to the special category of spirituality are abundant here: joy, grace, awe, wholeness, passion and compassion" (Stone-Zander and Zander, 2000, p. 24).

It occurred to me that Dyadic Developmental Psychotherapy (DDP) was about creating a world of possibility through the creation of intersubjective experiences. I have always loved the energy of the first session with clients. It has always been about the anticipation of the unfolding of a story, one where I may come to know it intimately, or maybe just a small piece of it. However, I can only come to know the story through the relationship with the author, a co-creation of a narrative.

Typically when children are referred to me for Dyadic Developmental Psychotherapy, the parents are exhausted by multiple attempts to ameliorate their child's behavior. Their relationship with their child is often strained and the child and family are often firmly entrenched in the world of measurement, feeling that they all measure up poorly to those around them. Workers may speak about strengths, but spend more energy on the obstacles. Parents are worn down by behavior and have lost hope of the possibility for positive relationships. The excitement of working with a new family is finding (or perhaps retrieving) for the child and for the family the possibility of a different experience of themselves and their relationships.

To give up focus on survival and turn it to imagination and creativity requires safety—no mean feat for children who have spent years being hurt badly by those who were supposed to look after them. I thought about the parallels between the adjudicator, Stone-Zander and Zander (2000), and the Dyadic Developmental Psychotherapy therapist. All use their voice, body, energy, and experience of the other to come to a new possibility of seeing and experiencing.

I was recently consulted about a five-year-old girl, whom the Protective Services wanted to place up for adoption. Sarah had been apprehended from her mother's care at the age of four due to many incidents of domestic violence, neglect, and physical abuse. Sarah had a younger brother, Peter, who was the favored child. Sarah was frequently shunned by her mother, yelled at, punished, and ignored. Both children had been placed in the same foster home. Her younger brother was soon to be placed with his biological father, and although he had acted as Sarah's father, he was not a biological relative so had not sought custody of her. Unfortunately, this again replicated the dynamic of her being the least favored or least wanted child. Sarah's birth mother continued to fight for both her children to be returned to her care, but in visits continued to find it difficult to give Sarah the love and attention she so desperately craved.

As her workers and foster mother described her behavior, it was readily apparent that any attempt at adoption would fail without intensive supports for both Sarah and any potential adoptive parents. Sarah, at age five, was already described as very controlling. Everything had to be on her terms or she would have temper outbursts. She was frequently aggressive toward her brother, sometimes sneaking into his bedroom and hurting him while he slept. In addition to the aggression toward her brother, she had been aggressive to the family pets on more than one occasion. One of the first tasks was to reframe her need for control and aggression as being adaptive. As a little girl Sarah had learned that she needed to be the one in charge since her parents were so unable to care for her. If she could make things go her way then she could minimize her fear and sense of powerlessness. By the age of four, Sarah had also been witness to a great deal of violence. Her aggression toward smaller children and animals may be seen as her way of understanding that to be vulnerable was dangerous and her rage at the experience of powerlessness and vulnerability was now directed at individuals or animals smaller than she.

Sarah had been living with her foster parents, Marie and Dennis, for almost one year at the time of the consult. She was demanding of Marie's attention and would be clingy and whiny if directed to be independent or if Marie had to attend to something other than her. [*Editor's note. What Dr. Phillips is describing may be examples of an ambivalent pattern of attachment. The behaviors learned in relation to a neglectful and preoccupied parent are those that will engage that parent. Once this pattern is set, it becomes a "strategy" for managing all other relationships. In order to get the attention of a parent with a preoccupied state of mind with respect to attachment, the child must exert a high level of energy.*] She was not able to play by herself; she no longer hoarded food, but demanded snacks at regular intervals and always seemed hungry. Marie reported that she had never seen Sarah cry, only angry. Sarah had a high pain tolerance and rarely sought help if hurt. Her focus tended to be on receiving material items when out shopping and she was intensely jealous if Marie paid any attention to Peter or her birth children. Marie also worried because Sarah was very indiscriminate in her affection. Despite the challenges, Marie loved Sarah and felt prepared to foster her as long as it took to get her ready for an adoptive home.

Sarah would not be able to tolerate another move and any placement would need very strong, patient, and informed parents to succeed. The recommendation from the consultation was to begin Dyadic Developmental Psychotherapy with Sarah and Marie and to involve whoever would be caring for her permanently when the time was right.

It took very little time to be aware of Sarah's lack of trust in adults and her fear that drove her absolute need for control. My first job was to create some safety for her. As she entered my room she was full of anxious energy. She was quick to notice different aspects of my office and moved rapidly between different thoughts or ideas, rarely finishing a question or train of thought. I matched her energy with my voice, answering her questions and commenting on her great curiosity, while internally maintaining a sense of calm and curiosity about this young girl who had been through so much. I then asked her to sit beside Marie on the couch. This was in part to see how she would respond to my direction and in part to assess whether she could use her foster mother to help her regulate.

Therapist: Sit right there next to the couch next to your mum.

[Sarah does as asked, hands between her knees, shoulders hunched.]

Sarah: Are we in the picture? (noticing the video camera)

Marie: Yes, you love being in pictures, don't you?

S: (nods her head)

T: This way I am going to tape our work together so I don't have to take any notes. I find it difficult to write and speak at the same time.

S: I know how to write.

T: Do you? Are you learning that at school right now? [*Editor's note: This is a clear example of the Dyadic Developmental Psychotherapy component of follow-lead-follow.*]

S: (nods her head)

T: Don't you find that it's hard to write and speak at the same time? If you write you stop speaking or if you speak you stop writing.

S: (nodding emphatically) I speak and I write with my homework.

[Sarah moves quickly away from this topic of conversation and starts talking about something else. I allow a little break, and then want to see how she responds to more direct interaction with me and the use of touch. I need also to ensure that I continue to support a building alliance and sense of safety.]

T: (leans toward Sarah and touches her feet) I love your socks. Do you think they would fit me?

S: (tucks feet behind her and leans into Marie) [*Editor's note: This indicates that Sarah is able to use Marie as a secure base.*]

T: You don't want me to have them; you are hiding them behind you. I love them. They even match your stripy underwear! [*Editor's note: Here the reader will observe an example of PACE. Sian is playful and accepting of Sarah.*]

S: (giggles)

T: How cool is that! You are a stripy girl. [Sarah gets off the couch to go play and starts talking about her friend.]

T: Where are you off to? Oh I think this is my chance to get those lovely socks!

S: (jumps right back onto couch next to Marie)

T: Don't you think, Sarah, we could switch socks? (I begin to take my boot off)

S: NO! (smiles and leans further into Marie)

T: But they are so cool. You had better keep them hidden up there, because I might want them!

S: NO!

T: NO! (clapping knees, matching vitality) You don't want me to have your socks!

S: I will never let you.

T: Never, never, never, never!

[By trying playfully to get her socks, I have been able to use the playful and accepting aspects of PACE to continue a beginning alliance. I have also been able to use play to get her back on the couch, asking for help from her foster mother. If I had asked her directly to get back on to the couch she would have resisted and we would quickly be into a power struggle. We move again into chatting about her different collections.]

S: And I collect a house like that. (points to the doll's house)

T: You have a doll's house like that?

S: (looks down and pouts for a second then turns to Marie) Do I?

M: Well, the one on the porch, the one I let you play with.

S: Yeah . . . (moves away from Marie)

T: (reaches out and touches her knee; she looks back, but tolerates the touch) Do you know something I notice?

S: What?

T: It's really kind of cool. When you don't know something you ask Marie to help you.

S: (looks and tries to climb on Marie's knee)

T: So, good for you, asking for help if you don't know.

[Asking for help is certainly something that Sarah has very little practice with so I want to highlight that she has this relationship to support her. It is very difficult for her to tolerate even a tiny increase in emotional intensity and she regulates by switching the subject again.]

S: Are we going to take a picture? Is the camera on?

T: Yes.

S: (makes goofy faces)

M: She's so smart.

(We play with making faces for a minute.) [*Editor's note: Being playful, particularly during the developing an alliance phase, can help create the safety and security necessary to create a safe base for later exploration. In this instance, Sian's use of self to engage Sarah is quite evident and a clear example of how the therapist must be emotionally present, engaged, involved, and authentic.*]

T: What a big tongue you have! (everyone laughs) Is that to lick all the icing off chocolate cakes? Is that why you have such a big tongue like that?

S: Mmmm. (nods)

T: Wow! Stick it out again! [I want to see if she will tolerate my direction during play.] Look at that big long tongue. It's a big long tongue if ever I saw one! Can you touch your nose with your tongue? [*Editor's note: Another illustration of PACE.*]

S: (tries)

T: Oh, you almost can, but it's not quite long enough!

S: I can . . . mmmm, I can touch my hand with my tongue! [Sarah doesn't like the notion of not being able to do something, again needing to be in control to regulate her sense of vulnerability so looks for something she is able to do. I follow her lead.]

T: You can touch your hand with your tongue? So can I!

S: (touches tongue to palm of hand)

T: Maybe your hand tastes good?

S: Guess what Angela did one day. She ate play dough.

T: Oh! I thought we were talking about tongues and hands? Why did you think about Angela?

S: (gets up and again gets in close to Marie and holds her face in her hands, pushes her aggressively back into the couch)

[Sarah seemed to get dysregulated and move into shame when I brought up something she hadn't done or maybe she perceives me to be disappointed? Although I reacted to the aggression internally, I didn't mention it. I think this was because I was unsure whether we had enough alliance for Sarah to tolerate the shame that she would experience if I set limits at this time. It also seemed very much like a regular interaction between the two of them. Hurting Marie in response to her own shame or dysregulation is a theme that continues to come up in this and subsequent sessions.]

[*Editor's note: It would appear that Sarah's response to shame is probably grounded in an adaptive response "learned" in her previous homes, as a way of coping with and expressing dissatisfaction.*]

M: Tell her who Angela is?

S: My friend.

M: Her best friend at school.

S: (still with her face very close to Marie's face) You talk strange. (gets off the couch)

T: Oh! Wait, wait, wait, wait, where are you off to, Miss Bouncy? Come and sit next to your mum on the couch. (complies and leans on her lap) Is it OK if I call her your mum? I know that sometimes she is Marie and sometimes you call her Mum. [*Editor's note: Sian's comment and question to Sarah is an illustration of the reflective function. Sian is demonstrating observing experiences and reflecting on experiences.*]

S: Nooo! Marie! (bouncy, gets away from Marie)

T: So I should call her Marie, not Mum?

S: No!

T: I should mix it up?

S: No! (flops over Marie)

T: Oh my goodness, it's so confusing! What should I call her?

S: Marie.

T: I should call her Marie. But you call her Mum sometimes.

S: Because I forget her name. (holding Marie's face and directing her with her hands)

T: You forget her name? So is it OK sometimes if I call her Mum.

S: NO!

M: (to Sarah) She can call me whatever.

T: She's not my mum.

S: My mum! It's my rules!

T: Oh, is that right? You would like to come here and make it your rules! Well, what happened to my rules? I am going to have a little bit of fussing if you say it's going to be all about your rules! This is my office; *I* get to make the rules! (Sarah looks worried, nervous giggles, fingers in her mouth) I think you might be a little worried that I am angry that you want to make them your rules and didn't know that I was teasing you. Or maybe you are worried that I might make big rules that you don't like. [Here I am aware that Sarah is worried and I want to be curious and reflect on what she might be worried about.]

[*Editor's note. This is a nice illustration of the affective/reflective dialogue and the reflective dimension.*]

S: (shouts) Why can't you make me see my mother? Let me see my mother!

T: (in a very quiet voice) Oh, you think I can make a rule so you can see your mother. You miss her and you would like to see her.

S: (nods, fingers in her mouth)

T: You are wondering whether I can help you with that.

S: (quietly) Yeah.

T: Oh! How come you don't see her anyway?

S: I live with Marie.

T: I know; how come?

S: Because. I love my mother. (gets on Marie's lap and gives her a hug)

T: Oh! You say you love your mother, but you give Marie a big hug and a squeeze. Now I am really confused. Who do you mean when you say your mother?

S: (quiet, looks to Marie and whispers in her ear) What's her name?

M: What is your mum's first name? Stacey.

S: I love Stacey!

M: Stacey is your real mum.

T: Oh, so you have a first mum and a foster mum.

S: Yes I do, you silly brain.

T: Yes, I am trying to get it straight. I have just met you and I don't know you yet.

S: I am Sarah.

T: Yes, Sarah who has a first mum and a foster mum.

(Sarah wriggles away from Marie)

T: Hey, hey, come and sit up close to Marie. (leans in close) I am wondering something. How come you don't live with Stacey anymore?

S: Because they fight. [Sarah says this very matter-of-factly with no apparent affect, so I want to highlight the seriousness associated with domestic violence and lead her using my voice and body language.]

T: They do! Big huge fights? Throwing things and stomp about fights?

S: (nodding) They hit things. [Notice her use of present tense when she is remembering.]

T: (whispers) Oh, what happened to you when they did those things?

S: (jumps up and turns around away from me) I cried.

T: (whisper, with lots of empathy) You cried. It's really scary, isn't it, when people fight like that?

(Sarah is looking away still, but nodding, then suddenly makes the big feelings go away.)

S: (to Marie) When are we leaving for lunch? (chats to Marie about going to McDonalds)

T: Marie, I notice your girl doesn't want to think about those times when she was so scared when she lived with her first mum [I want to acknowledge how frightened Sarah must have been, but it was clear that she needed to distance from her feelings so I direct my comments to Marie in a way of talking about Sarah rather than directly to her.]

(Sarah distracting, trying to jump back onto couch)

T: Oh, you need some help! Say, "Marie, help me, help me!" [I revert to using PACE to help Sarah return to a sense of safety.]

S: Please help me, Mother.

M: (pulls Sarah onto her lap, laughing; Sarah pulls away onto her knees, but still close)

[In this first part of our beginning session, I am very aware of Sarah's anxiety and her huge need to control her foster mother and the interactions with me as a way to stay safe. I use my voice in very different ways, sometimes matching her bouncy energy and at other times whispering, conveying empathy for her struggles. She finds direct, emotional interaction very threatening and can only manage a few seconds at a time. I allow her to take breaks when she needs to but don't want to lose track of her narrative and keep returning to it, trying to get to know her story. I use follow-lead-follow to build a rhythm between us and to build our alliance. Since she responds well to that rhythm, we are able to move quite quickly into exploring her experiences.]

S: I called her Mother.

T: I know.

S: How do you know?

T: Because I heard you; you said, "Help me, Mother!"

T: Hey, I thought of something. (leading) Your first mum and dad used to fight. Did anyone help you then?

S: (shakes head) Mmm mmm.

T: You were all by yourself. (lots of empathy)

S: Jesus helped me.

T: Oh, I am so glad you had someone to help and you weren't all by yourself.

S: But I am kind of scared when my mother used to fight. [Sarah returns by herself to her experience, which suggests that we are maintaining an alliance and that allows her to tolerate a little more emotional intensity.]

T: I bet! You were so little (using a little voice, gesturing low to the ground) and they were really, really big. (changed voice) I bet they were loud. (Sarah engaged, still in her body when my voice animated)

S: I was screaming.

T: You were screaming too? Everyone was screaming?

S: I yelled, "Mama, stop!" then I cried.

T: Did she listen when you yelled stop?

S: No. (gets up off couch and turns away) Then I cried a lot (flops down on Marie), then Jesus helped me. (Points at some artwork) Who painted that?

T: Phew, you have such a bouncy mind, I bet it helps you not feel the hurt when you think about something else. [I want to accept that she needs to move the focus away to something less emotionally intense, and want to highlight how adaptive having a bouncy mind must have been when she needed relief from the difficult times.]

S: Can I paint after? I love painting!

T: Hey, I am trying to understand something. I am getting the idea that you didn't always live with Marie. How old were you when you came to live with Marie?

S: (holds up four fingers)

T: Four!

S: No, two, no wait, my brother was two.

M: Mmm.

[Sarah remains quite distracted and anxious and her language is incoherent, jumping from subject to subject. She jumps on Marie and then grabs a copy of her foster mother's book, *Building the Bonds of Attachment* by Daniel Hughes, and demands to meet Katie, the character in the story.]

S: I want to meet Katie. I want to go see her. [*Editor's note: What the reader will see in the next few interactions is Sian and Sarah co-create a new meaning for Sarah regarding her experiences with her birth family. This new meaning is positive, growth facilitating, and significantly reduces Sarah's sense of shame.*]

T: You do? You want to go see her. How come?

S: Don't know.

T: (whisper) You know why, Sarah? Because Katie is five years old just like you.

S: Where does her live?

T: She is a story about a girl just like you who had the same kind of life you had. It's a story about Katie when she was just your age—not one, not two, not three, not four, but five. (holds out five fingers)

S: I have five. (holds out her hand)

T: (she allows me to put my palm against hers; I hold her hand and count her fingers) You were not one, not two, not three, not four, but five. [She starts to get dysregulated. I use an excited voice to draw her back in.]

[*Editor's note: This is a good example of co-regulating a person's affect by matching the vitality affect (the volume and energy) but not necessarily the categorical affect (mad, sad, glad, or scared, for example).*]

T: You know what else! You know what else! You want me to tell you? (Sarah nods; I whisper) Katie had a mum and a dad who fought too.

S: (excited) But where does she live?

T: In the story she goes to live with a family who takes care of her so she doesn't have to be scared anymore.

S: But where does she live?

T: In your imagination.

S: Does she live in the book?

T: Yes, when you read the pages of the book, you get to know Katie. She is a girl just like you.

S: (opens the book) Can you read it?

T: Shall I try to find a part that's just like you? (flip through the book) You know, it will be hard to find a part just right, but I have another book about someone just like you. Scoot up next to Marie and I will read it to you.

(Marie pulls Sarah onto her lap.)

T: Isn't it a great place for stories, mummy's lap?

S: Yeah.

[I want to start co-creating a more coherent narrative for Sarah. Our interaction about Katie is a beginning and I want to expand the exploration by reading *Teenie Weenie in a Too Big World* by Margot Sunderland (2003). It is a lovely book that I often read in a first session since it outlines how Teenie Weenie feels powerless by a "Too Big World" and wants to give up. He is persuaded to take risks by a character who believes that when doing things together the "Too Hard" becomes possible. Sarah is immediately absorbed by the pictures and tolerates sitting on her foster mother's lap as I read.]

[*Editor's note: While this is an excellent book, I am convinced that what engages Sarah is Sian's excitement about the book and Sian's genuine emotional engagement. This clearly illustrates the Dyadic Developmental Psychotherapist's use of self to build and maintain the alliance necessary to enter the exploration and integration phases.*]

[Sarah begins to notice differences in the pictures, often minute details and I see how hypervigilant she is. She is able to tolerate me making bridges between the character in the book and her life, as long as we are both directing our attention to the book and I am co-regulating the intensity of the interaction. It is also an opportunity to co-create a different meaning to her early experiences so that we can develop a more coherent narrative for her.]

[*Editor's note: What the reader will observe is early integration. The co-regulation of affect and co-creation of meaning develop a more coherent autobiographical narrative, which is an example of integration.*]

[As soon as we were finished, however, Sarah becomes dysregulated and reverts back to tangential thoughts and incoherent language.]

T: Hey, back here! (gestures for her to lie on Marie's lap; she complies) Thanks for the break; I'm just going to chat to Marie for a while. Here, I will take your hand. I love these little stars on your shirt. (points to them)

S: I love you!

T: You love me! You do. How come?

S: I like . . . I love you for this for all time.

T: Oh, my goodness, but you have just met me; you don't even know me! [I then want to reflect on what she might mean.] Oh! Do you think you might be saying you kind of like it here? Do you think that maybe you like me to hold your hand and count the stars on your T-shirt? You kind of like that. You weren't sure you were going to like it and maybe you are starting to feel safer? You didn't know what to expect when Marie told you you were going to talk to someone and now you know it's not so scary.

S: But I heard someone coughing.

T: Oh, you thought you were coming to a doctor's office like people do when they are sick?

S: (nods and then changes the subject again) Did someone leave their wallet here when they came? (points)

T: I don't know what that is. (Sarah gets off the couch to get the thing she's looking at.) You know you are so observant! Thank you for showing me that. You know what that looks like? That looks like a little bit of a hair band that has broken. You know the kind that goes on your head like that? (puts it on her head) It may be that someone sat on it or it was in someone's purse and fell out.

S: If I had this headband, I wouldn't bring it here so it wouldn't get broken.

T: You know what I notice?

S: What?

T: This piece of headband matches your ribbon and the stars on your shirt.

S: (bounces delightedly) How do you know that?

T: (playfully) You aren't the only one who can be observant you know!

S: It matches this too!

T: It does!

S: (goes to doll's house and brings something from it)

T: You know you are a tricky one, aren't you. You will try anything to try and play with my toys! (everyone laughs) Nice try; sit back down! You thought you were going to get me, but you didn't. (Sarah and Marie laugh together) Such a tricky monster!

S: I tricked you! There is a spider on your back.

T: There is not a spider on my back! (makes a big show of turning around) Marie, is there a spider on my back?

M: Noooo. (Marie and Sarah laugh)

T: Oh, you are such a tricky girl! Back on there. (gesture to lap) I was talking to your mum. You are distracting me! You know that! You are! Right back there because I was talking to your mum and you are distracting me! (lies back on her lap) There you go. Oh, Marie, I was getting so distracted by headbands, spiders and stories and (starts to rub Sarah's back) and stars. So Marie, this girl of yours, she's had a hard go of it the first few years of her life. Her mum and dad used to fight and fight and fight. And I understand that sometimes they would yell at Sarah.

S: (starts to snore loudly)

T: Marie! She's tricking me again, isn't she? (to Sarah, using PACE) Well, I am sure glad you feel relaxed enough to go to sleep. (snores again; I choose to ignore her and talk to Marie) [*Editor's note: Another illustration of PACE, the playful dimension.*]

T: Does she ever tell you about those times?

M: Yes, she does. (turns to Sarah) You have shared some stories with me. Remember those stories? (Sarah jumps up and hugs Marie again, holding her face tightly.)

S: I have to tell you something. I dream that my mother got dead. In my dreams . . .

T: Do you? (lots of empathy) That must make you really sad. (leading)

S: And one time I had a dream about daddy dying.

T: Ohhhh. (lots of empathy in my voice)

S: (a little dysregulated and language is not as coherent as she describes her dream)

T: (paraphrase what Sarah has just said) So first you got really, really scared that your daddy was dead and you sang to him and he woke up? Oh, what a relief!

S: Hey, what happened to the stairs? (of doll's house)

T: Hey, nice try! I am on to your tricks. I am getting it. I start talking about hard things and you try to distract me! I am on to your tricks. (everyone laughs; Sarah holds my hands, starts to play with my hair)

T: (gestures to get back to her mum's lap)

S: You have hair in your face.

T: You are right! I need a haircut badly. Maybe by next time you come I will have had a haircut.

M: (laughs, pats her leg). Lay down. (She crawls onto Marie's lap, but has a hard time, half on, half off.)

T: What a wriggle wart! She probably wants to say "Hold me, Marie, hold me; I am having a hard time getting onto this couch!" [*Editor's note: We observe the verbal-nonverbal dialogue in these exchanges.*]

S: Oh, the crocodiles are going to get me!

M: (playfully pulls her up)

T: You better stay right up there!

S: (gets up and kisses Marie; her interaction with Marie is much softer and not as aggressive as it's been before and I want to bring it up to make Sarah more aware of the difference)

T: Hey, how come you gave Marie a kiss right then?

S: Cos.

T: How come?

S: Cos I love Marie. (the two of them hug, lovely, no attempt to hurt Marie this time)

T: You do! Wow! You love your Marie.

S: (kisses Marie again)

T: You kissed her again!

S: (Sarah kisses her again; in response Marie and Sarah are playful.)

T: Does she give you lots of kisses . . . ? And another one!

S: (gives her lots of kisses, no hurting)

T: Is that how you show that you love her?

S: (Sarah and Marie snuggle)

[Sarah tolerates the snuggling for a very brief time and then moves away from the intimacy physically by getting off the couch and intellectually by focusing on a variety of different topics. Again I let her have her break and then pull her back to her narrative. I am very aware of using follow-lead-follow to hold Sarah in the rhythm of the session.]

T: (to Marie) Do you notice that when I start talking about mummies, that Sarah gets more curious. She finds it hard, I am guessing, to talk about mummies. [I am now using reflection to comment on Sarah's need to lead and I also want to ensure that I highlight the adaptive nature of her distraction, using the word curious rather than something with a more negative connotation.]

M: Yes, she changes the subject.

S: How did that truck get there?

T: See! What a girl; since you are so curious I want to talk to your mum for a bit. Lie down. Do you want to go sunny side up or sunny side down? [Again using PACE to maintain connection rather than compliance.] Up? OK, flip over then. Belly button has to point to the sky. (laughs)

So this girl of yours, you say that she has shared some stories of her hard times, her hard, hard times when she was a little girl.

M: Yes she has.

T: Wow! I am so glad you have had Marie to share those hard times with.

S: (changes the subject again)

T: (playfully teases her, then says) I want to do an experiment. I want you to look out of that window while I talk to Marie. I want to see if when I talk about mummies, you change the subject. Ready?

[I want to continue to develop Sarah's narrative and do so by talking about her to Marie. This serves two objectives: it allows Sarah to integrate a different experience of her life and also helps Marie understand Sarah differently and have empathy for her.]

T: (with lots of empathy and rhythmic voice) So Marie, Sarah's first mummy Stacey used to get into big fights with Sarah's dad. They would scream and the kids would be so scared and sometimes they would have to go and hide. Sarah would have to take her brother sometimes and hide him too and lock him into her room so he wouldn't get hurt. That was so much for a little kid to do. She was so little. Sometimes I understand that Sarah's mum used to be mean to her. Sometimes she would say, "I don't love you, you are just a stupid little kid!" I can't imagine what that would have been like for Sarah—so hard, so very hard. (Sarah covers her ears, but doesn't say anything.) Her mum would say mean things to her and she must have felt really, really bad! Probably, Marie, it was really hard sometimes for Sarah to believe that anyone loved her! Wow! How hard! [*Editor's note: This section is a wonderful example of talking for the client and doing that to weave a new, growth-enhancing narrative.*]

S: (giggles briefly)

T: My experiment worked! It is so hard to remember that she is helping herself forget by giggling! Good for her that she knows how to make the hard things go away! Marie, do you think that Sarah's mum used to say things like "You stupid kid!" and "I don't love you anymore!"

M: (nods)

S: (nods, still looking away out the window)

T: She did? Then it would be really hard for Sarah to know that anyone loved her. (quiet empathy) And then! Maybe Sarah started to think that she was a bad kid! Her mum was so mean to her. (more energy in my voice) Oh Marie! Maybe she thought it was her fault that her mum was so mean? Oh, wow, if that's true that's got to be hard! If she thinks it's her fault. She was such a little kid and she was trying to make sense of her mum. Why her mum would say such mean things to her like "Shut up. You are such a stupid kid. I don't have to listen to a snotty-nosed kid!" And Sarah thought it was her fault. Oh, Sarah, I am so sorry that you thought it was your fault. [*Editor's note: In this example the reader will observe the reflective element of the affective/reflective dialogue. In addition, as in a number of previous exchanges, Sian creatively uses the nonverbal elements of narrative (tone of voice, facial expressions, touch, cadence, prosody, and gestures) to both engage Sarah and to co-regulate her.*]

S: But it was my fault. (turns back around)

T: Oh, you thought it was your fault. (lots of empathy) Oh my!

S: Then after, I locked my brother in my room so he didn't get into a fight with mama again.

T: You were trying to make sure Peter was OK.

S: Mama did the same thing to Peter.

T: She called him stupid too?

S: Mmmm. (nods, turns around and cuddles right into Marie's side, fingers to her mouth, very vulnerable looking)

T: Oh! (Lean in) I'm so sorry! That would have been so hard for you both.

S: (accepting Marie's hugs and stroking her leg) Me and Peter thought it was our fault.

T: I am sure you would have thought it was your fault; you were such a little girl, so little. (voice falls away)

S: We were both little. . . .

T: Yes, just a little boy and a little girl. (gesture with hands)

S: Was I this tiny? (holds finger and thumb a little apart)

T: Only way before you were born.

S: (jumps up) Now I am this big.

T: (emphatically) Yes! (match vitality affect, then I use a very low, quiet voice to get her back to her story) But when you were this big (marking on her body how tall she would have been) and this big and this big, your mother said such mean things to you.

S: (jumps back onto couch and looks out window again)

T: Oh, my goodness me, it was so hard for you, for you and for Peter. (whispering) You thought Mummy didn't love you because you were a bad kid; that must have been so hard. Oh Sarah, I am so sorry you didn't have enough love. It was such a hard time.

(Sarah was about to change the subject again, when I jumped beside her on the couch and pretended to be her, talking for her.)

Sian, it was so hard; you don't understand how hard it was. I thought it was my fault. I thought she didn't love me because I was a bad kid.

(I jump back to my chair, whispering.) You thought Mummy didn't love you because you were a bad kid; that must have been so hard.

[Sarah is sad and sitting still beside Marie. I am guessing that this is the first time Sarah has allowed herself to experience the sadness rather than the anger at her life.]

T: Marie, can you tell your girl that you are sorry that she had such a hard time?

M: I am sorry that you had to feel that you were a bad kid. I am sorry you had to go through that with your mum. (stroking her hair)

S: (regulated and listening; throws herself into Marie without hurting her and starts to cry just a few tears)

M: You deserve love. (hugging her and rubbing back)

S: (one big sob and then pulls away)

T: I am so sorry it was so hard.

M: I am sorry too, honey. (tucks hair behind Sarah's ear)

S: It's OK. (bounces off couch) I would just look out the window! What would happen if someone broke your window?

T: (playfully) Wow! You just made all those hard feelings go away! How did you do that? Are you trying to change the subject because it is hard to remember how hard it was for you when you were little and your mum was so mean to you? [*Editor's note: The use of PACE (being playful) in this instance allows Sian to reflect on the experience and help both her clients develop greater insightfulness.*]

S: Well, what would happen?

T: I would fix it.

S: How?

T: I would call someone and say "Would you please come and fix my window?" [Here I want to model reliance on someone for help, since Sarah's experience is having done all the hard things by herself.]

S: Cool truck.

T: Hey, you are doing it again! You are trying to distract me! (everyone laughs)

S: When are we going to get our picture taken . . . (very demanding voice)

T: Oh! Are you saying you want to be the boss again and you have forgotten who is the boss in this office? Is that what you are doing? [*Editor's note: By observing and commenting on what is occurring right now, Sian is able to co-regulate Sarah's affect; this is an illustration of developing the reflective function.*]

S: (laughs, tosses head playfully) I forgot that you are the boss.

T: That's right; don't worry, I will remind you if you forget again.

(Sarah fusses about being thirsty and wanting a drink.)

T: Are you saying "Sian, I don't want you to talk anymore about how hard it was when I was little." Is that what you would like to say to me?

S: (nods)

T: Go ahead, you can say it. Say "Sian, enough talking about hard stuff!"

S: I just don't like it when my mother said that stuff to me!

T: (emphatically matching her affect) You are right about that! Thanks so much for telling me! I don't like it either! I don't like it that she said that to you!

S: (shoulders slumped) It just makes me cry. Peter was crying on my shirt and I was crying on his shirt too.

T: (quietly) Yeah, you were trying to help each other out. I bet you were crying.

S: (looks down) We were both crying at the same time. And once, Peter followed me, but he tripped down the stairs.

T: He was so little. (low voice with lots of empathy)

S: I carried him on my back. (looking at me)

T: Did you? You were so strong! (quietly, introducing a different experience of the powerlessness she must have felt)

S: I was angry at Mother for the whole time.

T: I bet you wanted to say, "Don't you dare call me names like that!" (angry voice, then softer voice) I bet you wanted to be the boss. [*Editor's note: By talking for the child, in this instance, Sian is able to substantially deepen the emotional experience.*]

S: Yeah.

T: And maybe you wanted to say, "Stop it!"

S: I was going to say, "I hate you, Mother." (wipes at eyes; it appears that she is crying, but I didn't want to address it for fear of it being too much focus on her vulnerability and I want to encourage her staying with her experience)

T: Were you? Did you ever say it?

S: I was going to feel like it, but I didn't want to hurt Mother's feelings.

T: Ahh! That's so hard, isn't it; isn't it hard when you have big feelings like that but you are still worried if you say it that Mama would get even madder or sadder?

S: Yeah, it is hard for me to understand. (completely regulated)

T: (thoughtfully) It's hard for lots of people.

S: I can't hear you because my ears are full of rain like the Jonas Brothers.

T: The Jonas Brothers have ears full of rain!?

[Here Sarah breaks away, again needing a break, so I give her the break she is looking for. She puts something back into the doll's house.]

T: Thank you for doing that.

S: I am a good girl, aren't I?

[I missed this opportunity to comment on how maybe she might think that I thought she was a "bad" girl because of her revealing of vulnerability and the part of her narrative that involved being angry at her mother. Instead I redirect her back to telling her story. Although she is able to return to talking about her past and can identify her feelings about it, she has already been able to touch affect that she has never revealed to Marie before. She has responded really well to follow-lead-follow and has done a fabulous job of returning to some very painful aspects of her past. Each time she returns to her past experiences, she seems able to tolerate it for longer and need less support to bring her back to her narrative. This suggests that we have been able to create a sense of safety for her that has allowed for this exploration. It would have been enough to finish the session, at this point we have been together for about forty-five minutes, but we keep going. The decision to keep going was made because Sarah was responding so beautifully to the rhythm of the session and I didn't have the sense that she was too tired or exhausted by the work she was doing. Intuitively, I felt that Sarah wanted to tell more of her story.]

T: Hey! Hey! So where were we?

S: On the mummy part, that bad part.

T: That part where you wanted to say, "I hate you, Mummy, for doing all those horrible things to me!" That one? Did you ever say it?

S: Yeah. No! I would never say that to my poor mother! (gets off Marie's lap).

T: Hey, where are you going?

S: Just looking at the toys.

[I realize that she needs more of a break and return to some playful matching of her affect. After a few minutes where she is playing with toys I want her to return to the couch to get support from her foster mother and am contemplating wrapping up the session. I use more playfulness to redirect her.]

T: Quick, say, "Marie, I have fallen off the couch and I can't get back up."

S: Crocodiles!

M: (playfully starts to pull her up beside her)

T: Thank goodness Marie was here to help you!

S: (giggles; tries again to change the subject and I playfully tease her about it) Marie, could you tickle my feet?

T: Thanks so much for asking Marie to tickle your feet.

M: She loves her feet tickled.

T: I bet that sometimes helps her when her mind is thinking about hard things. It's so good that she has you to help her. Marie, I think your girl has some very angry feelings towards her first mum. (Sarah lying with feet in Marie's lap)

M: Yes, she is very angry.

S: I feel it too. (pauses) I am so mad at my mother.

T: (grabs Sarah's foot) Maybe you want to stomp and stomp (punctuate with her foot) and say "stop being so mean!" (leading)

[We played around briefly with her being able to stop bullies by bonking them on the nose and referring back to the book we had read earlier, where the character and his friends started to be assertive with those who were hurting them.]

T: (say with a sigh) But I bet you couldn't do that when you were just a little girl; you were just too little.

S: Yeah (sighs, perhaps mirroring my voice), just too little. It just makes me angry. (gets off the couch, Marie pulls up her pants on the way)

T: (bigger voice) I see that! So mad that your pants are falling down. (giggles, but stays with me; Sarah starts to bounce) So mad that you can't even sit still sometimes there is so much mad inside wanting to get out. So mad that I bet sometimes you can't even concentrate on having fun because you're so mad!

S: I want to play!

T: I know, you want to say to me, "Sian, don't you get it yet; I don't want to talk about this mummy stuff. I just want to play!"

S: (getting very bouncy and silly)

M: (pulls her up onto her lap and cradles her, but she is very wriggly)

T: Hey, do you guys know how to sing lullabies?

M: Do you want to sing, Sarah?

T: (direct Sarah to snuggle back on Marie's lap; she sits beside her and cuddles under her arm)

S: Marie, will you sing?

M: Do you want to do Rock-a-Bye Baby? (pulls her onto her lap)

S: No! I want to sing. . . .

T: Are you wanting to be the boss again? (Marie and Sarah giggle)

M: Are you bossy? (lovely interaction, looking gently into her eyes; no irritation from Marie, but Sarah finds the intimacy too difficult and shouts)

S: No! It's my turn! (climbs out of Marie's lap)

T: Hey (playfully), I'm the boss! Here is how it's going to go! Marie is going to pick a song; put your bum on her lap so she can sing to you.

S: No, I want to sit here. (beside her on arm of couch)

T: Oh no! Oh no! She is going to make me work hard again to remind her who is the boss in this room! (Sarah giggles and rolls over onto the other side of Marie.)

T: That doesn't count; your bum was on her lap for less than a second!

S: (giggles, sits in Marie's lap, her back on Marie's chest, looking away from her, but is quite stiff; it is evident that she is out of her comfort zone and unsure of the intimacy)

[I can recognize that this is really difficult for Sarah and wonder whether to allow her to take a break or to see if I can structure it and make it safe so she can access some help from Marie. I decide to proceed with getting her to be in her foster mother's lap so that she can experience being held in her vulnerability.]

T: OK, I am going to be a sculptor and I am going to move you around the way sculptors do. Put your legs over here. (I move her legs to the side and we play around for a minute moving her into the position of an infant looking up at a mother.)

T: Your eyes have to be on Marie's eyes.

S: (giggles with a fair bit of anxiety)

M: (starts to rock her while looking in her eyes, Sarah still giggling nervously; Marie starts to sing and Sarah looks increasingly more uncomfortable, so Marie asks her if she would prefer to sing to her)

S: I have a song! (Sarah moves to the other side of Marie again.) I want to sit like this; it's more easier. I like to curl up like this. (facing away from Marie)

T: Hey! (playfully) Who is the boss?

S: You are. (This time she says it with sadness, not playfully)

T: I want you to be able to look up at Marie's eyes.

S: (cranes her neck back to look up at Marie)

T: (playfully, but being directive) You can't do it that way; you will hurt your neck; scoot around.

S: (pouting, looking down) I just don't like looking at Marie's eyes.

[Now I finally get that this is too much for her.]

T: It's too hard. (whispering) Any ideas how come?

S: Because I just don't like when I do that.

T: Thank you so much for telling me that, Sarah. I was asking you to do something that was too hard. I am sorry. It was too hard; I made a mistake. (all the time Marie is stroking her hair nonverbally, very engaged with Sarah)

S: That's OK. (sad)

T: Any ideas how we could do it?

S: Wellll (more energy, has made the difficult feeling go away) maybe you could put the song on.

T: How could you sit so you are all safe and snuggled up?

S: Like this. (gets on lap and Marie pulls her in close and starts to rock her; Sarah is looking away from her)

T: There, does that feel better?

S: Mm mm. (wriggles off and Marie playfully catches her and pulls her back on)

S: (notices the light on the computer; even though she is distracted, she is not so dysregulated)

T: Are you ready?

S: (snuggles back into Marie) I just don't want to look in your eyes.

M: You don't want to look in my eyes?

S: (gets all bouncy again)

T: Oh, Sarah, this is so hard; you are doing this all by yourself; it's hard to ask Marie for help with these hard feelings. We talked about so many hard things today. (I list a number of hard things we have talked about.)

S: (still bouncy)

T: You are saying you don't want to be close with Marie right now; it's too hard. Let's do the song another day.

S: No! I like songs.

T: I think I made another mistake by asking you to snuggle with Marie to listen to my song. I think you are telling me you would rather bounce right now because we talked about so much hard stuff. You might want to say to me, "Sian, I don't want to think about any more hard stuff today." You are right, girl! Too much hard stuff!

M: (turns to Sarah) How are you feeling?

S: Scared! I am scared of you! I am scared of my mother! And what's going to happen to me when I live with my aunt. [There was a recent plan to explore a kinship placement.] I don't want you to bring my mother here; that's why I'm scared of you!

T: Did you think I was going to ask your mother to come here and talk with you and Marie? Oh, I am so sorry that you were scared of that. Thanks so much for telling me! Nope, that's not going to happen.

(Sarah gets off the couch.)

T: (start clapping arms together like crocodile, Sarah jumps into Marie's arms and we all giggle; we take a break by playing Crocodiles—Sarah deliberately gets off the couch and I act like a crocodile and she jumps into Marie's arms; we do this several times and then I catch her) I don't think Marie can save you now. She is mine, Marie! (Marie and I play tug of war with her; she initially enjoys it, but then starts to get overstimulated and I stop the game).

T: We will be finished soon. Here is a blanket for you to hide under while I talk to Marie. (I give her a blanket to help her manage the story I want to talk about to Marie; this way she can choose to move away from the intensity of her story if she chooses without bouncing off the couch.) Marie, thank you so much for bringing your girl here today to meet me. It was lovely to get to know her beautiful big brown eyes. She has so much energy and she is so curious and she was able to tell me about how hard it was for her sometimes before she came to live with you. Did you notice that your girl has such a hard time with big feelings? She tries so hard to keep those big feelings away. And did you notice that the bigger the feelings, the more bouncy she becomes? When she has big worries like where she is going to live or worries about her first mum or she's got big angry feelings towards her first mum, she's probably bouncy, bouncy, bouncy. She probably doesn't want to listen or do things. I bet that's how you tell when things are on her mind.

M: For sure, sometimes she tells her mum that she is angry at her.

T: She does? She's brave enough to tell her mum she's mad at her! But she is only five; how does she do that?

M: At some visits, they have their fights. She tells her she hates her and then she comes home and is mad.

T: But she's only five. (hold out five fingers, Sarah puts her hand on my hand and holds it there while I say) She's able to say, "I don't like it that you say mean things to me and didn't do such a good job of helping me."

M: Then her mum gets upset.

T: Oh (direct my comment to Sarah), that's that part about feeling bad about telling your mum how you feel. [I want to link what we are talking about now to an earlier part of the session to highlight the coherence in the narrative.] That's a tough, tough thing. Your mum doesn't make it easy to tell her things, does she?

S: Yeah! She is always screaming a lot and I can't understand!

T: I bet you can't when there is so much screaming.

S: Sometimes my brain is not useful!

T: Not useful?

S: Sometimes I want to get rid of this brain because it is not helping me.

T: Oh, I guess I can believe that because there is so much up in the air for you that you don't have any control over. You can't be the boss over it and make it work out the way you want to!

Marie, when Sarah was little she couldn't be the boss. She couldn't make Mummy and Daddy stop fighting. I am guessing that she really wants to be the boss now so she doesn't have to be scared. (Sarah playing quietly beside the couch) If she can make things happen the way she wants things to happen, then she doesn't have to be scared. Ohhhhh, how smart is that. How smart is your kid!

M: Very.

S: I want to live with my mother! [Sarah is throwing out another theme that we could have potentially explored, but I want to end with the reframing of needing to be the boss and its link to being scared. There have been a few times in the session where Sarah has made reference to her ambivalence towards her mother and I make the decision that it can wait until a subsequent session. I do, however, want to accept her comment and so say.]

T: Oh, is that kind of confusing? Wow! Thanks for telling me that; that's got to make you all kinds of confused inside.

S: When are you done talking so I can play!

T: (playfully) One more thing! (more serious tone) Thank you so much for telling me about your thoughts and feelings and letting me know a little about your life today. Now it's time to play!

It is always remarkable to me how quickly children respond to attunement, co-regulation of their affect, and the creation of concordant intersubjective experiences. With this kind of structuring of the session, Sarah was able to return time and time again to her narrative and I was able to introduce the themes of feeling that she was a bad kid and that she felt her mother's inadequacies were her fault. We were also able to reintroduce the concept of needing to be the boss as a strength that made sense given how much was out of her control when she was little. Sarah didn't fully integrate this different experience of her need for control in this session, but at least it was an introduction to how behaviors that were typically perceived by others and Sarah, as negative, were actually positive adaptations to her environment. She is very articulate for a five-year-old and was able to tell me very clearly how scared and angry she was during the fighting. She was also clearly able to tell me when I was lacking attunement and asking her to do something that was too hard!

There was not as much interaction between Marie and Sarah as I would have liked, although Marie was attentive, warm, and engaged nonverbally. It was clear that I needed to have had another session with Marie to help her understand more clearly what to expect from a Dyadic Developmental Psychotherapy session. Marie would need help in the coming weeks recognizing how she could help Sarah with her fear by taking more control and supporting Sarah in allowing her to make more decisions for her. As we began to address this, Sarah became worried and, consequently, more angry and demanding as she tried to regain the control that Marie was beginning to exert. Marie was also able to respond to Sarah with greater empathy and understanding of her fear, which allowed for the development of a more secure base. [*Editor's note: This illustrates the primacy of parents and how important it is to work with parents first so that the parent can facilitate and support the work with the child.*]

This initial session utilized a number of Dyadic Developmental Psychotherapy components such as follow-lead-follow, co-regulation of affect, co-creation of meaning, talking for and talking about, PACE, creation of a coherent narrative, and some affective/reflective dialogue. The main goal was to develop an alliance with Sarah and to create a sense of safety through attunement and co-regulation of her affect. However, the session also shows how exploration and integration can occur early and the lovely positive feedback loop between safety, exploration, and integration.

Chapter Five

Developing the Alliance (and Much More): A Surprising First Session

Mary-Jo Land, CPT

Sally is an almost five-year-old child adopted at the age of three years. She lives with her mother, father, and sister Mia, who is nine. Mother is an insurance broker while Father is a machinist. Both parents are highly committed to Sally and to working to create a deep attachment with their daughter. Mother, somewhat more so than Father, takes the lead in learning about Sally's needs and getting resources for Sally. Both parents are committed to learning about therapeutic parenting. Mother is especially keen to have all of the professionals involved with her daughter aware of how Sally's life experiences impact her current functioning in school and daycare. Even though the adoption is finalized, the child protective agency provided for my services through a post-adoption subsidy. Mother was able to shift away from typical behavior-focused parenting while Father was more influenced by the opinions of the extended family who were proponents of "typical" rather than therapeutic parenting. This created some conflict between the parents.

Sally was born to a young mother with a history of involvement with Children's Aid Society (CAS). This young birth mother was attempting to make a go in life with Sally's birth father but their continued use of illegal substances and failure to utilize the services offered to them precluded their continued care of Sally, resulting in her apprehension by the CAS. A few times, Sally stayed with her maternal grandmother for weeks at a time during her first year. She was apprehended from her birth mother when the police were called for a domestic dispute between her birth mother and her birth father. When Sally was twelve months old, at Christmastime, she was placed in a foster home. For the next year, Sally lived in the foster home; however, her birth grandmother submitted a plan to take custody of Sally. This plan was abandoned when the CAS learned through the police responding to another domestic violence call that grandmother was allowing Sally to have access to her birth mother. The agency petitioned for Crown Wardship (termination of parental rights) and placement for adoption. Sally's last visit with her grand-mother was just before Christmas and her second birthday.

Sally remained in the same foster home where she lived with a few other foster children, some of whom had fairly dysregulated and socially inappro-priate behaviors. At nearly three years of age, Sally was eligible for adoption and matched with her adoptive family. There was an extended visitation schedule that ended with placement just prior to Christmas.

The pattern for this child throughout her first three years was instability and inconsistency in caregiving. Her birth mother was unable to provide adequate care. She had several caregivers and several homes before her adoption with all of her major transitions occurring at Christmastime. Sally was witness to domestic violence and police intervention in her home. She was placed in a foster home where there was a less than optimal and calm environment. Sally went back and forth between her foster home and her adoptive home over the course of several weeks despite her increasing distress. Sally clearly wanted to remain in the adoptive home after her first few visits; she was consistently upset and protesting when returned to her foster home.

Sally's adoptive parents approached me because they were concerned about their daughter's behavior. She was often aggressive with other chil-dren at school, very controlling at home with her family members, anxious in many situations, and highly anxious in general as demonstrated by pick-ing her skin, biting her nails, sucking on clothing, and twirling her hair. She also exhibited several idiosyncratic repetitive behaviors with her fingers and hands. At times, Sally would cling to her parents when out in public, while at other times she would leave their side and be unaware of their location. At home, Sally was often behaviorally out of her own control and demonstrated periods of intense anger and at other times deep sadness. Sally had hours and sometimes a whole day of intense emotion and hyperactivity. Some of her more inappropriate behavior was clearly imitative of children in her foster home even after almost two years of placement. One year after her placement in the adoptive home, as Christmas approached, Sally's behavior deteriorated. As the next winter approached, Sally's behavior grew even more concerning. The family began to search for assistance for their daughter. [*Editor's note: The history and current functioning in relationships at home, school, and in the community suggest that Sally has a disorganized pattern of attachment—complex trauma.*]

I met with the adoptive mother and father twice for two hours. The first session was primarily to take the history and the second was to discuss the ef-fects of this type of early experiences on a child's development. I introduced therapeutic parenting and provided a reading and resource list. Primarily, I asked the parents to focus on re-regulating Sally's emotions in the context of her life experiences rather than good/bad behavior.

The following is the third session, but the first with Sally present in the session.

TRANSCRIPT OF SALLY: SESSION 1

As Sally and her (adoptive) mother enter, creating safety begins right away thanks to my large dog, who is heard barking. As I squat to take her coat, I assure Sally that he is away and will not come upstairs. As she comes into the office, we chat about the deer she saw as she came to my house. Mum and Sally sit at opposite ends of the couch.

Creating an Alliance

MJ: (squatting in front of Sally and looking at her shirt) What does it say on your shirt?

(Sally looks down at the letters she can't read yet but might know what is said there. She stretches it out for me to read.)

MJ: (pointing to each word, without touching her) "If no one saw me, I didn't do it!" That's a funny shirt! [verbal-nonverbal dialogue: I am using a close proximity, a near touch, and a bright, smiling face, with a cheerful, fun tone of voice.]

Sally: (big smile, letting me know it is OK to be that close to her)

MJ: Who's this little monkey? (touching the monkey on her shirt) Is that a little monkey like you? (with smiling, high-pitched voice)

Sally: (smiling, giggling) No, I'm not a little monkey!

MJ: You're not a little monkey?!

Sally: (smiling) No!

MJ: (still squatting in front of Sally, agreeing) You're not a little monkey! What's this beautiful thing on your hand? (pointing to and touching a butterfly sticker on her hand) [*Editor's note: Here we see an example of follow-lead-follow. The therapist is building an alliance with Sally and creating psychological and relational safety by following Sally's lead. Mary-Jo's playful and engaging interaction helps begin to put Sally at ease.*]

Sally: A sticker.

MJ: Where did you get that sticker? (voice is soft and wondrous)

Sally: At dance.

MJ: At dance! Did you go to dance today? [I am wondering about her sense of time.]

Sally: No, I went on Friday. [I note that she knows that she goes to dance on Fridays and therefore has some sense of days of the week and her routines.]

MJ: Yesterday. Wow, would you like to show something that you learned at dance? Maybe you could teach me something you learned at dance. [I back up, expecting her to jump at this opportunity since she is often very active and rambunctious at home.]

(Sally looks down into her lap.)

MJ: (much more tentative) Would you like to show me one thing? (standing up and inviting her)

(Sally shakes her head. I realize I completely miscued with her. My expectation of an outgoing, highly active child is not accurate at this moment. My efforts at creating an alliance are going off track.)

MJ: No? (softly) Are you feeling a little shy? (squatting down again) [*Editor's note: This comment by the therapist is an example of reflection. By reflecting back to the client what the therapist feels the client is experiencing, the therapist can enhance the client's own reflective function. In this instance, Sally may not even know what she is feeling until the therapist verbalizes this for her.*]

Mum: That's unusual. She's not normally shy.

MJ: (brightening) That's OK. Maybe later, before you go, you could show me one thing.

(Sally looks down at her sticker.)

Mum: What kind of dance do you do?

Sally: Tap.

MJ: (I drop my voice almost to a whisper, working to get the alliance again.) But you're feeling a little shy right now. And that's all right. (Sally nods, looking in my face. She and I attend to her sticker which she takes off and on.) [*Editor's note: This is a good example of the use of PACE and reflection to develop and maintain the alliance. This is in preparation for deeper exploration to follow later in the session.*]

[I want her closer to her mother as I see that she is feeling shy. (Here I am working to keep her affect regulated by Mum's closer proximity and touch.)]

MJ: (in a bigger, animated voice) So, you are sitting WAAAAY over here and your mum is sitting WAAAAY over there. I want you to sit close to your mum. So, Mum, why don't you sit here and Sally can sit right beside you. Sometimes I need to sit here. (Mum gets up and moves to the other end of the couch; I sit on the couch.)

MJ: Are you going to skooch in next to your Mum? (Sally cozies right up next to Mum and holds the arm Mum has put around her.)

MJ: (softly) Oh, that is so lovely! Do you love to hug your mum? (Sally nods) You do. (very softly) Wow, that is beautiful. (pausing to let the feeling of love and warmth be felt by both mother and child) [*Editor's note: By reflecting (part of the affective/reflective component of Dyadic Developmental Psychotherapy), Mary-Jo deepens the affective experience. This reflection amplifies the emotion, which is necessary for exploration and integration.*]

MJ: You know what I know about you? (Sally shakes her head) I know that in a couple of weeks it is going to be a big day for you, isn't it? (Sally nods) It's going to be your birthday. (Sally nods again, still cuddled up against Mum, with Mum's arm around her, but looking fully into my face.) And how old are you going to be?

Sally: (holding up five fingers) Five.

MJ: (with excitement) Five! Can I count how many that is? [I am making this an opportunity to touch in a playful way. I touch each finger and thumb in turn.] One, two three, four, five. You're going to be five years old! Are you excited about being five years old? (nods) What do you think you will have for your birthday? A party? (nods) Who would you like to be at your party? [I am fishing to see if she will list family or friends first. Who is top of mind?]

Sally: Chrissy.

MJ: Chrissy?

Sally: Yeah.

MJ: And who else?

Sally: Kimberly.

MJ: Anyone else? (Sally thinks) What about this lady sitting beside you? (with animation and smiles)

Sally: Yeah! Mummy!

Mum: And your sister?

Sally: Mia!

MJ: And Daddy? Would you invite Daddy too? (Sally nods)

Sally: Daddy! [This is a very verbal child using one- or two-word responses, whose anxiety is creating some regression. Sally touches my leg with her toe.]

MJ: Oh! What is this? Is this a little foot over here? (smiling, I wiggle her foot.) Is it a tickly foot? (I give it a tickle.) [Here touch and play create positive affect and close proximity which develops the alliance.]

Sally: No. (giggling)

MJ: Is it a tickly foot, Mum? [I want to show how Mum knows her girl, since she was obviously ticklish.]

Mum: Oh, she's ticklish all right. Aren't you? (Mum tickles her and Sally laughs. This shows me they enjoy tickling. Sally continues to laugh and to sit leaning against Mum with Mum's arm around her but facing me.)

MJ: So, Sally, I am just wondering if this little foot is as ticklish as this little foot? (tickling each foot in turn) [This is about creating an alliance with play and touch. There are a few more little bits like this, looking for her sticker (which we find together), admiring the braid in her hair and looking at the hole worn into the knee of her pants from playing. In this way, I am noticing her and attending to her. Sally snuggles back up to Mum.]

Sally: MMMMMummy.

MJ: Oh, you love your mummy. (Sally hugs Mummy's arm.)

MJ: You really like to hang on to your mummy, don't you?

Sally: (nodding) Uh huh.

MJ: That was something that I learned from your mum and dad: that you really like to hang on to them sometimes. [And sometimes she recklessly runs away from them in public.]

Sally: (squeezing Mum's arm) Uh huh. [*Editor's note: In this instance the reader is observing a deepening alliance being developed by the therapist as she explores the meaning of Sally's touch. This is a good illustration of how the phases of treatment in Dyadic Developmental Psychotherapy cycle back around in a spiral-like manner, going ever deeper, allowing for deeper exploration, integration, and healing once there is a beginning secure base.*]

(Pause while Sally hugs Mum.)

MJ: So, Sally, I was wondering if you know why you came here today. Why did you come to see Mary-Jo? (She looks a bit blank.) I don't know, that's a funny question. Huh?

Sally: I have a lot of problems. (very softly)

MJ: You have a lot of problems? (gently) Oh! I didn't know that. [That is not the language her parents use with her so I was really curious about what she meant.] [*Editor's note: This is a good illustration of the use of curiosity to find the meaning for the client of some experience. It is a good example of how when the therapist does not understand something or what was said, or what occurred does not make sense to the therapist, that the therapist then needs to accept what the client says, and be curious, until the therapist understands the experience*] *as the client does—empathy.*] What kinds of problems do you have, Sally? (she cuddles into Mum)

MJ: I love the way you cuddle with your mum when you think about your problems.

Mum: It is OK. You can talk with Mary-Jo.

MJ: I didn't know you had a lot of problems. What do you think your problems are? (Sally looks down, shrugs her shoulders) (gently) You're not sure? (slowly) What I know from talking to your mum and dad is that you have some really big feelings. I am not sure I would call them problems. I would call them really big feelings. [*Editor's note: In this comment Mary-Jo is beginning to co-create with Sally a new meaning of the child's behavior, a new meaning that is growth enhancing and that can lead to healing.*]

Mum: What did Mummy say? Do you remember? No? You don't remember? Remember I said Mary-Jo was going to help you with your mad and sad feelings?

MJ: 'Cus sometimes you have some really, really, really big feelings and it's hard to know why they are there. Yeah. Sometimes some really big ones. But you seem to know what to do when you have them 'cus right now you might have some big feelings of being a bit nervous or a little shy and you are hanging onto Mum's arm and getting nice cuddles. Maybe you would like to have Mum's arm all the way around you! Wouldn't that be better? All of Mummy, not just her arm? (Mum puts her arm around Sally) Yeah, let Mummy put her arm all the way around. That's it. Ohhh. Lovely big smile. (Sally snuggles in) That feels so good, doesn't it? [*Editor's note: In this instance the reader can observe the therapist helping Mum co-regulate Sally's affect before going back to the new meaning. This is one of the responsibilities of the therapist—to maintain a healing PACE of treatment.*]

Sally: Mummy. (giggles)

MJ: Ahhh. Very nice. Does that feel good? Does that feel good to be cuddled up with Mum?

Sally: Yeah. (pause)

MJ: So, sometimes you have some really big feelings. But you know I learned another nice thing about you from Mum and Dad. I learned that you sometimes, at night, you like to go and listen to Mummy read Mia stories. You like to hear Mummy's voice while she is reading to Mia, don't you? After you have had your story, you like to go and listen to Mummy's voice. (Sally nods, sitting up straight, looking very intently at me.) So a little later we will have Mummy read you a story, OK? (Sally nods, still interested.) So here is what we are going to do today. We are going to do a few little things. We are going to have some fun and we are going to talk a little bit about those big feelings. (Sally nods) Mum, did Sally have any big feelings this week?

Mum: (nodding) Sally had a LOT of big feelings this week.

MJ: She did?

Mum: It was a big feeling week, wasn't it? (Sally nods)

MJ: It was. Wow. (Sally grabs hold of her mum's arm.)

Mum: Can you explain some of your big feelings?

MJ: Were they fun big feelings or hard big feelings?

(Sally looks ashamed) [*Editor's note: Although feeling some shame, Sally seems to have begun to accept the new meaning of her behavior. The new meaning, which is not pejorative, acts to reduce the amount of shame Sally experiences.*]

Mum: Do you want Mummy to explain? (Sally nods) Were you feeling a bit angry? (Sally nods) And there was lots of sad.

MJ: So there was LOTS of sad (I hold my hands way out to the side, measuring) and a little bit angry? (moving my hands in closer together)

Mum: Well, there was quite a bit of angry too.

MJ: Quite a bit of angry too? Wow. That must have been hard for you.

Sally: Mmmmm. (sitting up, giggling)

MJ: What's funny now?

Sally: She's tickling me.

MJ: Mummy's tickling you! Oh, my goodness! Oh, my goodness, Mummy's tickling you.

Sally: Mummy. I love Mummy. (hugging her arm again, smiling)

MJ: You love Mummy!

Mum: You want cuddles again? (Mum puts her arm around Sally again. Sally snuggles in.)

MJ: So, Mum, maybe you could tell me a little bit about. . . . Maybe we could talk a little bit about the angry feelings. [*Editor's note. When it is difficult for a child, the therapist, as Mary-Jo does here, can move to "talking about" the child. This will often reduce the child's stress and help keep the child regulated.*]

Mum: (to Sally) Do you want to talk about the angry feelings or do you want me to talk about the angry feelings? [I want Mum to talk about the angry feelings because Sally is experiencing enough vulnerability; I don't want to increase her shame.]

Sally: Mummy.

MJ: It's OK if you tell me about the angry feelings, Mum. (light tone)

Mum: (in a tone that is storytelling-like, not at all punitive) Sally was quite angry this week. She had big attitude, I guess. She was beating up on her dolls, and punching them and growling. . . .

MJ: Oh? (with curiosity) Oh boy.

Mum: And having temper tantrums . . .

MJ: Wow!

Mum: And she gave the teacher some attitude. [Here I want to move away from the label "attitude." Here in this session, I want to focus on creating the alliance so I am looking for strengths and positives in the middle of these big feelings.]

MJ: (gently) You were hurting your dolls. (Good eye contact here with me, leaning against Mum, with Mum's arm around her; Sally stays like this for some time.) I am so glad you were hurting your dolls, and not someone else, instead of a person. I am so glad it was dollies that do not feel when they are getting beat up. That would be better than a real person, right? (Sally nods a lot) Yeah. (softly) You were really angry. (Sally nodding) It's those big, big feelings. They just come sometimes? (Sally nodding) And you don't know what to do with them. But what you did was a little bit of beating up of your dollies. (Sally kisses Mum's hand and returns her gaze to me) [*Editor's note: This interchange is a good illustration of the nonverbal elements of the verbal/nonverbal dialogue. Mary-Jo's skillful and insightful "reading" of Sally allows Mary-Jo to keep Sally well regulated as Mary-Jo engages in exploration with Sally of an emotionally difficult experience.*]

Mum: And that's what Mummy and Daddy explained to her, that that is better than hitting her sister, but she can also come and get cuddles and hugs.

MJ: (animated) Oh! Oh! Just like you are doing now! Getting cuddles when you are feeling a little bit of big feelings. [Sally is now waving Mum's limp hand at me, smiling. I will accept that she wants a break and will follow her lead on this.] Is Mummy's hand waving at me? (Sally giggles and waves it more.) Hello, Mummy's hand! (I imitate the waving with my own hand, laughing.) Hi, Mummy's hand! (we all laugh; Sally skooches in closer to Mum, hugging her arm, giggling) Mummy's hand is silly, eh?

Mum: (tries to get on track again) Yes, there were a few days this week when Sally had some really big sad feelings. [Sally keeps waving and I keep playing with that.]

Sally: It's wobbly. It's falling off.

MJ: Oh no! We wouldn't want Mummy's arm to fall off. That would be terrible.

Sally: Yeah. (laughing)

Mum: Then I couldn't cuddle you!

Sally: Then you would have to use the other hand!

Mum: That wouldn't be very good!

MJ and Mum together: Mummy needs two hands/arms to cuddle you. (laugh)

MJ: Mummy and I think the same about that!

(Sally gets up on her knees and gives Mum a full face-to-face hug.)

Mum: Remember when we were cuddling on the rocking chair?

Sally: That's what we did last night.

MJ: (quietly) When you were having some angry feelings? Or some sad feelings?

[Sally is waving Mum's hand again, but this time I am ignoring as I like where this discussion is going.]

Mum: She was having lots of sad feelings.

MJ: There were sad feelings too. Oh, so there were angry feelings and there were sad feelings.

Mum: Lots of crying. So we cuddled.

Sally: In the rocking chair.

Mum: In your room. [I had asked Mum in the intake sessions to put their rocking chair, which was not used much, into her room and rock her nightly with her stories and when she is upset. Mum is letting me know that she did this.]

MJ: If you need to do any rocking (pointing to the chair beside me) this chair doesn't quite rock but it bounces. So sometimes if you and Mummy want to sit here you can. (I bounce the chair.)

Sally: (pointing at the chair and giggling) That's funny. (cuddles up to Mum again)

MJ: Mmm. You're a giggly girl. [*Editor's Note: Here the reader will observe Mary-Jo using PACE to keep Sally regulated and engaged. This represents a move into exploration by deepening the alliance.*]

(pause)

MJ: So, Mummy, what were the sad feelings all about?

Sally: I don't know.

Mummy: I don't know. She wouldn't tell me. She woke up in a sad mood and she was crying and angry and frustrated all day.

MJ: Oh my.

Mum: There were two different days this week that she was sad all day.

MJ: All day. And did Sally know to come to you to get some hugs and some cuddles? [Again, in intake we talked about using comfort to regulate feelings. Sally is leaning up against Mum.]

Mum: No. She was just not happy all day. Right? (looking at Sally; Sally nods)

MJ: Mmmm. Was Sally having some thoughts that were upsetting?

Mum: I tried to ask her. But either she didn't want to talk about it or she couldn't.

MJ: No. Maybe she just didn't know? [*Editor's note: Mary-Jo is co-creating a new meaning for Sally's behavior by reflecting on it (affective/reflective dialogue), with Mum. This helps Mum develop her reflective function and insightfulness regarding Sally. Helping caregivers develop their insightfulness, reflective function, commitment, and sensitivity are important elements of treatment in this approach. The parents are the keystone to good outcomes.*]

Mum: Sometimes she can talk about it and sometimes she can't. Sometimes Sally is VERY good at talking about it and sometimes . . . she can't.

MJ: I wonder if today is one of those days when she is good at talking about things. (Sally is playing with Mum's fingers; she smiles at me.) Do you think today is one of those days when you are really good at talking about it?

Sally: Uh huh. (nodding, smiling)

Mum: Daddy and Mummy tried to explain to her that it's not about getting in trouble. We like to know what's wrong so we can help. Right?

Sally: (playing with Mum's wedding ring) Does this come off?

Mum: Nope.

MJ: Oh! It's stuck on there!

Sally: It stays on forever? (with amazement)

Mum: Yup!

Sally: I want to wear one of your rings. [A discussion follows about ring size and having her own rings. I allow this diversion, giving her a break for thirty seconds. She snuggles up to Mum.]

MJ: So, I wonder, Mum, if some of these big, big feelings are feelings that come from . . . (Sally burrows into Mum and puts Mum's arm around her.) Oh!

Mum: That feels better.

MJ: I wonder if there was a time in Sally's life when she had so many big, big feelings that she just didn't know what to do with them. And now, they just keep coming back and coming back. . . . [*Editor's note: In this example the reader will observe the exploration phase of treatment. This exploration is possible because the therapist has begun to create a secure base within the treatment setting. The alliance has been developed and is maintained so that exploration can occur.*]

Sally: (leaning against Mum, facing me, looking very sad; she nods)

Mum: Sometimes, the winter makes Sally sad too.

MJ: (very softly) The wintertime.

Mum: Why do you think the winter makes you sad? What are you thinking about?

Sally: Mmm. I don't know.

Mum: You don't know?

MJ: Do you think, Mum, that Sally might be thinking about the times before she came to live with you? (Sally is looking into my face, sitting still, Mum's arm around her, leaning against Mum, holding her hand.)

Mum: I think so.

MJ: You think so? I think Sally thinks so too. (Sally is nodding) I think she is thinking about some of those times before she came to live in your wonderful family. (Sally continues nodding, looking into my face.) You think so? Are you thinking about some of those sad and scary times? (Sally nodding, looking into my face.) There were a lot of sad and scary times. A lot of times when you just didn't know what was going to happen. You didn't know where you were going to live. You didn't know who was going to look after you. (Sally nodding, sitting still, focused on my face.) Sometimes you thought you were going to live with your grandmother. (At this, Sally looks away and down.) And sometimes, you thought you weren't and that was a sad and scary time. (Sally turns and snuggles into her mum; my voice is slow and quiet.) I wonder whether sometimes you miss some of those people you used to live with. (Sally turns back to look into my face and nods.) Yeah? Can you tell me who you miss? People who you don't see any more? (Sally looks down) [*Editor's note: In this instance the reader can observe the beginnings of integration occurring. The integration phase of treatment the reader sees here is built on the exploration that has occurred, which is firmly grounded in the alliance Mary-Jo has created with both Sally and Mum. This is a good illustration of how many of the phases can occur within the very first session.*]

Mum: Who do you miss, honey?

Sally: (turning to Mum and hugging her) I just miss you. (looking very sad)

Mum: I'm right here.

MJ: Oh.

Mum: Do you miss Diane? (foster mother)

MJ: She said she misses you. I wonder if that means that you worry that you might not see Mummy, that you might miss her sometime in the future? (Sally nods, looking back at me) This mummy is never, never going to go away. You are with this mummy and this daddy and this sister for ever and ever. (pause) You don't have to worry about not being with this mummy. (I rub her leg reassuringly; she is looking very sad.) Do you sometimes worry about that? (Sally nods) Yeah. You do? (Mum hugs her) Mummy and Daddy love you so much. You want to sit on Mummy's knee? You want to get closer to Mummy? (Sally nods) That's lovely. Is your arm OK? It's kind of stuck back here. Do you want to tuck it under Mum? (She moves in closer to Mum but turns to look at me, expectantly.) So I think that's where some of those big, big feelings come from. (Sally nods and settles into Mum to hear her story.) I think they come from thinking about the old days . . . the days before you came to this family. (Sally continues nodding) There were so many big feelings back then . . . and I think you didn't have this mummy's arms around you to help you with those feelings back then . . . and you wanted this mummy's arm around you to help you feel better when you were sad . . . when you were scared . . . when you were angry. (Sally nodding, Mum stroking her hair gently) You were confused; you didn't know what was going on. (Sally nodding and looking very sad; I shift to talking with Mum to reduce the intensity of emotion that Sally is experiencing, giving her a break.) You know, Mum, I think your daughter had a lot of hard days. [*Editor's note: The outcome of the exploration and integration phases here is that the therapist is co-creating with Mum a new meaning for Sally's behavior. The outcome of this is healing.*]

Mum: (emotionally) I think she did too. (stroking Sally's hair)

MJ: I think she didn't know who she was going to live with.

Mum: I think she was scared a lot of the time.

MJ: I think she was.

Mum: (to Sally who is moving to sit up) I think you were scared when you lived with Gramma and Diane. Do you want to sit on my lap? (Sally nods; Mum puts Sally on her lap, hugging her, facing me.) Is that better, honey? (Sally nods, still looking sad, still engaged intently but not speaking.)

MJ: Do you remember visiting with Gramma? Some days it was fun and some days it was scary? (Sally nodding) Do you miss Gramma? (Sally shakes her head no decisively) No, you don't. [I guessed wrong here and Sally was able to correct me. I thought she was grieving the loss of her grandmother and foster mother, but I was wrong.] You don't miss Gramma? (Sally shakes her head) Because it was scary? (Sally nods) You had a lot of scary times, eh? (Mum is rocking her and rubbing her back) But you are not going to go back to see Gramma. (firmly) [*Editor's note: This interchange illustrates how if the therapist is accepting of the client's experience, and is not trying to push an interpretation on the client, that the client will be able to correct the therapist. This is the core of the Dyadic Developmental Psychotherapy component of the co-creation of meaning.*]

(pause while Mum rocks Sally)

MJ: Your daughter's face is a little sad, Mum. (Mum can't see her face; she is still lying with her back against Mum's chest, being hugged and rocked by Mum, looking at me.)

Mum: I'm sorry she's sad.

MJ: (quietly) Those were hard days. [*Editor's note: This is an example of empathy.*]

Mum: Remember Mummy said I was sorry that you had to go through that, that you are safe with us now, right? (Sally turns into Mum and smiles)

MJ: Ohhh, that gave her a big smile!

Mum: You're safe with us now.

MJ: Mmm, big smile.

Sally: Mummy. (Mum turns Sally to hug her face to face, smiling, rocking.)

MJ: Oh, heart to heart hug. Oh yes.

Mum: Big hug.

MJ: Oh, that's beautiful. Mummy and Daddy love you so much.

Mum: This is how we were hugging last night, only you were laughing, not sad. Remember?

Sally: Mm, mm.

Mum: Do you remember what you said? (Sally looks to her mum) Do you remember? (Sally looks blank) You said no one ever cuddled you like that before. (Mum now has her cradled in her arms, rocking and looking in her face.)

MJ: (sadly) No one ever cuddled her like that.

Mum: That must have made you really sad, didn't it? But now you get cuddles like that, don't you?

MJ: Oh what a big smile.

Mum: And sometimes, you, me, Daddy and Mia cuddle. (getting animated)

MJ: Everybody?! (animated) (Sally is sitting up now between Mum and me.)

Mum: Everybody.

MJ: Everybody cuddles.

Sally: (looks at Mum) (with resolve) And if I move we are all going to move.

Mum: That's right! Explain what you are talking about because Mary-Jo doesn't understand. (Sally climbs back into Mum's arms, arms around Mum's neck, hugging and rocking.) We were talking the other day about moving and I was explaining to her that she is never going to move and that if she does move, we all move together.

MJ: Ohhh. Are you moving?

Mum: No. I was explaining we are one family. She's never going to move families. No more moving families.

MJ: Is someone at school moving?

Sally: (shakes her head) No.

Mum: I think it is just "moving" time of year. [Wow, great, Mum! She is really getting how Sally's repeated moves at Christmastime cause Sally to feel like she is about to move at this time of year.]

MJ: Yes. Moving time of year. Brings back those memories of moving.

Mum: Yes, you didn't like it when you had to go back and forth. (Sally gets up and starts walking) Where are you going? Do you still want cuddles? (She nods and sits down next to Mum on the other side.) What were you telling Mummy the other night at dinner? Do you remember? That you didn't like it when you were going back and forth to Diane's.

MJ: Ohh.

Mum: That scared you, didn't it, because you didn't know?

MJ: You were worried about moving a lot.

Mum: She was very confused because she would spend the day with us, then the night with them, going back and forth, every night. I think it confused her a lot. It must have been really scary.

MJ: That was very, very scary and confusing. (Sally is sitting beside Mum, with Mum's arm around her.)

Mum: Right? Does the winter and the snow remind of that sometimes? (Sally nods) Yeah? [Sally gets up again, standing. I think she has had enough. We have talked about this hard stuff for ten minutes.]

MJ: Did Sally come to your family during the winter and the snow? [co-creation of meaning]

Mum: Yes.

MJ: Was that last winter?

Mum: Two winters ago.

MJ: Two winters ago. Wow, Sally's got a really good memory.

Mum: Yeah.

MJ: I think Sally's getting a little restless.

Mum: Yeah.

MJ: So I have a little game we could play. (Sally looks at me excitedly) Oh! (laughing) Are you excited? (with animation; Sally hugs Mum again) Your mum knows you waaaay better than I do. I made a little snack for you but I don't know if you like it. So, Mum, does your daughter like tangerines?

Mum: Yes.

MJ: She does. You know her so well. Does your daughter like blueberries?

Mum: Yes.

MJ: We are going to play a little game with tangerines and blueberries. Do you know what it is called?

Sally: What?

MJ: It's called Birdie Feeding!

We are now halfway through the session. The rest of the session is spent doing three different activities:

1. Birdie Feeding: Mummy Bird feeds Baby Bird one piece of food directly into her mouth, controlling the rate of feeding and the size of the portion, while Sally sits on her lap, face to face. I hope that Sally looks into her eyes and I encourage this but do not require it. From the history, I knew that Sally often gorged her food, especially when anxious. I wanted to use this nurturing and fun way of eating and playing to create joy in the session. During this feeding Sally hugs Mummy and tells her she loves her. We talk about how Sally likes and eats healthy food in this family. Mummy tickles her a bit. I talk about Sally's beautiful blue eyes. We talk a little bit about Sally's gorging food from not enough food in her home when she was little. I suggest Birdie Feeding if she is gorging. Mum told me about her change in diet by rejecting her old diet and accepting the new healthy diet. We talked about getting hugs and cuddles when the big feelings come and how Sally didn't know to do that when she came to live with this family. This is done in a light tone, more storytelling-like.

2. Story in the Bouncing Chair: Mum has Sally sits on her lap and reads *The Bean Seed* by Robert Spottswood (2005), which we don't process very much because I think she has had enough deep work for the first session.

3. Rocking in a Blanket: We talked about how rocking can be really soothing if Sally has really big feelings. If Sally is too upset to allow intimate
   hugging, she may be able to tolerate rocking in a blanket. I had Sally lie
   down on a blanket with her head toward me and her feet toward Mum, so
   she could see Mum. I picked up two corners and Mum picked up the other
   two corners and we rocked Sally in the blanket, very gently.

This session was successful in my opinion because Sally was able to begin
to develop an alliance with me, was able to respond to the strategies used by
Mum and me to regulate her affect, was able to begin to explore and she was
able to co-create some new meaning for the hurt and confusion of her past
experiences. Sally left wanting to come again after she experienced more joy
than sadness or anxiety through the session.

Chapter Six

Hello, Norma Jean!

Craig W. Clark, MFT

Carol met Norma Jean after attending a meeting at the local children's shelter. The moment she first saw Norma Jean's beautiful face, with her stunning deep blue eyes that were full of light and life, she felt the renewal of her heart's desire to have a child of her own.

Carol is a thirty-three-year-old single woman who currently has no adult partner. She is a psychotherapist, employed by the county Department of Family and Children's Services (DFCS) in their child mental health unit. Norma Jean was almost seven and in desperate need of a home. It was the second time in just a year that she was forced to call the children's shelter her home. She missed her family. Only her younger brother was brought to the shelter. Her other siblings were placed elsewhere. Her parents could only visit for an hour every other week. She was feeling lost, sad, and confused, but mostly it was anger that she shared with others when she just couldn't take it any longer.

Carol was adopted at age two and a half. She has one older sister and two brothers, one older and one younger (adopted). Her father was hard-working, but emotionally distant and strict with his children. Her mom worked part-time in a small flower shop to make a little extra money. She was not always available to watch over the children. When this happened, it was the older sister who was the surrogate mom. Carol's older siblings were both in their mid- to late teens when Carol was twelve. This is when her older brother began to be sexually involved with Carol. She was always afraid to tell her parents, fearing her father's anger and what she imagined he would do to punish his son. By the time Carol was fourteen, she could not quell the feelings that had been aroused in her and she began a sexualized relationship with her younger brother, who was then twelve. Her mother discovered this sexual behavior between Carol and her younger brother. Her father beat her in front of her siblings. She has never forgiven her father or her older brother, whom she never exposed.

Norma Jean lived with her birth parents and a younger brother for the first four years of her life. The family had become homeless and frequently changed camping locations. At age four she was removed by Child Protective Services and placed in a children's shelter. Two weeks later, Norma Jean and her younger brother were placed with an emergency foster family. This placement failed after ten days due to the difficult behaviors of the children. They suffered frequent, extended tantrums, and acted out sexually between themselves and the other two children in the home. Norma Jean and her brother were returned to the children's shelter where they remained for another two weeks. At the shelter, they were physically aggressive to adults and peers. Norma Jean became a noted behavior problem at school, where she was hard to control and destroyed school property. The problems escalated until the school suspended her.

During this second stay in the shelter, Norma Jean's DFCS caseworker learned that Carol was a potential foster mother for Norma Jean. The siblings were separated the following week and Norma Jean was placed with Carol. She was nearly seven years old at the time of placement.

Norma Jean's behavior toward Carol was often very violent. She would swear, hit, kick, and bite whenever she felt she would not get what she wanted at that moment. This behavior was very much a problem because she was tall and strong for her age and apparently could not stop her aggressive behavior once it began. In spite of her struggles to control Norma Jean's behavior, Carol became very fond of Norma Jean and came to believe that she could help her to resolve her trauma and modify her aggressive behaviors. Carol asked the caseworker to change the placement to a foster/adoptive placement. Carol and Norma Jean finalized the adoption seven months later.

There were two prior therapists before they came to me for Dyadic Developmental Psychotherapy. The first treatments were with a play therapist and the second therapist utilized a cognitive/behavioral approach.

The session presented in this chapter is the twentieth dyadic session in a six-month period. Additional individual sessions were held with Carol to provide support and help with parenting issues.

CASE TRANSCRIPT AND COMMENTARY

Craig: Hello, Norma Jean, how 'ya doin today?

Norma Jean: What's that? (looking at couch and chair together)

Craig: I moved it a little closer, so you could sit there and Mom could sit on the couch.

Norma Jean: Hee heee hee. (giggles, jumps onto chair, takes off her shoes and places them on the chair, giggles and looks at me)

Craig: Is that a present for her [Mom]? Let's see, the shoes belong on the floor. Let's put them right here. (places them nearby under a side table, out of the way)

Norma Jean: (lies down on the couch as Mom enters the room, taking up the entire length and covers herself with a blanket). They're not mine. (referencing her shoes; she has now covered her entire body with a blanket, including her face)

Carol: Hello. (Mom to Norma Jean, as she sits down in the chair)

Craig: (with heightened expression) Uh, where did she go??? (we now have a peek-a-boo game enacted)

[Note: In this session I am attempting to use the rearranged furniture to encourage closer proximity of the parent and the child while allowing for an option of being seated separately. In previous sessions where they shared a small couch, Carol and Norma Jean have found it difficult to monitor and maintain physical proximity that offered intimacy while affording each person to feel in control of their sense of safety and trust. By leaving her shoes on the chair where her mom will sit and lying down on the couch, Norma Jean seems to be nonverbally expressing her desire to keep her mom from finding a place in the room. At the start of this session, Mom is checking her cell phone and turning it off, making very little contact with either me or her daughter. I experience resistance and mild defiance from Norma Jean and have not yet connected with the parent. We are all seated at some distance from each other.]

[*Editor's note: This is a good illustration of the difficulties a therapist may face in a session. Norma Jean is somewhat dysregulated and Carol appears somewhat disengaged. This may be a microcosm of their relationship dance. Craig now has the task of creating a safe base and engaging both mom and child in a therapeutic alliance.*]

Carol: Where's Norma Jean? [*Editor's note: PACE is being illustrated. By being playful, Craig engages Norma Jean and models for Carol how to engage her child. This will serve to create the safety necessary to maintain the alliance and, later in the session, begin exploration.*]

Craig: I heard that she was here, and that she has had a very special event.

Norma Jean: No! (lifts blanket and looks at Mom, speaking emphatically)

Craig: No special event. (said with even affect, with a slight questioning tone)

Carol: No special event. (distracted with a large envelope) Well, what's this? What would you call it then? (pulling out photos)

Norma Jean: I would call it super, super dumb. (covers her face with blanket again)

Craig: Well, wait a minute, what is this? (rolling over to be closer to Norma Jean and puts on reading glasses to see the photos)

Norma Jean: No, no. (moaning, pleading tone as the photo of Norma Jean and her mom is passed to Craig)

Craig: It's OK if you want to take a break under the blanket. (soothing tone) Mom and I will just visit for a minute. [*Editor's note: When a child is becoming dysregulated, "talking about" can reduce the level of affect and allow the child to become calmer. Clearly Norma Jean is not dysregulated now, as she is coherent and, in her own way, engaged with Craig and Carol.*]

Carol: Well, OK. (agreeable)

Norma Jean: I can still hear you two. (lifting blanket to look at me).

Craig: Well, we'll be quiet. (reaching over to gently touch her on the head as she lays back down, Mom watching, focused on the interaction) How's that?

Norma Jean: (throwing off blanket, reaching over to grab the photo from Craig) That's mine!

Craig: Wait a minute, is that you? (said with amazement, pulling photo away from her reach and making eye contact with Norma Jean, who is smiling back at Craig)

Craig: Let me look again . . . haaah (with amazement), is that really you? (steady eye contact with Norma Jean and incidental hand-to-hand contact with our hands as they are draped on the edge of the couch) Two front teeth, two eyes, blue eyes . . .

Carol: Yes, beautiful blue eyes. (looking toward Norma Jean)

Craig: Hair cut very stylishly, yes. (compares photo to Norma Jean with each statement of similarity) Nice smile.

[Note: I am setting a rhythm with each statement and moving up vocal pitch and intonation in an attempt to establish and encourage greater intersubjectivity. Norma Jean glances between the photo (of herself with adoptive mom) and me, now with greater focus and calm attention.]

Craig: I think I know this girl; and who is that woman standing over her . . . Oh! That looks a lot like Carol. (with amazement)

[Note: I now move a little closer, focused on Norma Jean's face to further establish our intersubjectivity. Norma Jean has looked away and thrown her left arm back in a semi–back arch move. I pause, maintain my proximity to her and make brief contact with her right hand, providing expression of concern about her reaction. She has been expressing her anxiety since entering the room and now it has reached a level that requires co-regulation or she will elevate her affective responses and will escalate and prevent expression and exploration of her narrative.]

[*Editor's note: In a difficult and complex case such as this one, it is imperative that the therapist continually monitor the state of the alliance as Craig is doing. In this portion of the transcript we are primarily observing how Craig is working in developing the alliance and maintaining the alliance phases.*]

Carol: That is an awesome mom!

Norma Jean: She's not awesome! (pointing her finger directly at Carol)

Carol: I'm not?

Craig: (sighs audibly, turning back from photo to face Norma Jean)

Norma Jean: You're good. (smiling at Carol with eye contact)

Carol: Oh. OK.

Craig: Is good, good? [*Editor's note: Craig's use of curiosity is another way to keep a child both focused and regulated.*]

Carol: Um hm. (agreeing that good is good) Here's another handsome picture. (I start to hand photo to Carol)

Norma Jean: Urgh. (complaint, lurches forward to grab it roughly) Ahhhh! (lays back down, pulling up blanket in protest)

Carol: Do you want to show him that one?

Norma Jean: No! (pulling away from Carol, scrunching further into couch)

Carol: You don't??? (with incredulity)

Craig: Well, I've got one that is very nice. (soothing tone of voice) [*Editor's comment: This illustrates the use of verbal-nonverbal dialogue. Using tone of voice, facial expressions, cadence, and other nonverbal cues, Craig is able to co-regulate Norma Jean's affect.*]

Carol: We got to make those; they took that picture of us and we made those frames. Then Norma Jean wanted to put a picture of her birth family in the one she made for her Mommy Sophie. So I made a picture of her mom, her brothers and sister . . . so that's who is in that picture.

Craig: So I see. So that's the one she's protecting. (referring to photo Norma Jean is hiding under blanket)

Carol: Yes.

Norma Jean: But you don't know who's in it! (peeks over at Craig, while Craig looks at another copy of the family photo)

Craig: (Norma Jean peaks at Craig from under blanket) No, I don't. (said with resignation) Maybe you'll show me sometime, when you're ready. (said with affirmation)

Norma Jean: What?!

[Note: I used a paradoxical statement about the future possibility of her showing the photo when she is ready, suggesting that the client will act to share the photo in the future when she feels enough trust and safety.]

Carol: This morning, we got to read a book in her class; I got to read a book in her class. (hands more photos to Craig) And so we passed around these pictures as we told the story. (Norma Jean now looking out from under blanket, observing the interaction)

Craig: Well, let's see what's going on here. (looking at another photo) This looks like Norma Jean sitting in a judge's chair?

Norma Jean: No.

Craig: That's a pretty nice chair you've got there! With a big seal on the wall, says state, the Great Seal of the State of California.

Norma Jean: A seal?

Carol: That's what they call the emblem . . . the round, sticker kind of thing that's on the wall.

Craig: That's not you? (heightened curiosity)

Carol: See, Norma Jean. (holds up another photo) The great Seal of the State of California. (leaning forward toward Norma Jean, holding out photo; Norma Jean looks from a distance and does not take the photo from Carol)

Norma Jean: Oh.

Carol: That's what that is.

Craig: Oh, I see . . . Norma Jean, what was it like to sit in that chair? [*Editor's note: In this exchange we observe another example of Craig setting the rhythm and tone by using curiosity as a means of co-regulating Norma Jean's affect.*]

Norma Jean: Cool.

Craig: Was it a nice chair? [*Editor's note: Now Craig uses the follow part of follow-lead-follow to try to maintain the very fragile alliance being built between him and Norma Jean.*]

Norma Jean: Yeah.

Craig: Yeah. . . . Did you get to stay in it very long?

Norma Jean: No.

Carol: We just went up there to pose for pictures.

Craig: Now when you were up there, who were you looking out at? Who was over there when you sat in that chair? Who did you see? (Norma Jean looks at photo with Craig)

Norma Jean: LOTS of people! (begins to look away)

Craig: Oh really, like who?

Norma Jean: I'm not going to say ANYTHING! (with rapidly heightening affect, squirming on couch, squealing repeatedly, grabbing for remaining photos being held by Mom)

Craig: Oh, you didn't want to tell me about that? I'm sorry. (gestures with hand to add emphasis) Did you tell me you didn't want to say anything? [*Editor's note: This is a nice illustration of interactive repair and that the therapist must assume responsibility of breaches in the developing alliance.*]

Norma Jean: Nooo! No, no, no . . .

Craig: You know what? You know what Mom has?

Norma Jean: Yeah, I'm gonna read it.

Carol: Mr. Craig, Mr. Craig. (trying to interject while Norma Jean is escalating affect)

[Note: Carol enters narrative with an urgent, elevated affect. She attempts to distract me from continuing to follow this narrative, perhaps because she is sensing that her daughter will get out of control.]

Craig: You know what, Mom . . . wait a minute. (touches Norma Jean on shoulder as she leans forward toward Carol, reaching out to take document) [*Editor's note: Craig uses touch in a very sophisticated and titrated manner in this session to regulate an emotionally volatile child.*]

Carol: Listen to Mr. Craig. (pulling document away from Norma Jean, as Norma Jean leans forward, glaring at Carol)

[Note: Carol is attempting to co-regulate her daughter's affect by withholding the document and telling her daughter to follow my directions, but Norma Jean may feel that her mother is not empathizing with her feelings of vulnerability. The effect is to leave the child feeling vulnerable and she implements control language as a defense.]

Norma Jean: Give it.

Carol: Just listen to Mr. Craig.

Norma Jean: Arragh! (screeching voice, like a very young child in protest) I'm gonna read it!

Craig: I'm gonna ask Mom to hold on to it for a minute and I'm going to ask you to tell me what is going on with you right now. (gently touching Norma Jean on shoulder; she responds by looking toward Craig) You look frustrated. (said with voice of concern) [*Editor's note: The previous power struggle between Carol and Norma Jean was escalating toward dysregulation. Craig's intervention illustrates several points: the use of touch and other nonverbal means to regulate the child, intervening in a nonproductive interchange to model a more positive manner of relating, and the creation of a concordant intersubjective experience to increase regulation. The session is still in the maintaining the alliance phase.*]

Norma Jean: Nothing! You're BEESWAX! (looks away, then turns sharply back to look directly at Craig, then away with face in hands)

Craig: I'm concerned. (said with much vocalized empathy) I'm concerned because, you look like you're a little bit disturbed or upset, unhappy or grumpy, or . . .

[Note: I use empathy to help co-regulate Norma Jean's affect and moderate her defensive response. She may feel very isolated due to her mom's attempts to control her perceived oppositional behavior without expressing empathy for her emotional distress. Norma Jean may interpret my continued interest in this narrative of the adoption ceremony as intrusive and insensitive to her, as yet unexamined, and unconsciously (Schore, 2009), nonverbally expressed conflict about alliances with her birth family.]

Norma Jean: I've had enough sleep though!

Craig: You did, didn't . . .

Norma Jean: I did not have enough sleep.

Craig: Is that what's going on . . . you're feeling tired? A little out of sorts?

Carol: She didn't fall asleep until after 11:30 last night. She just couldn't sleep.

Craig: What was keeping you awake, do you know?

Norma Jean: Don't. I told you I'm not going to answer any more questions! (said with anger/frustration; Norma Jean sitting up, agitated, so I place a hand gently on her shoulder)

Craig: No more questions; I tell 'ya what. What would make you comfortable right now?

[Note: Because the client is moving toward increased dysregulation, it would be better to help the client access her inner-state feelings at this time, so a statement rather than a question would be "It must make you worry when you can't sleep."]

Norma Jean: I said no more questions (looks away toward Mom, but avoids eye contact with her; Mom sits very still, with a sad look on her face)

[Note: This situation with Mom looking sad and silent and with Norma Jean headed toward increased affective dysregulation is an example of the challenge that is faced when both the parent and the child simultaneously experience their own unresolved issues and defend against increased vulnerability through use of defenses: evidenced by Norma Jean's use of avoidance and control, and Carol's disengagement.]

Craig: Oh, I thought that was about other stuff. I didn't know that pertained to right now too. 'Cause, I was just trying. . . . You know what, Norma Jean, when you come here, I try to make it comfortable here for you. (Norma Jean leans way over toward me, sticking her tongue out while making direct eye contact with me; Mom sits very still, observing the interaction.) You're sticking your tongue out at me right now. (said with a matter of fact tone of voice) It's like you don't believe me? [*Editor's note: In this intervention by Craig we can observe the use of the reflective function by the therapist to increase both Carol's and Norma Jean's insightfulness and to co-regulate both parent and child. By sharing his intentions, Craig is helping co-create a new meaning for the interaction; a new meaning that may be quite different than Norma Jean's perceptions of an adult's intentions.*]

Carol: I think maybe she wants you to grab it. (said in an earnest, serious manner)

Norma Jean: Heh, heh, heh. (giggling and playing with blanket at her feet, leaning toward Mom; they make eye contact, smiling at each other)

Craig: Well, I don't usually grab tongues, you know. (said with minor incredulity) [*Editor's note: This is a good illustration of being playful.*]

Carol: You're not that kind of a doctor. . . .

Craig: But I don't know if, umm (while lifting blanket and touching Norma Jean on her shoulder with hand wrapped inside the blanket, in a semi-tickling contact), if that meant something by your sticking your tongue out like you were.

Carol: (nods in agreement) Like we used to do when I was a kid.

(Norma Jean turns toward Craig, quite close to each other, and they both stick out their tongues at each other; Norma Jean laughs and turns away after just a couple of seconds to play with her feet, breaking off visual contact with both adults.)

Carol: Like, nah, naah, naaah naaaaah! Like you want someone to go away.

(Norma Jean now sticks tongue out at Mom, shaking her head with emphasis; Mom responds by staring back at Norma Jean with a serious expression.)

Carol: Let me stick my tongue out at you, tease you.

(Norma Jean turns to Craig, sticking out tongue in a playful manner, shaking her head for emphasis; Craig responds in like manner, mirroring Norma Jean.) [*Editor's note: As we can see, this is probably a rather worried child who may be fearful of the effect of emotions on her. One could call that "resistance," but resistance has a negative connotation and leads one to feel negatively toward the person "resisting." Since this fear probably reflects a lack of trust, based on past experiences, there is a very shallow alliance and little secure base evidenced. Craig is using humor (the P in PACE) and touch in very skillful ways to keep Norma Jean engaged and to begin to create a therapeutic alliance.*]

Norma Jean: Heh, heh, heh.

Craig: It's kinda fun, isn't it! (with a subdued, but still playful affect)

Norma Jean: Yeah. (giggles)

Craig: Do you like the blanket? Ooops, that's another question. Sorry. Let me say it this way. It looks like you like the blanket! (Craig touches her on the shoulder; Norma Jean grabs a framed photo, handing it to Craig.)

Craig: And it's one of my favorite blankets. Thank you. (for handing him the photo) And it looks like you like laying on the couch, because that's where you usually come sit, anymore . . . and you sit there.

Carol: (touches Norma Jean's hand)

[Note: Carol's comment suggesting that I would grab Norma Jean's tongue could be interpreted as a threat and served to further escalate her daughter's trend toward dysregulation. It also put me in a situation that needed me to clarify my appropriate physical boundary and to use acceptance and playfulness to help co-regulate the child's anxiety. Carol's reaching to touch her daughter's hand is a desired example of a nonverbal expression of empathy by Carol. In these previous few minutes of the session, Norma Jean has responded positively to my use of PACE as evidenced by her self-regulatory calming and refocusing on the photo that she had initially refused to let me see or to discuss. These changes in affect re-attunement and intersubjectivity are therapeutically helpful.]

Craig: So I kinda moved the furniture around today to make it more comfortable for you and your mom and me to be here . . . so well, sometimes Mom is sitting way over there against the wall in the big chair, and you're sitting over here (on couch) and you're sitting quite a ways apart (Norma Jean, now rocking more with her eyes closed, suddenly kicks at Mom's hand and pulls her foot away from Mom's hand and laughs while pointing at Mom; Mom spontaneously pulls her hand away from Norma Jean, who laughs more and flops onto her back.) This way, Mom's gonna be closer. . . . Oh, did you make Mom move? (Norma Jean giggles, pulling blanket up over her face) You did, huh?! (Norma Jean giggles more) As soon as I said closer, she put her foot up there. [*Editor's note: In this interchange we see Craig using the follow dimension of follow-lead-follow while accepting Norma Jean. However, Norma Jean is continuing to find the interaction upsetting and may be experiencing some shame and anxiety. In this initial phase of building the alliance, Craig is working hard to co-regulate Norma Jean's affect by relying on touch.*]

Carol: I know.

Craig: So maybe that's as close as you want her right now. Is that it? Oops, that is another question. Oh, was that an OK question?! (Craig places hand momentarily on Norma Jean's shoulder; Craig looks at photo) Oh! This is beautiful!

[Note: Further examples of using playfulness and nonverbal gestures of empathic reassurance through gentle, nonintrusive touch, integrated into the ongoing effort to explore the adoption ceremony narrative that is the autobiographical center of this session.]

Carol: I know. Isn't that a beautiful family!

Craig: This is beautiful. And someone made the picture frame so beautiful—very creative.

Norma Jean: I didn't do that. (peeks out from under blanket)

Craig: Did Mom help you with this? [*Editor's note: Knowing what actually happened, Craig ignores Norma Jean's distancing and continues to try to engage her and maintain the growing alliance.*]

Norma Jean: Un huh. (nods yes)

Craig: So, uh, wait a minute, there's that girl with the cute hair and the cute smile. That's somebody I know. [*Editor's note: Being playful and gentle teasing can be helpful in developing the alliance, but with this child it does not appear to have the desired effect.*]

Norma Jean: Noooo!! (scowls in protest).

Craig: Guess not. Looks like . . . It looks like somebody I know. [*Editor's note: Accepting Norma Jean's response and following it allows Craig to enter into her experience, create concordant intersubjectivity, and begin to engage her.*]

Norma Jean: It's my twin.

Craig: Your twin! *Jeanine*? (said with surprise)

Norma Jean: (responds by shaking her head no)

Craig: No? (said with soft, quiet voice)

Norma Jean: (smiles, making eye contact again with Craig) That's my name!

Craig: (responds by sitting more upright, reinforcing eye contact and shared intersubjectivity) I thought you were *Jeanine*! (playfully)

Norma Jean: (shakes head, yes)

Craig: You've changed your name? (surprise)

Norma Jean: (nods yes, smiling and eye contact with Craig and then with Carol)

Craig: That's a pretty name. Shall I call you *Jeanine* now?

Norma Jean: You can.

[Note: Norma Jean is pleased to share her new adoption name, Jeanine, and her agreement for me to use it is a sign that we are once again attuned and are re-engaged in concordant intersubjectivity. The new name also opens another avenue for exploration of her adoption story. What follows is a nicely relaxed and playful engagement with the client.]

Craig: Well, I can. I will try. Sometimes I might slip up and you can just look at me, like Craig, you should know better. Kinda like that. (Norma Jean a.k.a. Jeanine smiles at Craig, giggles gleefully)

Norma Jean: Or like (playfully makes a stern face at Craig).

Craig: Yeah, like that.

Norma Jean: (giggles, pulls hands up to chin)

Craig: Yeah, like you do there. Then I'll go (I point to my head), then I'll go, "Uhhh, Craig, so she has a new name! And it's *Jeanine!*" It's a very pretty name. [*Editor's note: By being playful and accepting, Craig is able to enter into Norma Jean's experience and this becomes a good way to begin to create the alliance. Until there is a secure base in treatment and an alliance, exploration will have to wait. However, creating an alliance, in and of itself, is therapeutic. Craig is demonstrating for Carol how to avoid conflicts and arguments with her daughter, and this is very important work.*]

Norma Jean: Heh, heh, heh. (giggly, smiling broadly, looking at Craig)

Carol: It's actually her old name as well. Right?! (to Norma Jean)

Craig: Hm, *Jeanine*. A new old name. (I nod my head in agreement, looking at Mom)

Carol: It's a new old name.

Craig: A new old name. (echoing Mom's statement)

Carol: Has lots of special meanings. (comment directed at Craig)

Craig: Yeah.

Norma Jean: Yeah. (said louder) It has LOTS of meanings. (comment directed at Mom)

Carol: Lots of things.

Norma Jean: My birth mom said it is the name of an angel. [*Editor's note: In interchanges like these we can see brief forays into the exploration phase and the beginning work of co-creating new meanings and a coherent autobiographical narrative.*]

Carol: Haah, ooooh! (breathily) (eye contact with Norma Jean)

Craig: You know, I didn't know that.

Carol: (Norma Jean, smiling, eye contact, nodding yes, with Carol; Carol has a pleased look) But it's a very fitting name. (looking at another photo, I ask, "Who's this other lady here?")

[Note: I have a choice to make here in the narrative. I could further explore the meanings of the name, the facts, beliefs and motivations of the birth mother for comparing Norma Jean to an angel, or explore with Carol her feelings that are brought up with Norma Jean claiming the name or exploring how she experiences any "angelic" qualities of Norma Jean, etc. Instead what I chose to do was to let these options remain unexplored at this time in order to further establish the secure bases of the therapist with the child.]

Norma Jean: Judge.

Craig: I thought this was the judge? (with playful incredulity, points to another person in the photo)

Norma Jean: No-oh. (smiling broadly, pulling hands up to chin)

Craig: You could've fooled me. Judge always sits in the big leather chair. That's . . . your twin!

Norma Jean: No-oh. (shares eye contact and smiles with Mom)

Craig: This must be somebody who came to the adoption party.

Norma Jean: No-oh. (giggling)

Craig: No-oh. (in agreement)

Norma Jean: He's talking about this one. (takes photo from me and shows it to Mom, pointing to one of the people in the photo)

Carol: Oh, I knew who he was talking about. That's judge . . . Judge De La Rosa.

Norma Jean: My promise to Jeanine.

Craig: My promise to Jeanine?

Carol: Oh, I know what she's talking about, because the judge asked me to repeat after her, and these are the things I said. Can I read it to you? (said to me)

Craig: Please.

Carol: My promise to Norma Jean: I, Carol, solemnly swear to treat Jeanine in all respects as my natural child.

Norma Jean: . . . as my natural child (echoing Mom, smiling broadly at both adults)

Carol: I am prepared to accept this gift of a child to raise and will share my life with her, help to mold your mind, nurture your body, and enrich your spirit. I will never betray your trust. . . . (Norma Jean gets up from couch, wraps the blanket around her like a shawl, steps on and over the arm of the couch, and goes over to the shelves to look at toys.)

Craig: Oooops. Where 'ya goin'?

Carol: Uh oh . . . is this too much, babe? [*Editor's note: This is a good illustration of Carol's reflective function. She is attempting to find meaning in Norma Jean's behavior and make that explicit for Norma Jean. Over time, this will develop Norma Jean's reflective function.*]

Norma Jean: No.

Carol: No?

Craig: Maybe it's a lot. Maybe we should slow down.

Carol: Okay, I can . . . stop. (with empathy, understanding voice)

Craig: We can slow down. (said slower)

Norma Jean: (continues to wander in the back play area of the room)

Carol: Well, I know . . . Jeanine . . . (Norma Jean makes no response to Mom)

Craig: Oh, is there a Jeanine here? (playfully)

Carol: Yes.

Craig: No, I think that's Jeanine over there with the blanket. Hello, Jeanine. (I am trying to regain her attention)

Carol: Norma Jean . . . Jeanine. Norma Jean, Jeanine, NJ. Hi . . . you know I know there's really something you wanted to talk about today. (Norma Jean turns toward Mom; Norma Jean returns holding a marionette puppet.) Oh, you've got puppets, the marionettes. Ohhh . . . is this too much? (holding out the other documents) Do you want me to stop reading? (Norma Jean does not respond to her mom's questions and keeps focused on untangling the marionettes.)

Craig: Well let's just slow down a minute here, and see. [*Editor's note: Craig is managing the emotional temperature in the room and is helping regulate Norma Jean by slowing down the pace of the session. This is an example of the differential use of components of Dyadic Developmental Psychotherapy in the maintaining the alliance phase.*]

Carol: OK.

Craig: I don't know . . . the puppets are all tangled and a mess today.

Norma Jean: Yeah?

Craig: Yeah.

Norma Jean: Could you help me? (hands one of the puppets to her mom to untangle)

Carol: I would love too. Great minds think alike, huh?

Craig: Umhum.

Norma Jean: Yeah.

Carol: You were asking, just as I was saying . . . yes!

Craig: Jeanine. Somehow that name doesn't work.

Carol: I tell you; sometimes it works really well.

Craig: Sometimes it works really well; it's, it's a new name, so maybe it takes time for everybody to get used to it. Oh, except it's a new old name.

Carol: Yeah.

Craig: I didn't know what the old part was. Was that your given name of a long time ago?

Carol: Her birth name.

Craig: Your birth name of a long time ago.

Norma Jean: (shakes her head no)

Craig: Wait a minute; you're shaking your head no? (said with surprise)

Carol: It wasn't your birth name, Norma Jean?

Craig: Where did the name come from?

Norma Jean: That's a question! (looks briefly, accusingly at me)

Craig: You are so right.

Carol: (breathily) You know . . . ?

Craig: No questions. (agreeing with Norma Jean) [*Editor's note: This is a wonderful example of interactive repair, demonstrating that this can occur in a quite brief and defined manner.*]

Carol: You know what, Mr. Craig? If you want to ask me questions, I'd be happy to answer them and then if I give the wrong answer, she might decide (said with play-acted frustration) to tell us.

Craig: Oh, OK. I got it. Well, you're right. But I first wanted to acknowledge the fact that, Norma Jean, you've been so good about catching me asking questions after we agreed that it would be OK not to ask questions. . . . (intentional pause) You're so smart that way. You listen so carefully.

Norma Jean: That's a question! (makes eye contact with me)

Craig: No, it wasn't. That's a statement: you listen so carefully. AND another thing I notice is, you've gotten really good at telling me when I am doing something that I agreed I wouldn't do, so congratulations! (Norma Jean drops onto knees on floor between me and Mom, focusing on her mom's puppet.)

[Note: The marionettes serve to increase the intersubjectivity of the parent/child dyad which has not been developed to the needed level so far in this session. Also, the marionettes have the potential to allow the clients to deepen their shared adoption narrative through externalization of feelings by having the marionette characters speak for them. The clients focus on untangling the marionettes for the next few minutes. Carol reveals the fact that Norma Jean has been stating over the past few days that she misses her birth mother.]

Carol: You know what else, Mr. Craig, along the same lines?

Craig: What?

Carol: She got really good this weekend, at letting me know, I'm missing my birth mom.

Craig: Ohhh.

Carol: She rather . . . just like she did just now, rather than having a fit or acting all silly, she came up to me a couple of different times this weekend and she said, I'm missing . . . my . . . mom!

[Note: What follows for several minutes is that we focus on untangling the marionettes. By taking this break I am focusing on regulating the ebb and flow of the emotional content of the session. I was thinking that by engaging in a common task together we will deepen our alliance and be able to move into the exploration phase and begin discussing her birth mother.]

Craig: So, Mom, that makes sense in a way.

Carol: Perfect sense.

Craig: Thinking about moms. Getting a new mom and becoming a new daughter legally to somebody. That's a lot of changes.

Carol: You and I . . . I just thought of something, Norma Jean. (with much excitement of discovery) You know what? You and I officially have something in common.

Norma Jean: What? (said in a low voice)

Carol: We're both adoptees . . . that's pretty cool.

Craig: Now she knew that about you before?

Carol: Yeah, but we were . . . yes, she did. But now for the fact that we're both now officially adoptees.

Craig: Ah, huh.

Carol: That's really different!

Craig: Ah, huh, ah, huh.

Carol: That's different than before. That's pretty cool, I think! (Still both mom and daughter remain mostly focused on the puppets.) [*Editor's note: The use of the puppets provides some distraction and enables both Carol and Norma Jean to enter into the exploration phase and remain regulated. This is a lovely example of how Craig modulates the level of affect in the session to keep the experience emotionally meaningful without becoming overwhelming.*]

Craig: How old were you when you got adopted?

Carol: I was about three when I was finalized.

Craig: Now Norma Jean, how old are you?

Norma Jean: Seven. (now trading puppets with Mom, no eye contact with me)

Craig: Seven . . . wow!

[Note: I used more expression in this response about Norma Jean's age to attempt to have her focus on me and engage her in a playful manner so we can continue with this topic of them sharing being adoptees.]

Norma Jean: (giggles at Mom's puppet, which she now holds). Doesn't that look like real?

Craig: That looks like a real person. You did a good job of straightening out his strings there.

Craig: So if you're adopted as a baby of two or so, little babies don't know about that idea of adoption. So I was wondering about when you, kinda, figured it out.

Carol: I was about Jeanine's age when I understood it. My parents started telling me when I was four and a half because they wanted to get another child and the social worker said, "Have you told her yet that she's adopted?" And they said, "No." And she said, "If you are planning on telling her, it's now or never." And they said, "Oh no, we're gonna tell her," so they started telling me . . .

Craig: Uh, huh.

Carol: . . . when I was four and a half. So I just kinda grew up with it. I just kinda feel like I always knew. That it was just a normal part of my growing up. But I figured out what it meant when I was her age.

Craig: Wow.

Carol: All of a sudden it just dawned on me . . .

Craig: It made sense . . .

Carol: I am related to someone else out there.

Craig: Yeah. (with empathy). How did you feel about that; you remember? [*Editor's note: In this interchange between Craig and Carol, we see Craig beginning the exploration phase with Carol. By doing this in front of Norma Jean and about something that directly relates to the child, Craig can gently begin exploration with Norma Jean and see if she is ready for that.*]

Carol: Umm, curious and excited. Um, and sad that I didn't know who that person was.

Norma Jean: You didn't know the person? (said in a funny skrunchy little kid voice)

Carol: No. I just knew little things about her. I knew . . .

Norma Jean: He's dead. (said as she laid her marionette on the floor)

Carol: . . . that she was going to be a nurse. And, that only partly turned out to be true.

Craig: Ah huh.

Carol: Not by . . . my parents weren't trying to keep a secret from me or anything; they just went with the information they were told.

Craig: Right. That's what they were told.

Norma Jean: Right.

Carol: Yeah. So . . . but I remember my little brother having lots of emotions as he was growing up. And even as an adult, lots of mixed emotions about being adopted. Being happy to grow up with our family (his adopted family) and sad because he wanted his birth family.

Craig: Um hmm, so it took a long time for your little brother to kinda figure that all out.

Carol: It did! It did and that's why I understand why Norma Jean might feel the way she does. About wanting . . . [*Editor's note: The preceding discussion is a good illustration of "talking about." In this instance, Carol and Craig are talking about Carol's experience and those experiences also apply to Norma Jean, which allows Norma Jean to integrate the material in a nonthreatening manner. The interaction can help Norma Jean develop a more coherent auto-biographical narrative by identifying with her mom, Carol, and internalizing their shared experience.*]

Norma Jean: Let's have a show.

Carol: . . . her birth family. And wanting her birth mom. Cause even though my brother's now thirty-one . . .

Craig: Norma Jean, you've got to sit down on the couch. (Norma Jean was sitting on her knees on the couch; she complies.) That's good, Norma Jean.

Carol: . . . he still misses his birth family.

Craig: Really?!

Norma Jean: High five! (Norma Jean playing with puppet on couch, focused on puppet but listening to conversation between Carol and me)

Craig: Yeah.

Carol: My birth mom moved away just before my fifth birthday and we lost track of where she lived.

Craig: Wow, that must have been hard not to see her anymore. (with empathy and eye contact being made with Carol)

Carol: Soo . . . I can understand Jeanine's desire to see her mom . . .

Craig: I bet you guys have talked about all that.

Norma Jean: We have. We have.

Craig: Does it seem to help Norma Jean for you to tell her that story?

Carol: That seems to be a good question for you to ask Jeanine.

Craig: Well, I can't. I'm trying to not ask her more questions right now.

Carol: Oh. Oh, that's right. I forgot.

Craig: We've, we've got a very low threshold for questions today.

Carol: Today . . . got it.

Craig: Maybe you could ask.

Carol: Yeah.

Craig: Maybe you could ask instead of me. I'll ask you, what do you think and you could check it out with her.

Carol: OK. That sounds . . .

Craig: And maybe if you made a guess . . .

Carol: Yeah.

Craig: Maybe she could just

Carol: I . . .

Craig: Say close . . .

Carol: OK, I'm gonna make a guess.

Craig: Or not close.

[Note: Carol and I talk over each other during the previous couple of minutes. I am trying to establish Carol's presence and full participation in this adoption narrative. She appears hesitant in this role.]

Carol: Norma Jean, I'm gonna talk for you. (Carol makes eye contact with Norma Jean for first time in a few minutes) OK and you can tell me if I'm right.

Craig: Or you could say no or something. (gesturing and reassuring Norma Jean) [*Editor's note: "Talking for" Norma Jean will allow Carol to do for Norma Jean what Norma Jean may not be able to do for herself at this point: create a coherent narrative and express her underlying affect and make meaning of the experiences.*]

Norma Jean: (responds to Craig with a lean back of her torso and a snort sound but maintains eye contact and a slightly mischievous smile)

Carol: And I don't know how to do this . . . I've decided . . . I have no clue. (referring to marionette she is trying to make work; hands it to Craig) Ummmm, Mr. Craig.

Craig: (receiving the marionette, turns and hands it to Norma Jean) Norma Jean, here, you can play with it.

Carol: Mr. Craig, I'm acting as if I'm Jeanine, OK? Um, Mr. Craig, you help me sometimes when my mom tells me about her little brother being adopted. It's not the same, because I'm older and I grew up with my mom and dad. . . .

Craig: Umm.

Carol: . . . and I was like four or a little older than that when I got taken away, so I knew them and I lived with them. So, it's different in that way, but it helps me to feel good that my mom knows what it feels like to miss her birth mom and wish to be with her.

Craig: Right. . . .

Norma Jean: Was it real . . . wait. (verbalized dialogue between the marionette puppets that Norma Jean is playing with)

Carol: Does that sound right, Norma Jean?

Norma Jean: Yes.

Carol: That sounds right. . . . (trailing voice)

Craig: So the last part . . . that it's helpful that you know your birth mom, Sophie?

Carol: Moma Sophie.

Norma Jean: MOMA SOPHIE.

Carol: (repeats) MOMA SOPHIE.

Craig: Moma Sophie.

Carol: It helps Jeanine to make her mom special by using this name instead of just calling her mom.

Craig: Moma Sophie is a pretty name, like Jeanine is a pretty name and a very special name. (attempting to further connect the current narrative with Norma Jean)

[For the next few minutes we discuss the puppet. I wanted to provide Norma Jean a break to keep her regulated and continue with our exploration.]

Carol: It dawned on my adopted brother one day that he had a birth father. That's how he felt, that he was real. Like all of a sudden, the Velveteen Rabbit became very real to him. . . .

Craig: Yeah, yeah. That story . . .

Carol: . . . and he started collecting rabbits after that.

Craig: Wow!

Carol: Because it dawned on him . . .

Norma Jean: And he has lots of rabbits.

Craig: And he was how old?

Carol: Ah, in his mid-twenties.

Craig: Twenties??

Carol: Yeah.

Craig: So it's taken a long while to . . . to come to terms with having . . .

Norma Jean: Look. (trying to get us to look at her puppets)

Craig: . . . another mom . . .

Carol: Yeah, yeah. (trailing voice) So that much more, I appreciate Jeanine's courage and her love for her birth family.

Craig: Yeah. (said quietly)

Carol: . . . because they are very special. (said softly to Norma Jean, who does not look up from her play with the puppets)

Craig: Maybe, partly what goes on when you get adopted . . . here's my guess about what goes on when you get adopted. Especially a girl your age, Jeanine, is that you think that it's not fair, or it's not right for some . . .

Norma Jean: Puppet show. (said to Carol as a request for her to play)

Craig: . . . for the judge (with more emphasis as Norma Jean has been distracted by her mom picking up the wizard puppet) to say, "Well now some other woman's your mom now!"

Carol: Ungh . . . good point!

Craig: 'Cause it seems like somebody else is tellin' ya what to do and how you should feel. (Norma Jean gets up from couch and goes to back of room) So that would be my guess as part of what goes on. Especially when it comes right down to being in the room and the judge is there, and the papers all get signed. . . . *[Editor's note: The content is becoming quite emotionally intense for Norma Jean and so she is moving away. Craig appears to sense that, while difficult for Norma Jean, she can still stay regulated and engaged. This is a good example of how once there is an alliance, the therapist can, in the exploration phase, be more direct and directive because the client (Norma Jean in this instance) knows that the therapist's intention is to be helpful.]*

Norma Jean: Um hm . . . (focused again on the wizard marionette)

Craig: . . . and the pictures all get taken, and it's a lot to take in. (said in a continuous rhythmic pattern) And it's really probably too much to take in all at once. (Norma Jean returns to couch)

Carol: Yeah, I never thought about it that way, that . . .

Craig: Yeah.

Norma Jean: I want a puppet show. (interjecting into conversation)

Craig: The judge is the one who gets to say . . .

Carol: Yeah! (agreeing with me)

Norma Jean: I want a puppet show.

Carol: Umm, yeah.

Craig: She's still trying to get her strings. Maybe you can help her with the strings, because you did a good job with yours? (said to Norma Jean)

[Note: We again take a break and spend some time talking about the puppet and untangling the marionette's strings.]

Craig: Hey, were any of your friends, umm, there with you? (referring to the adoption ceremony) *[Editor's note: After following Norma Jean by focusing on the marionette and untangling the strings, Craig can now lead back into the emotionally intense dialogue about Norma Jean's adoption and what that means. This is a good example of how the therapist manages the ebb and flow of the affective/reflective dialogue; moving into and out of emotionally intense subjects. This allows the child to stay well regulated and experience the positive aspects of the exploration and integration phases. Craig is slowly helping Norma Jean develop a more coherent autobiographical narrative as they co-create new meanings for events and reflect on these experiences.*]

Norma Jean: Huuugh. No! (looks right at me)

Carol: You didn't have any friends at the adoption? (surprised) I'm gonna tell some people you know on you! (kiddingly)

Norma Jean: Hee, hee. (giggles)

Craig: No friends! (incredulous and in fun) It must have been terrible! (making eye contact with Norma Jean)

Norma Jean: Everyone!

Craig: Everyone. (affirming voice; sitting up tall and maintaining eye contact)

Norma Jean: Everyone I saw, they were my friends.

Craig: And so you did have some there. You weren't alone.

Norma Jean: Nooo.

Craig: It wasn't just you, the judge and your mom . . .

Carol: Matter of fact, we had some great pictures of her; and who else, Jeanine?

Norma Jean: Tina and Sarah. (her friends who are adopted too)

Carol: Tina and Sarah. (in a singsong voice)

Craig: Oh, OK. Yeah, that's good.

Norma Jean: Tina's a freak!

Craig: Why? [*Editor's note: Because the work of the exploration phase has been going on for a while and Norma Jean is probably becoming tired, we see Craig relying more on the follow part of follow-lead-follow to keep Norma Jean regulated and maintain the alliance.*]

Norma Jean: Because she messed up my project.

Craig: I'm sorry to hear that.

Norma Jean: . . . my project. (trailing voice) Hello. (voice of child puppet to wizard puppet as the show begins)

Carol: Hello, little girl.

Norma Jean: It's a boy.

Carol: Hello, little boy.

Norma Jean: Hello.

Carol: Say . . .

Norma Jean: You're off the ground. (to Mom about her puppet not contacting the floor)

Carol: Oh, I'm a wizard, I can float.

Craig: Well, it's a wizard . . .

Carol: I'm a wizard, I can float!

Craig: Yes, he's a floater.

Carol: Do, du, doo . . . (puppet dances)

Norma Jean: Can you make me float?

Carol: Yeah, sure. Boink! (touching boy puppet) I have touched you with my magic wand! Now you can float. (both puppets are floating and swaying) But you must float gently, or your strings will get tangled.

Craig: Hee, hee, heeh . . . (looking on and enjoying the show)

Carol: I hear, young lady, or young boy, that you are just having a visit with your birth mother, Norma Jean.

Craig: Well, you don't know this, but he is adopted as well. That's true!

Carol: (chuckles) Is that true, young man?

Norma Jean: Yes. It is true!

Carol: And, how would you like visits to take place?

Norma Jean: That's a hard one. (turning away from Carol and Craig and placing her hand to her head in an expression of frustration) I'm not answering that one.

Carol: Oh. You're going into hiding. Is that too hard of a question?

Norma Jean: This could always be a walkway. (with difficulty, squeezes behind the big chair and the office wall)

Craig: It's a little tight there.

Carol: Mr. C . . . [*Editor's note: In the following interchange we see Carol and Craig engaged in an affective/reflective dialogue to reflect back to Norma Jean what may be her experience of the moment and to demonstrate that they understand her.*]

Craig: Yes.

Carol: Do you think that was too hard of a question?

Craig: I think that might . . .

Norma Jean: Oh, no . . .

Craig: . . . over the top.

Norma Jean: . . . questions!

Craig: Oh, wait a minute. Mom and I have an agreement that we can ask questions from each other.

Carol: Yes.

Norma Jean: But no questions . . .

Craig: My agreement was with you, but I . . . Oh, careful, careful, careful. (Norma Jean in danger of knocking over a table as she attempts to escape to the back of the room) I tried not to ask questions from you today.

Carol: But I did not agree, however. I am the wizard!

Craig: It's OK with Mom and I. (Norma Jean is back over near us and making eye contact with me; she is carrying a floor cushion with her.) Oh, good. You've got yourself a cushion.

Carol: I did not agree to that, for it is important for me to ask questions in order to help.

Craig: Um hmmm.

Norma Jean: No it didn't. (boy to wizard)

Carol: As the great wizard does.

Craig: It's almost time to finish up.

Carol: As the great wizard does!

Norma Jean: I don't want to use this one. (dissatisfied with her puppet)

Carol: Do you want to trade places with me? And you could tell me what you would do as the wizard about this special visit. (they trade puppets—Carol has child puppet, Norma Jean has wizard)

Norma Jean: You can't float!

Carol: Oh. OK, I can't float. Hi, wizard. I'm the little boy now. And we were talking about my visit with my birth mom.

Craig: Because he's adopted.

Carol: Yep. He's all turned around. (trying to untangle strings on the boy marionette)

Craig: He's all turned around. Yep.

Carol: That's what it feels like sometimes.

Craig: Yes, that's what it feels like.

Norma Jean: You did it wrong and that's why.

Carol: I did?

Norma Jean: Do you want to float in the air?

Carol: No. I want to visit my birth mom. What do you think about that, wizard? Do you . . .

Norma Jean: Well, I think . . .

Carol: Do you think . . . what do you think?

Norma Jean: Just tell me what you were going to say. (in a younger child voice)

Carol: I can't remember.

Norma Jean: I can make you float.

Carol: You can?

Norma Jean: All I have to is . . . all I have to do is that. (taps boy with his wand)

Carol: So am I floating now? Is that OK?

Norma Jean: Yeah.

Carol: Do, doo, doo . . . (dancing)

Norma Jean: Doo, doo, dooo . . . (in rhythm with mom). It's kinda hard floating in the air, huh?

Craig: Well, I have a question for the little boy. Little boy, did that help? Did the wizard help? Since you can float, maybe you don't have to worry about your birth family anymore?

Carol: No. Floating's nice, but I still have all those feelings in my heart about my birth mother, Norma Jean.

Craig: Oh. So floating isn't helping so much right now with that problem.

Carol: No. What do you think, wizard? How can I deal with these feelings in my heart for my birth mom?

Norma Jean: Well, maybe you need to sit down and get some coffee for yourself.

Carol: Oh, coffee. Caffeine? That will help? I think that will make me go doo, doo, to dooo. (very fast dancing)

Norma Jean: (chuckles) Oh, ohhhhh! (laughs and points as boy puppet gets tangled)

Carol: That's what it will do for me, all right. I think that I will get all tangled and twisted up.

Craig: He looks kinda twisted up there!

Carol: Yeah. Yeah. I'm not so sure that coffee is the answer. What else have you got, wizard?

Norma Jean: What do you need?

Carol: Well, in my heart, I have all these big feelings. And see, I was just adopted this week. And now my mom is my mom by law, but I still have a birth mom and I'm having all kinds of feelings about it now. (a pause ensues before the wizard responds)

Norma Jean: Well, what do you think you might be able to do?

Carol: That's why I came to see you, wizard! You're supposed to know the answers to everything!

Norma Jean: No, I'm not.

Carol: You're not?! I thought wizards knew e-v-e-r-y-thing. Are you adopted, wizard?

Norma Jean: Yes I am!

Carol: What would you do if you were in my situation? How would you deal with your big feelings about your birth mom?

Norma Jean: I'd just forget about them! (sad, serious tone)

Carol: Huh, forgetting about them, though. I'm not a wizard, but I am not so sure that's the best answer.

Norma Jean: Well, I forget about them. My cape matches my shoes. (very child-like small voice, said almost to herself)

Carol: Oh, are you forgetting about them now, by talking about your cape and your shoes rather than what we're talking about?

Norma Jean: Actually, can you please . . .

Craig: I have an idea! (puts on Minnie Mouse puppet and joins the conversation)

Carol: Ahh.

Craig: Hi! (waves puppet at Norma Jean)

Norma Jean: Hello. (playfully now, not so sad)

Craig: Hi. How are you?

Norma Jean: NO questions!

Craig: I've been thinking about . . . I've been hearing your conversation because I was sitting over on the couch and I have an idea.

Carol: What's your idea?

Craig: I think it might be gooood to send maybe a picture and a note to my birth mom, if I knew how to get ahold of her that way.

Norma Jean: We already know how!

Craig: Then I would send her a note and a picture and tell her that I've been thinking about her and maybe missing her some. [*Editor's note: By using imaginative play, Craig is able to continue in the exploration phase and keep Norma Jean well regulated and focused.*]

Norma Jean: I'm your wizard dad.

Craig: What do you think? (said to boy puppet held by Mom)

Carol: That's a great idea! Wizard, what do you think?

Norma Jean: Well, that's a good idea!

Carol: Do you think that's a good idea?

Norma Jean: Yeah. Can we just play Pinocchio? (asking Mom)

Craig: Yeah, we could play Pinocchio, but if someone was just adopted and they wrote a letter to their birth mom and sent her a picture then she might like that.

Carol: I think so, and you know what? I think I would be OK and I think my mom would be OK if I said I love you, Mom, and I do miss you and I just want to let you know I'm doing OK.

Craig: Wow! I think that would be really good.

Carol: I think I feel really good about that. What do you think, wizard?

Norma Jean: Well, I think that's an excellent idea. (in wizard-like voice) I'm gonna have some coffee. OK?

Craig: Can I join you guys? That sounds like fun!

Norma Jean: OK.

Carol: OK.

Craig: You guys look like great people. I'm really glad I met up with you!

Norma Jean: I've got some coffee. You want some coffee?

Craig: Oh, thank you.

Carol: Ummm, yumm, yumm! (starts dancing) Is this decaf or regular?

Norma Jean: Regular.

Carol: Oh, my goodness, whooo! Hmmm, I wonder . . .

Norma Jean: You have a tag on yourself. (pointing to boy puppet)

Carol: Oh no. I'm tagged!

Craig: That's pretty funny. How did it get there? What's it say? It says something collection. It never got taken off.

Carol: Made in China. (all laugh together)

Craig: So he's a Chinese boy.

Carol: He doesn't look Chinese. He looks like a scarecrow.

Norma Jean: Yeah, he does. You're a scarecrow.

Carol: You're a scarecrow.

Norma Jean: Wizard, thank you so much. And thank you so much Mrs. . . . Minnie therapist or whoever you are.

Craig: Yes, this is Minnie Mouse.

Carol: . . . for that wonderful idea about writing that letter to my birth mom, because I think that might just help me.

Craig: Well, I hope it works and maybe you guys can let me know if that's what you do because I'd be interested.

Carol: Yeah. I had kinda wondered about having a visit with her, but I know that last time I had a visit with her, it just . . . it was kinda hard (Norma Jean gets up and goes to back of the office) and I just didn't know what to do with all my feelings.

Craig: Oh . . .

Carol: Wizard . . .

Craig: Well, sometimes we have more feelings than we know what to do with.

Carol: That is so true!

[Note: We now continue to play with the puppets. By co-regulating Norma Jean's level of arousal, we can continue to circle back to the use of the puppets for imaginative play to discuss grief and loss issues. We then end the session.]

Carol: Ready to go with me? (Mom holds out her hands. Norma Jean holds hers out to reach Mom.) Come on. [*Editor's note: At the end of the session we see that Norma Jean needs continued comforting by her mom. Despite this child's very impaired capacity to regulate her emotions and limited reflective abilities, Craig has been able to move from maintaining the alliance into the exploration and integration phases in a measured and titrated manner that will lead to healing.*]

Craig: Bye, guys.

Norma Jean: Carry!

Carol: Tell you what, we'll go out into the lobby and we'll talk about it.

Norma Jean: NOOOOO! (like a baby)

Carol: Com'on, we've got to go out there. (gently pulling her out of the chair)

Norma Jean: Mommy. (protest voice, but walks out of room with Mom)

Craig: Jeanine, I'm going to give you a head's up that there's probably other people sitting out there.

Carol: So, let's be quiet.

Norma Jean: (grabs light switch on way out of office and turns off the lights)

Craig: Just so you know. All right. Bye bye. (said with concern and care)

[*Editor's note: In conclusion, this transcript illustrates the use of several of the components of Dyadic Developmental Psychotherapy with a family and child who is easily dysregulated and who is quite difficult to engage. Craig's work with Carol and Norma Jean demonstrates how important it is to focus on the alliance and is a good representation of work in maintaining the alliance phase of treatment.*]

Chapter Seven

Pekka: The Silent Boy Who Has ADHD

Pirjo Tuovila, M.Soc.Sc., Lic.A.(Psych.)

Pekka is a twelve-year-old boy who has lived in a professional family foster home with his older sibling for half of his life. [*Editor's note: In the United States this arrangement would be called a group home.*] The professional family home consists of the parents and eight other foster children. Six of the children are siblings from three different homes. In the daytime, seven outside workers—four caregivers, two for cooking and housekeeping, one for gardening and building—come in to help the parents. Pekka meets his birth father once every two or three weeks. The father and his new family live some distance away; it is a 1.5-hour drive to their home. Pekka's birth mother lives very far away and Pekka last saw her about two years ago. The mother also has a new family, and she does not keep in touch with Pekka at all. Occasionally, she sends e-mail to the older sibling, though.

Pekka's parents were divorced quite early in their marriage and the children were left with the father. Both parents had serious mental health problems. Moreover, they were heavy drinkers and substance abusers. It is very likely that Pekka was prenatally exposed to both alcohol and drugs. Economic problems and violence characterized the family's everyday life. The siblings' childhood was chaotic; they were abused, and seriously emotionally neglected. They lived in a children's home for a year before they were placed in the professional family home where they now live. The father has managed to put his life more or less in order, but he would not be able to take care of these children, so they will continue in foster care until eighteen or even up to twenty-one if they want to stay longer.

Pekka has been examined in a neurological clinic as well as in a children's psychiatric clinic. He was diagnosed with ADHD at age seven. Since age nine he has had medication for this and other disorders (i.e., attention deficit and hyperactivity disorder, depression, and rapid mood changes). He has partici-pated in two neuropsychological rehabilitation programs. At school he was placed in a special class that had only ten students but already the whole last year he attended a normal classroom.

I have seen Pekka for over a year in twenty-five sessions. The frequency of our meetings has varied from two to three times a month, but we have also had a break of five months. When we first started, Pekka's ADHD problems seemed primary. He was stealing, lying, had no friends, was very aggressive and impulsive, and often ended up fighting with other children. He was very accident-prone and had no sense of danger. In his relationships with adults, he was described as annoyingly loud and resistant; he needed a lot of atten-tion, felt worthless and was convinced that nobody loved him, and he was given to outbursts of rage. There was some bed-wetting, too, and he woke up very early in the mornings; in all, he was an extremely anxious, unhappy, and troubled little boy. [*Editor's note: This pattern of difficulties and the multiple diagnoses that may result are a hallmark of complex trauma. This boy's history of various treatments, without much success, highlights the importance of conducting a thorough assessment that includes screening across a range of domains including attachment, behavioral regulation, emotional regulation, cognition, defensive patterns, physical/biological, and self-concept (Becker-Weidman, 2007).*] He had many practical skills and digital dexterity so he managed well in daily chores, but at school he was a clear underachiever. He was quite attached to the parents of the professional family home, especially his foster mother Liisa, although she had little time for Pekka, since the home had three other children who were hard to care for. Pekka liked to attend therapy and he enjoyed the times that he could spend with his foster mother.

As therapy has progressed, Pekka's problems have diminished in many ways and at present he is doing quite well. In the family home he still runs into problems with a younger child who is very difficult, but otherwise daily life goes well. In the treatment, we have now reached the stages of explora-tion and integration. We shall break up for the summer after a few more ses-sions, and will continue in the fall, though less frequently.

The therapy session described here is the twenty-fifth. At the beginning of the session we hear what Pekka has been doing. He has participated in the fi-nal round of the floor bandy tournament, at school his teachers are being laid off, and we wonder how Pekka will deal with such an exceptional situation. Pekka himself has nothing special in mind that he would like to talk about. He is in a good mood, and initially he takes an active part in the discussion, but is a little bit restless.

We are finishing the family tree that we have been working on over a long period of time. Pekka last met his birth mother two years ago at her wedding. The mother lives very far away with Pekka's younger half-sisters and her new husband (not the children's father). As to his mother's family, Pekka only meets his maternal grandmother a few times a year. We fill in some new information on the side of his birth mother in the family tree. Foster mother Liisa recalls that Pekka's birth mother moved several times after she had left the children. At the time Pekka had been only two years old. Liisa points out to Pekka where he and his older sibling have lived. Pekka seems to remember that at some point the children lived just with their mother. It is important that Pekka can build a conception of his own history and early childhood and their meaning for his later development and inner working models. Developing this coherent autobiographical narrative takes several sessions and requires repetition of facts in intersubjective relationships, since only part of it all will be stored in his memory at one go. This enables a deeper exploration of events, co-creation of meaning, and co-regulation of affect together with an adult. In this way the reflective function can develop during affective/reflective dialogues. The process thus enables creation of a coherent autobiographical narrative. I can feel that there is a strong positive intersubjective connection between Pekka and Liisa, and I can proceed to deepen and explore the theme together with them. Pekka leans against Liisa as she is speaking in a calm, quiet voice.

Liisa (the professional foster parent): Your mummy and daddy lived together, and you never lived with just your mother; you lived together with Mummy and Daddy, and afterward with just your Daddy. You have visited your mummy sometimes during holidays, but you never lived with her, really.

Pirjo: What do you remember of the holidays that you spent with your mummy? [*Editor's note: Here we see the therapist intervening to deepen the emotional experience by evoking a more detailed memory and recounting of the memory.*]

Pekka: (moves closer to Liisa, under her arm and leans against her while fiddling with a case of felt pens; the theme brings emotions on the surface, Pekka is looking for safety close to Liisa and needs to do something with his hands.) I can't remember anything else, just that I was with Mummy on my holiday.

Pirjo, referred to in the rest of the transcript as Therapist or T: So you remember nothing of what it was like there? [*Editor's note: This is a good example of the follow part of follow-lead-follow.*]

P: (shakes his head and throws the case of pens on the couch) [He may feel a bit ashamed and frustrated because he can't remember. Liisa comes to help and brings Pekka back to a better relationship, thus immediately repairing a possible breach (interactive repair). After getting help, Pekka remembers things amazingly well.] [*Editor's note: It may be that the safety created by Liisa and the concordant intersubjective experience she creates with Pekka is what helps him "reintegrate" and reduce the shame he may have been experiencing.*]

L: When your mother lived in Andersen and then in Bulbo, I wonder if you got to visit her in Bulbo three times and in Andersen twice?

P: Just once in Andersen.

L: So there were not many day visits, were there?

P: In Andersen Liisa was with us.

L: Oh yes, I remember.

T: When you now think of that time with your mummy and all that happened and that your Mummy has moved so many times, how does that feel to you? What do you think, what did that mean to you?

P: (very softly.) I don't know.

[Note: I now try to help Pekka to understand and reflect on what the absence of his mother and her frequent moves have meant to him and his conception of himself (exploring the initial meaning of events and internal working models).] [*Editor's note: It may be that too many questions had been asked of Pekka and that this led to his "I don't know" response.*]

T: Hmm, your mummy has moved a lot and has not been able to do all those good things that mothers are supposed to do, like take good care of her children. (Pekka picks up the family tree to have a closer look at it or to hide behind it. A shame reaction could arise: "My mummy did not take good care of me because I was a bad child.") Pekka, do you think that has had an impact on what you think of yourself and what you feel, and what kind of a boy you are?

P: (Pekka lets the family tree come down and says very softly) How can you know?

[Note: I accept Pekka's answer and try again to repair his possible feeling of failure as he cannot answer my question (interactive repair).]

T: You don't need to know that, but perhaps we could think about it together.

P: (spreads his arms and raises his shoulders)

[Note: In order to strengthen the connection between Pekka and Liisa, I turn to Liisa. I know she is very good at raising the emotional level with her own comments. By being curious and exploring things we at the same time increase intersubjectivity, insightfulness, and the development of the reflective function.] [*Editor's note: In what follows we see a good example of "talking about," which is one method of reducing shame and deepening the affective dimensions of the interaction. Furthermore, we observe here the iterative nature of the phases of treatment. Pirjo is attempting to maintain the alliance while exploring a difficult subject and producing integration and healing in the next few moments.*]

T: Liisa, what do you think? What has it meant for a little boy?

L: Well, surely he could think that "I am not really a valuable child because they move with me from one place to another and I must remain in one place and then leave again, come and go. Then perhaps I begin to doubt that they really love me; I wonder if my parents ever loved me really, as they did all those other things but did not take care of me."

T: Well, Pekka, what do you think of that; could that be true?

P: (nods in agreement, leaning against Liisa)

T: Have you ever told Liisa how you have felt about all this?

P: (stretching himself) I don't know.

[Note: Usually Pekka finds it difficult to verbalize his emotional experiences, so in therapy I try to help him in that. It is important that a child will learn to identify his own inner world of feelings and express his feelings verbally, and to share all that with his attachment figure. A shared experience deepens the emotion and attachment. The great advantage of DDP is that even if the child does not speak the words, he can still be helped by speaking for him. The child then accepts or rejects the words, and my experience is that they really do that. We start by talking, with empathy, about Pekka's possible experience and then move on to put words in his mouth. We do not force him to talk but accept his reactions as they are—using the PACE attitude throughout the session. Pekka expresses a lot with his body, getting closer to Liisa. I comment on this so that he will be more aware of what is happening between them and what it feels like. In this way he will have an intersubjective experience which is both mental and physical and very integrative. It is important that Pekka should be able to feel sorrow because of his losses and his longing, so we try to stay with this theme for some time. Experiencing sorrow is the counterbalance for aggression.]

T: Hmm, you could really tell us now. It sounds so very, very sad, the way you have felt restless and unsafe, and you must really have felt that you were a worthless child, not lovable at all. Could you say something about that to Liisa? [*Editor's note: Here we observe the therapist engaging the child so that he can directly express himself. This is accomplished by first reflecting back to the child what the therapist experiences as the child's experience. The model being followed is that first the adult does "it" for the child, then with, and then the child can do "it" alone.*]

P: (looks at Liisa in a questioning manner, and says quietly) I don't know. (curls closer to Liisa and she puts her arms around him)

T: That sure is difficult, I know. It's so good that you are close to Liisa. She is holding you so gently, it must feel so good. It also tells you how Liisa feels. Would you like me to help you speak? [*Editor's note: This is a good illustration of the acceptance part of PACE and the follow element in follow-lead-follow.*]

P: I don't know.

T: It must feel awfully hard and difficult. (Pekka nods)

T: Oh, it's so hard. Really, it's a truly difficult situation when a small child is separated from his mummy and must move from one place to another and go to different places without knowing what will happen and what is where and who will take care of him. It's really so hard! That should not happen, but it did happen to you. Hmm. . . . You must have thought, "Why doesn't Mummy come?" Perhaps you thought that you are a bad little boy and that's why Mummy is not coming any more. (Pekka is tapping Liisa's hand to show his agreement and emotional bond with Liisa in the face of a difficult thing; Liisa continues the dialogue)

L: Pekka, I really believe that you have missed your mummy terribly since she went away. Hmm, that's probably why you remember living with her when you were actually living in the family center in Bulbo. From the center you then visited your mummy when you were on holiday. You must have been about four years old then.

T: Hmm, OK.

L: (turns Pekka so that she can see his face and have eye contact with him) Pekka, you must have been four years old then—Matti (Liisa's grandchild) will soon be four. Just think, what would happen to Matti if he were separated from his mummy? What does he always say when he comes to visit us at night and sometimes sleeps over? [*Editor's note: The beginning construction of a coherent autobiographical narrative involves the co-creation of a new meaning for these experiences. This is an example of the beginning integration phase.*]

P: When is Mummy coming?

L: Yes, that's what he always asks—"When is Mummy coming?"—because little boys and girls often miss their own mother, their real mother.

T: They miss their mother terribly, even if their mother didn't do everything right and well!

L: Mother is really important!

P: (sits up, moves away from Liisa and looks at the family tree again as if to build a visual image of what we are talking about) [Being contained by Liisa and the therapist, he is better able to integrate his own traumatic experiences safely (integration of trauma). Information received through many sensory channels strengthens the emotional experience.]

T: Hmm (pointing at the biological mother in the family tree), here's your mother Maria, who has not been part of your life much, not even later. How about now; when did you last see Maria? (Pekka leans back and yawns; he clearly needs a small break so I try to ease the emotional tension before we continue.) [*Editor's note: The therapist is responsible for maintaining a healing pace of treatment and managing the ebb and flow of the affective/reflective dialogue.*]

L: It must have been after their wedding in May.

P: (energetically) On Mother's Day!

L: That's right, on Mother's Day! You remembered that day so well!

T: Pekka, you have such a good memory! This can be so tiresome when you must think and ponder so much. By the way, Liisa, did you notice how big Pekka's mouth was when he opened it really wide? I was afraid he might drop his chin. (Pekka examines the family tree)

T: I wonder if you could tell Liisa how really, really sad you are about all that has happened to you, Pekka, the tiny little boy who was then really, really small. (Pirjo shows with her fingers the height of the small child; Pekka keeps looking at the family tree intensely.) Should we try?

P: (mumbles something)

T: Pekka, would you trust me so that if you feel too afraid to say it, I could speak for you? But could you now look at Liisa for a moment and pay attention to what she looks like when I speak for you? (Pekka leans back and turns to look at Liisa)

L: Is that OK, shall we look each other in the eyes?

T: Yes, then you will see what Liisa looks like! (Liisa strokes Pekka's cheek; Pekka looks at Liisa, then looks away, then presses his head against Liisa's neck.) You may repeat after me, Pekka.

P: (mumbling) No . . .

T: (sounding amazed) You don't want to repeat after me? Oh, this is so hard. . . .

P: No.

T: Will you correct me if I say something wrong? (Pekka shakes his head) Help me. How shall I know if what I say is right or wrong?

P: I don't know.

T: Oh, how hard this is! I wonder what makes it so hard? Can I still try and speak for you, Pekka? [*Editor's note: During the exploration phase and after a secure base and alliance have been created, the therapist can become a bit more directive. The creation of a secure base and deeper alliance lead to the client experiencing that the therapist is wanting to be helpful. As the child feels that the therapist's intentions are positive, the child can tolerate deeper exploration of stronger emotions. However, it is always important for the therapist to be vigilant that the therapist is not pushing the child and merely achieving compliance at the cost of shared intersubjectivity.*]

P: Yeah.

T: Pekka, is it too much if you look Liisa in the eyes when I speak; is that too difficult, too painful? (Liisa strokes Pekka's head and cheek; Pekka says nothing so I turn to Liisa again)

T: Liisa, do you think that looking is too hard for Pekka? Would it be better for you to be hiding, Pekka?

L: (in an accepting voice) You can stay here under my arm! [Pekka lifts his knees on Liisa's lap and turns to face her and leans against her. In this way he shows that he is preparing himself, but he still looks for support from Liisa to bear the difficult emotions. I help Pekka to become conscious of Liisa's presence and her safe lap. This emphasizes the ability that mother Liisa has to care for him and the fact that she is very different from mother Maria.]

T: Would it be easier for you if Liisa put her arms around you? I bet it would! I imagine, Pekka, that you might say to Liisa something like this: "I am so very sorry for losing my mummy and seeing her so seldom. I always missed my mummy so much, I never knew when I would see her next and I didn't really know where I was going when I went to meet her. It's been so very hard and sad for me, and I have cried a lot. But then at some point I stopped crying; I just thought that was it. And then I felt that I was not a good and lovely and lovable boy; I was a boy whose mother did not care for him, so there must be something wrong with me. I was so small and so alone." [Pekka presses himself closer to Liisa, showing that he is now involved in the process and is experiencing something that will repair his pain that he has been carrying by himself for so long. Liisa is holding Pekka, stroking him gently. The basic experience of being a bad boy is slowly abating.] "And Daddy could not help me either, as he had his own problems. So then I just tried to go on and manage somehow. It was so terrible! I cried so many times, alone and sad. . . . And then I stopped crying, because I felt it did not help me at all. I just waited for things to get better and then I moved to live with you, and my life did change into something better. You always tried to tell me what was going well and what I should try and correct. And you believed I was a good boy, not a bad child to whom all sorts of bad things happen. . . ." Hmm . . . Pekka, was that something you could have said?

P: (mumbles and nods)

T: (delighted) Oh yes, it was! I'm sure you wish your mummy could have held you as gently, when you were having a hard time.

[Note: I do not force Pekka to say anything himself, because speaking would be too much for him at this stage (the PACE attitude). Like a small child, he has shown with his body that he is involved and that there is a deep emotional connection with Liisa. We continue to strengthen that connection to make it even more profound and do this by talking about what could have happened if Pekka had arrived earlier in the family home which we have done also before. In this way we help Pekka build himself a feeling and experience of what he would have needed and what would have been possible for him—another kind of story can be built for him, a story that can repair him. That story contains no abuse or neglect. There is healing power in this very intensive intersubjective experience: a caring adult is participating with her own strong feelings. Eye contact strengthens the experience; that is why I try to help Pekka look into Liisa's beautiful bright eyes that are full of empathy.]

T: Liisa, what do you think, if Pekka had come to you when he was much smaller; what would you have done differently from his mummy and daddy, something that they didn't know how to do? [*Editor's note: This is a continuation of further developing a coherent autobiographical narrative.*]

L: Pekka, if you had arrived in our home when you were younger, I could have taken care of you and you would never have been alone or afraid. You would have been safe with us adults, and you would not have needed to cry. (Pekka holds on to Liisa even harder) You would not have needed to cry because of your sorrow and because you missed something. You would have felt that you are loved and a child that we always hoped for, you would have felt that you were taken care of. All little boys and girls need adults to look after them and they need to feel that they are important for the adults. [Pekka glances at Liisa. Now he is ready to have eye contact with her for a short moment, as well as to share his feelings of shame and his profound emotional experience with her.] If you had come to us as a little boy, you would have felt at once that you were a valuable, very special and wonderful child for us. I became so sad and I felt like crying when I thought of you being so alone (Pekka puts both his arms around Liisa and sits close to her as if glued to her) and how you missed your own Mummy. You would have liked her to come back, but she never did, or she came and then left again. And as a small boy you just couldn't understand that.

T: Small children often think that their parents go away because their children are so awful. They can't think that the parents leave because they themselves have problems or they don't get on with each other, but small children feel they are to blame; they think it is their fault that Mummy or Daddy does not want to be with them. But Pekka, this is not the way it is!

L: We have talked to Pekka about this and we have said that it is not the child's fault. (Pekka mumbles something) It is not the child's fault, is it? (Liisa asks Pekka) Pekka, you know that small children cannot really be so bad that their parents must go away?

P: Mmm. . . . (shaking his head)

T: Do you really know that? (Pekka nods, but does not say anything)

T: Pekka, do you think you are brave enough to look at Liisa now to see what she looks like? (Pekka hugs Liisa) I wonder what you might see in her eyes. What are her eyes saying to you? I wonder what can be seen there?

[Note: I turn to Liisa again, so she can speak for Pekka, who then need not feel ashamed or feel that he has failed or that we do not accept his way of expressing himself.]

T: Liisa, what do you think, if Pekka was brave enough and looked in your eyes, what would he see there?

L: Pekka would probably see sorrow for what has happened to him. Hmm. . . . But Pekka, you would also see that you are a valuable and lovable boy and that Liisa is ever so happy to have you.

T: (reinforcing Liisa's words) Liisa is so happy!

L: (continues the therapist's sentence from where she broke off) . . . that you are now living with us, that you are Liisa's son and a good boy, Pekka! We have resolved all those difficulties!

[Note: We now proceed to talk about Pekka's coping skills. Eye contact with Liisa would help Pekka to see himself as a skillful boy, as we talk about him. Pekka has found it difficult to receive praise or positive feedback.] [*Editor's note: Probably because the praise and positive feedback are not congruent with his self-image. This is why it is so important to be quite cautious when attempting to "get" the child to say or do something in treatment when what is being asked of the child is discordant. The therapist must be extremely sensitive to this and avoid at all costs sacrificing the intersubjective experience for compliance. As described elsewhere in relation to parenting, "it's about connections not compliance" applies equally well to the therapist and the therapy setting.*]

T: Pekka is a boy with many skills; he's super skillful. He has come through many big issues and has really worked hard in order to change things, and now everything is going much better with him. There are still things that are really sad and sometimes disturb everyday life—not so much any longer, though. [An ambulance can be heard through the window, Pekka leaves his mother, turns to the window and looks out, then looks back at Liisa, and returns to her arms. The sound attracts his attention, which is common among children with ADHD, but he returns to Liisa and the connection is reestablished, which is another sign of his progress. He need not even comment on the sound or ask anything about it.]

L: Oh, Pekka, you are such a lovely boy! (Liisa strokes Pekka's face tenderly)

T: Why don't you look at Liisa when she is telling you what a lovely boy you are? (Pekka gives a slightly slanting look)

L: You are such a sweet and good boy, and I am so happy I have a little boy like you! (they hug each other)

T: What did you see in Liisa's eyes, Pekka?

P: All kinds of nice things!

T: What were all those nice things?

P: (very briskly.) All kinds of nice things!

T: What were those nice things like?

P: Just some things.

T: Well, may I try and guess what they were?

P: OK, go ahead! [*Editor's note: Here we observe that Pirjo's interventions have restored the intersubjective experience.*]

T: Well, for instance, that Liisa is really happy about you and Liisa loves you very, very much. And that Liisa is sad with you for all those painful and difficult things that you have had to experience without your own fault, and for all that pain that you have had. Liisa would really like to take them away, but it's not possible any longer; one thing can be done, though: we can see to it that you will not have to experience painful things anymore, because you have had plenty of them already—quite enough.

P: (sits up) That's right, no more!

T: Those are things that you could see in her eyes—just take a look!

P: (looks at Liisa with a faint smile on his face)

T: I'm sure you are now brave enough to look at what lovely things there are for you to see—ah, such lovely things.

P: (lies down on the couch, thus letting us know that this is enough)

[Note: By now we have processed Pekka's losses and experiences of sorrow, and related feelings, for quite a long time; we have also deepened his attachment to Liisa by means of shared emotional experiences. Little by little it is time to end the session. I sum up what we have achieved and expand Pekka's story and his experiences so they become something that concerns children in general. In this way it is possible to ease the emotional tension and Pekka and Liisa can go home in a more relaxed state of mind and continue with their everyday life.]

T: Was it tiring? [*Editor's note: The therapist's pacing of the ebb and flow of the experience is vital to helping the child achieve integration and healing.*]

L: Sure, quite tiring!

T: What a fine session we had! We have really worked hard today. We have talked about children and things that happen to them even though we would not like anything like that to happen to anyone, and how children then often begin to have wrong ideas about themselves, quite wrong. They feel they are to blame for all the bad things. [*Editor's note: In this comment we observe the reflective dimension of the affective/reflective dialogue. Pirjo is summarizing and describing the experience (therapy session) that they have all just experienced.*]

P: Hmm. . . .

T: Children can then grow really restless or really aggressive; some may withdraw into their own secret world—they don't even dare to look at other people but try to be invisible like little mice. (Pekka nods) Children react in different ways, but they all react when they have difficulties. Then we have talked about Liisa and how much she loves you and takes good care of you and thinks you are such a wonderful boy. And you know these people are not going to disappear and leave you!

L: And that's really important.

(At the end Pekka looks directly at Liisa, their eyes meet, and they hug.)

T: A little boy who has had it so difficult, and now things are already going well!

The above description is an example of a session in which elements of both the middle phase and integration phase are present. As this was our twenty-fifth session, it is quite clear that we had already in many ways processed and explored Pekka's problems, which reflected his difficult life history and internal working models. In other words, we have explored how the past lives in the present. We have given events and Pekka's behavior new meanings and have developed his reflective skills. The results of our work can be seen in that his behavioral symptoms have disappeared almost completely. Shared and co-regulated emotions have balanced his behavior in many ways and have improved his own skills of regulating his emotions. We had been working on the family tree for a long time and had with its help processed many painful things, memories and feelings. The family tree says something about the present, too, and provided a good basis for exploring Pekka's relationship with his father and father's new family. Pekka visits the family in accordance with the regulations of the Finnish system of child protection. [*Editor's note: Unfortunately, such regulations, common in many jurisdictions, often are not in the child's best interests. Visits are often set up based on the parent's needs and schedule, not the child's needs and best interests.*] In the session depicted here we focused on the meaning of the absence of the biological mother. Central elements in the integration phase are designing a coherent autobiographical narrative and building internal working models that will truly function. These two phases overlap and are difficult to differentiate. We still have a lot of work ahead of us, because Pekka has difficulties in identifying and verbalizing his own feelings and emotions. That is why we still need to talk a lot about him and ask him so that he can really reach his own inner world when encountering his more difficult and profound feelings. In this way we also try to help him express himself better in speech. That, of course, is one of the main goals of all therapy.

I hope the session described above gives new ideas for those who try to help children and their new parents/caregivers in processing and integrating the children's painful early experiences and memories. Dyadic Developmental Psychotherapy has proved helpful even in cases when the children as yet do not actively verbalize themselves.

Chapter Eight

Exploration and Integration: When Present and Past Meet

Kim S. Golding, B.Sc., M.Sc., D.ClinPsy.

I first meet Liam while I am at the house to work with one of the other children. He remains quietly in the background, curious about me but not wanting
to admit to this curiosity. Psychologists are for the other children, the ones
with issues, not for him. He is ten years old, tall and thin with a shock of black
hair. He appears, surveys me briefly, and then disappears. I continue my work
and leave without seeing him again. This becomes a pattern. I arrive, am
aware of him in the background, briefly, and then he is gone. Very different
from his sister, Taylor, younger by eighteen months—she likes to make sure
of me. Instantly my friend, she checks me out, chatting to me but not waiting
for any answers, monopolizing my attention until Jenny gently removes her
and I can get on with the purpose of my visit.

Jenny and Tom are long-term foster caregivers to Liam and Taylor. I have
supported them for many years and heard about Liam when he first arrived
as a bossy but appealing eight-year-old. His intelligence, his need to enter-
tain, and his need to be in control were evident from the very beginning. He
quickly made clear that he would live here but would not allow Jenny or Tom
to parent him. He was already aware of the danger of showing emotions. He
explained to Jenny that he kept his feelings locked in boxes, the keys flying
around so no one could unlock the boxes even accidentally. When he was
nearly angry one day he looked at Jenny with astonishment, surprised because she had nearly caught a key.

This self-reliance was hard earned and had kept him safe during his early
years living with his birth parents. They were a well-meaning couple who
loved their children but had no idea how to meet their needs or keep them
safe. Preoccupied with their own safety, fighting regularly, and with little
ability to budget or even keep food in the house, Liam had to learn from
an early age how to look after himself and his younger sister. Liam's birth

127

mother was wary of Liam; she had a history of poor relationships with the males in her life and she anticipated a troubling relationship with her son. She made age-inappropriate expectations of him, and when he failed at these he was physically punished. At the local school they remembered a quiet child always hungry and dirty, but making few demands on them.

Liam was six years old when a decision was made to bring both children into local authority care. Practicalities of finding urgent placements meant that his first and temporary foster placement was without his sister. He was to live there for eighteen months while care proceedings were initiated and decisions were made for the children's future. It was decided that Liam and Taylor would be placed for adoption together, and because of this another short-term placement was found for both of them. This is how they came to live with Jenny and Tom. Their task was to help the children live back together again—to prepare them for adoption. Liam soon had other ideas; he recognized some fragile security within this family and he decided he was going nowhere. This is where he wanted to stay. Jenny and Tom recognized something in both the children that set them apart from other children they had fostered. After some careful thought about the long-term commitment they were taking on they decided to offer the children a permanent home with them. And so, two years later, I came to meet Liam, a child I had heard about now becoming flesh for me as I made my visits to the house.

Jenny and Tom are experienced foster caregivers. Highly collaborative in their approach, they like to form a team around the children, which includes the social workers, school, and myself offering psychological support. Liam and Taylor were introduced to the idea of a team around them from early on in placement. They knew that we were all working together to support their safety and, although they were less aware of this, their emotional growth. It was therefore quite natural, when Liam started to struggle, for Jenny to discuss with him the possibility of talking to me. At first he was resistant to this idea; I seemed a nice person, but a psychologist was for the crazy ones. His sister might need to see me but not him. At this time his behavior was becoming more up and down. His usually robust control of his emotions was becoming challenged by a range of stresses, including the imminent prospect of leaving his primary school and moving to the big school. I became more aware of him during my visits to the home as he gently moved in on me. At first I got a smile and a quick hello, but soon I was getting the full charm offensive. Liam was making himself safe before agreeing to start working with me. He and Jenny talked it through and he decided he would engage in some therapeutic work.

INTRODUCTION TO SESSION TRANSCRIPT

I have chosen to illustrate the therapeutic journey that Liam, Jenny, and I engaged in with a transcript of one session. By the time of this session I have been working with Liam and Jenny for nearly eighteen months. We meet every two to three weeks, and will work for a further six months before therapy ends. Progress has been slow at times; more frequent sessions would have been helpful but could not happen because of practical constraints. At this point in the intervention Liam is very familiar and safe with Dyadic Developmental Psychotherapy and is becoming more prepared to affectively explore his experience. I can therefore pay less attention to ensuring safety (building and maintaining an alliance) and more to facilitating exploration. Safety is always the bedrock of the work but when Liam begins to feel unsafe the alliance we have formed over the preceding months helps us to return to safety quickly, leaving more time for exploration. Liam is beginning to lower his defenses and experience sadness and shame about his current and early experience. Jenny and I help him co-regulate these emotions, allowing him to stay longer with them. This means we can work together to co-construct his narrative, moving toward integration and eventual healing.

Over the course of therapy we have developed a pattern of having affective and reflective sessions alternatively. Initially Liam is more comfortable with reflection and less affect. As we get to the session described here he is beginning to stay with the affective while we reflect. We can have more affective/reflective dialogues.

SESSION TRANSCRIPT

We all sit on the settee together. Liam is in the middle; Jenny, on his left and slightly behind him, is ready to comfort when needed. I sit on his right, turned toward him. The session begins, as usual, with some light banter. I have recently returned from a holiday and we spend some time becoming re-acquainted with our relationship. We have a catch-up and all laugh together. I then gently move us toward the more serious work of the session as I ask Liam how he got on with the task I left him.

Kim: So how are you doing? I left you with some things to think about.

Liam: Yer, we didn't.

[Liam looks ahead. He is not yet ready to look at either of us as he experiences the initial anxiety of beginning a session. As we begin this dialogue he swings his leg up and down, a clear sign of the discomfort he is experiencing.] [*Editor's note: This is a good illustration that even when there is a strong alliance and secure base in treatment, as will be evident as the reader delves more deeply into this transcript, the therapist must rekindle the alliance at the beginning of each session because of the break in the relationship that has occurred. This rekindling can be quite brief.]*

Jenny: (with a teasing voice) Eh, excuse me, and we have discussed at several different intervals your reaction to certain situations. [*Editor's note: What the reader can observe in this statement is the use of the playful element of PACE.*]

L: What?

J: Maybe being a bit over the top. Maybe why that was?

L: I don't remember.

J: (while challenging she remains light and teasing) Oh yes, you do, because you shut me down and said you didn't want to talk about it and off we went.

[Although Jenny is not being angrily confrontational we are in danger of moving away from the Dyadic Developmental Psychotherapy process, from maintaining a connection with Liam within which he can feel fully accepted. If this connection is lost he will not be able to be curious with us. It would move us away from intersubjectivity. I don't want our focus to become about compliance (did he or didn't he do the task). Instead I want to move us toward exploring what has been happening for Liam. I therefore slow us down.] [*Editor's note: This is a nice illustration of the idea of "it's about connections not compliance."*]

K: Liam's finding it hard to remember. Let's go back a step. What did I ask you to do? [*Editor's note: By engaging the reflective function, Kim can co-regulate Liam's affect and also maintain his engagement.*]

L: Talk to Jenny about if there's something I'm a bit worried about. I'm worried about my foot. (Liam looks down and strokes his foot) As I was playing football today I stubbed my toe to the ground as I was about to kick it (looks at Jenny) and it bent back like that (demonstrates with foot) and it stretched just here and it just hurts a bit, when I move it.

K: (teasing): That wasn't quite what I asked you to do.

L: (looks to Kim) Oh sorry; (laughs) I'm getting sidetracked.

[Liam's attempt at distraction reveals that he is on the edge of shame. We are still a bit too focused on his compliance, and I stay with this too long.] [*Editor's note: Here we see a lovely example of Liam's reflective function. He is able to think about what he did and said and reflect on that in the moment. This is an essential element necessary for affect regulation and impulse control and clearly illustrates the good work that Kim has done in past sessions.*]

K: (smiling) I know this is hard for you, but let's have a think. What did I ask you to do? [*Editor's note: Here we see Kim inviting Liam into a reflective state.*

Liam's following her is one indication of the strength of the alliance and that engaging in the exploration phase is now possible.]

L: (patient voice, and looking at Kim) Talk to Jenny about feelings and why I am feeling about it.

K: Yes, what you were feeling. That was the point wasn't it?

L: Yep.

K: When you're using a major defense, what was the feeling you were defending against? Do you remember?

L: (nods, now a bit more engaged and looking more intently at Kim) Yes, I remember, I remember.

K: We thought that was the bit we had got to, wasn't it? We now knew you were using the defenses but we didn't necessarily know what you were hiding from.

(Liam nods in agreement)

[During this dialogue Liam is gently resisting moving toward more uncomfortable discussion. Given what follows I think Liam knows what Jenny will want to talk about. He tries to put off the moment when this will be raised. I try a bit too hard to focus him on thinking about the task I had asked him to do. Use of self to communicate what I am experiencing of Liam's struggle (You're finding it hard to remember; I know this is hard for you) prevents a disruption in the relationship, however, and Liam does stay with me. This is further helped by my nonverbal communication. I lean toward Liam, and use my tone and pace of voice to help him stay regulated. This brings us into a state of emotional attunement.]

[*Editor's note: This also restores the concordant intersubjective experience.*]

[Liam tries some distraction, but this is half-hearted and eases with my empathy and playfulness. The attunement we experience allows me to co-regulate his anxiety. Despite my not fully accepting his resistance, Liam's trust in me allows him to become engaged without dysregulation. He remembers. I can now use curiosity to take us a bit further. Throughout this Jenny is playful but insistent as she reminds him of how uncomfortable he had been talking to her about his feelings. I now move actively into curiosity and ask Liam about any particular incident when he used one of his defenses. Liam is reluctant to go there but then, resigned, he invites Jenny to focus him on the event that I suspect has been the backdrop to his resistance.]

K: So can you think of any examples since I last saw you? When you've noticed yourself going into a defense?

L: (shakes head for no and looks to Jenny) She has.

J: Let me just see if you can recall Taylor in your bedroom?

L: (looks at me, slightly embarrassed) Ah!

J: You and she watching a DVD.

L: She wouldn't do as she was told at all. (Liam is looking into the distance and thinking hard as he remembers the incident; he leans his head against Jenny as he thinks.)

[We can now move actively into an intersubjective relationship within which we share affect, attention and intention. We will maintain this intersubjective dialogue for the majority of the remainder of the session as Liam becomes deeply engaged in exploring his experience.] [*Editor's note: In addition, the alliance that Kim has built provides the foundation for the secure base in treatment that is necessary to enter the exploration phase. As exploration proceeds and integration achieved, this allows for deeper exploration, integration, and further healing while also strengthening the alliance. In this manner the phases of Dyadic Developmental Psychotherapy are iterative and cyclical. This transcript is a lovely illustration of this and Kim's work reflects the artful shifting among different phases and the creative use of various components.*]

J: (with curiosity) Right, and what happened? What happened to you? How did you feel? (pauses, and then says gently) What happened Liam?

L: Well, Taylor said she was going to get her pillow, as I set the DVD up. We were in my room. She said she was going to get a pillow, which I thought was reasonable. Just sit on the floor, whatever. But once she came in with a cushion she lay down on the floor. I said, "No, Tay, you sit up; you're not in bed. Sit up. If you want to sleep you go to bed." (indignantly) She just said no. Every time I told her she just kept saying no. She wouldn't stop and she just wouldn't do as she was told at all. She was a right pain. I was just shouting. In the end I just took her. . . . She started crying, just after I took her pillow off her. I chucked it out of the room and said if you want to go and lie down just go in your room. So she just started crying and Jenny came up.

(Liam has now moved to lean with his back against Jenny, looking at me; Jenny strokes his shoulder.)

J: (with empathy) But you'd really lost it, hadn't you, and you were very tearful and you were very angry, weren't you?

L: I don't remember being tearful. I know I was angry. Anger was the main thing.

K: (with curiosity) But Jenny remembers you having tears?

J: Yes, you were. Your eyes were full of tears. You were so angry and yet it wasn't a huge sin. I'd seen you deal with situations with Tay before.

[Liam has allowed Jenny to take him back to the episode. He quickly becomes very engaged in thinking about this with her. He talks intently, gesticulating with hands to emphasize the frustration he was feeling with his sister. Liam's developing ability to trust Jenny is very evident here, as with my continuing support he is allowing her to co-regulate his anxiety and take him to the nub of what he was feeling. It is important that Jenny maintains an intersubjective relationship with Liam, that they use this relationship to explore together the incident they are thinking about. This avoids this dialogue seeming like an interrogation or question and answer session. It allows Liam to stay actively present without too much shame or anxiety.

As is typical for Liam it is easier for him to remember feeling angry than upset; he keeps potential feelings of shame away by not allowing himself to remember the more uncomfortable feelings. Helping Liam stay with the fear and sadness will be the main work of this session. I begin to do this by focusing Liam on what was underneath the anger that he is describing. This is very difficult for him, but he does not resist me. We have a go together at thinking about why he might have been so angry. We start to co-create meaning, while Jenny and I continue to co-regulate the anxiety, sadness and shame which are under the surface of this narrative. Curiosity with acceptance and empathy helps Liam to develop some insight into what happened that day, and to remember the affective experience that accompanied these events.]

K: (curious tone) The question is why did you get so angry?

L: I don't know. She just wouldn't do as she was told, her new thing that she does. She just says no in this like baby, middle of baby and the age she is now, type of voice. It gets really annoying. (sounds annoyed) The more she says it the more I get annoyed and angry. [*Editor's note: Generally, most children don't know "why" they did something or feel a particular way, and so the most common response is "I don't know," which is what Liam answers. However, he then goes on to describe what occurs, suggesting that the alliance with Kim is strong enough for him to be willing to explore a difficult topic. An important distinction is between asking why (which generally is an expression of disapproval—for example, when was the last time your boss asked you, "Why did you do such a good job there?") and being curious about the person and the person's motivation or intent—"I wonder why it turned out that way?"*]

K: (matching Liam's intensity) She can be very frustrating, can't she? [*Editor's note: This is a lovely example of accepting the client's experience and of the follow element of follow-lead-follow. The reader will see that this leads to deeper exploration and beginning integration phase work.*]

L: (sounds frustrated) Yer, for me anyway. She just will not do as she's told now.

[Liam is experiencing the feelings being evoked quite strongly now. It is important that I use empathy. I share my experience of Liam, and his frustration with his sister, in order to help him stay regulated. We can then continue to explore this curiously.]

K: So, what were you actually angry about? [*Editor's note: By being curious, the therapist can eventually get the answer to the "why" question without actually asking why.*]

L: (indignantly) Her not doing as she's told. She wouldn't sit up; there is no point lying down. In the end I gave up and said all right then if you want to lie down go on my bed. You don't need to . . . don't lie on the floor. She just said no, again!

K: I'm thinking about the big response you had to that. That was a big response, wasn't it? To be that angry, I wonder what was fuelling that?

L: I don't know. I seriously do not know. She just would not do as she was told, at all.

K: What is the danger of her not doing as she was told?

L: Me getting angry, going overboard and going into that volcano we did. Swelling up because of all the stress and that, and then boom.

[As Liam re-experiences the anger and frustration he was feeling I nonverbally attune to these emotions. I talk with more intensity, also gesticulating with my hands. This helps me to match, with my regulated affect, the frustration that Liam is reliving, which threatens to dysregulate him. As I communicate that I get his experience, Liam is able to stay regulated.] [*Editor's note. In addition, what the reader is observing here is Kim's affect-regulating approach of matching the vitality affect (the volume and energy) but not the categorical affect (mad, sad, glad, scared, etc.).*]

[Using a follow-lead-follow approach I decide to be curious about the stress that Liam has mentioned, wondering if Liam had been feeling a bit more stressed than usual. Liam is comfortable following me into this deepening exploration. We can be curious together.]

K: Were your stress levels high, do you think?

L: Yer.

K: Why do you think you were stressed? What was adding to your stress as well as Taylor being a bit awkward?

L: The movie. This little bit I wanted to watch was on and I was too busy sorting Taylor out.

K: So she was stopping you watching the program, which you really wanted to watch?

L: Yer, just a little bit I wanted to see.

K: What does Jenny think?

J: I think you had been a little bit stressed. You had just been to camp. Although you came through the door and said it had all been fine.

L: (turns head toward Jenny, indignantly) It was.

J: You didn't talk about it much. I asked you lots of questions about it and I got the monosyllabic answers—Yep, okay, not much. Zip wire, orienteering, and that was about it.

L: It was really good except for Martin, who was in my dorm.

J: So what was the problem with that?

[Liam and Jenny spend some time talking together about the boys in Liam's dorm and some teasing that upset his friend. I let them talk for a while. This takes us a bit down a side alley. I do not think that this is a distraction, but that Liam wants to share with us his recent experience. He has not talked much about this with Jenny since his return. He is feeling comfortable enough to share with her some of the difficulties he was experiencing with friends. I sense this is important for both of them. After a while I want to see if this experience and the resulting stress might explain some of his strong reaction with Taylor.] [*Editor's note: The reader can understand what is occurring as the therapist's skillful monitoring of the pace of treatment—the ebb and flow of affect and content. It is very important for the therapist to keep the pace of treatment therapeutic and not allow dysregulation or a merely cognitive chat. This "side alley" is a fine example of that, and as the reader shall see in a moment, Kim brings the discussion back quite artfully.*]

K: So you were coping with being away from home, weren't you?

L: Well, yes, but I went to the outdoor center as well for three days and I'll be, if it's all right with Jenny, I'll be going to France as well with school in year 7. That will be about three to four days as well.

K: You like going away, but it's a bit more stressful when you are not at home, isn't it? Everything's a little different.

L: Kind of, a little bit.

K: It's unsettling for anyone, isn't it? Not being at home.

L: Yer but . . .

K: Maybe not too unsettling, but let's come back to—so when you arrived home your stress levels might have been a bit higher? [*Editor's note: Here Kim returns to the earlier theme from the "side alley" taken. This allows Liam to feel "felt" and accepted and so become more regulated.*]

L: Not really high but just, um. . . . Not lots and lots but on a scale about there (indicates with hands).

K: A little bit more stressed, eh? We all feel more stressed when we're not at home. Much as everyone likes a holiday, it's stressful.

L: You've got to get used to things.

K: Yer, exactly, so your stress levels are going to be higher and then you came into your bedroom and Taylor's being tricky, yer. Do you think maybe you got angry quicker because your stress levels were higher?

L: (nods) Maybe.

[I am not sure that this has taken us very far, and clearly Liam is unconvinced that his stress levels were a factor. There is a danger here that my own theory regarding the stress of the trip could dominate our dialogue. This could lead to us having different attention/intention, thus moving us away from the intersubjective experience. I therefore decide to pursue another angle as we seek what lay underneath his anger. This time I focus more on Taylor and what she was doing.] [*Editor's note: In addition, focusing on an outside element (rather than on Liam and his internal experience) allows Kim to regulate his affective level of arousal, maintain the alliance, and engage in further exploration.*]

K: (using my hands for emphasis) I wonder what you felt most angry about. Taylor often doesn't do what you ask, does she?

L: (nods) I think it's just the way she was saying no.

K: Something about the way she was saying no on that day. What was she making you think or feel?

L: Just do as you're told.

K: But she wasn't going to because when Tay gets into that mood she won't, will she? (Liam shakes head in agreement) So you must be used to that. You've had years and years of Tay doing that, haven't you? (Jenny nods in agreement) What was it about that particular day, do you think?

L: I don't know.

J: (in a curious, accepting and nonjudgmental tone) It was unusual because I've seen you—I know Tay really irritates you sometimes. I know she does, but you normally deal with her really very well or you refer her to me, but that particular day, I was surprised by your reaction. It was really quite aggressive and you were not only very angry but you were quite upset and I wasn't quite sure why that was.

[As Jenny and I maintain a nonjudgmental but accepting, curious and empathic stance we help Liam to move deeper into his experience with Taylor. Liam listens intently to Jenny. He doesn't look at her at this stage but sits with his back to her, leaning against her for support. Again my nonverbal communication, gesticulating with my hands, talking with a more intense tone in my voice brings us into a state of emotional attunement. This together with the affective/

reflective dialogue we are engaged in helps Liam to get more deeply in touch with his emotional experience. Liam becomes deeply engaged in puzzling this out. Our persistent PACE has allowed Liam to remain regulated and therefore enter fully into the process of co-creating meaning. He wonders about the visitors who were around at the time. As with the comment about his stress earlier I again follow Liam's lead; this is more fruitful and he then allows me to lead him to a deeper understanding.]

L: (still sitting with his back to Jenny, Liam now twists around so that he can look at her) Might be because visitors were here?

K: You had visitors that day?

J: Were there?

L: Yer, because I was taking her away.

J: Oh yes, that's right—you were watching a DVD with her in your bedroom, weren't you? I remember.

K: So you had some responsibility to keep Tay quiet so they could have a good time. Were you feeling a sense of "I've got to sort this"?

L: (turning to look at Kim) Yes, just shut up, and do as you are told.

K: Because this is important? (Liam nods yes) And you were helping the adults out by trying to keep Tay amused.

L: (looking sad) She just wouldn't do as she was told.

K: (quietly, with empathy) And she wouldn't do as she was told. (I pause as I nonverbally support Liam with this emotion) So what's the consequence of that? If she doesn't do what she is told? She is going to go back downstairs and she is going to spoil things (Liam nods) and you've taken responsibility to make sure that doesn't happen. (Liam nods and is again looking quite sad) So maybe some of your strong emotion to that was I'm not doing a good job here?

L: Mmm, maybe. (continues looking thoughtful and sad) Mmm. (nods again)

K: (quietly) So why is it important to do a good job?

L: (shrugs) Don't know.

K: Do you want the adults to like you? [*Editor's note: The reader is observing how the use of PACE, being playful, accepting, curious, and empathic, leads to the co-creation of a new meaning, which is an element of the integration phase.*]

L: I want to make a good impression.

K: (acceptance) Yer, you want to make a good impression and you want to help Jenny, help her make a good impression?

L: (looks thoughtful) Um.

[As with Liam's earlier feelings of frustration and anger I now emotionally attune to his sadness. I lean toward Liam, using closeness to convey empathy. I
talk softly and quietly as I match Liam's affect. Liam remains very engaged but
I sense that the strength of emotion he is experiencing is beginning to dysregulate him. I now use a bit of playfulness to help him stay regulated and Jenny
follows my cue.] [*Editor's note: The reader will be observing another good
example of how the therapist manages the pace of treatment and the ebb and
flow of affect so that the family will feel safe in the secure base of treatment. This
sense of security allows for deeper exploration. When exploration leads into integration and healing, the secure base and alliance are strengthened, allowing
for deeper exploration and further integration and healing.*]

K: The family on trial here? *(Liam smiles)*

J: What do you reckon? (laughs) We've failed at the first fence then, eh? (we all
laugh, and Jenny kisses Liam lightly on the back of his head)

L: Can I just stretch? (stands up and stretches) Sitting a bit, makes your back
hurt.

K: You can put a cushion behind you. (reaches for a cushion)

L: No, it's okay. That's all right, I'm fine.

K: Well it's there if you want it.

(Liam continues to stretch)

K: (teasing) This is a new distraction, by the way!

L: No, no distraction—seriously, my back was killing me.

K: (to Jenny) How old is this man?

J: I know.

(Jenny and Kim laugh with enjoyment of this dialogue, Liam smiles as he ap-
preciates the playfulness.)

L: (sits back down) Oh, I did my 800 meters today. (I look at him in mock disapproval) No, I'm not distracting. I'm just saying I did 800 meters. [*Editor's note:
This comment by Liam is a nice example of the reflective function. In order for
him to say "I'm not distracting . . ." he has to have a mental representation of
Kim, himself, and the relationship. He knows what Kim may be thinking and
wants her to understand his intention.*]

K: (smiling) It just popped into your mind.

L: (laughing) Yes.

[The playfulness allows Liam to take a needed break, as he stands up and
stretches. I continue to gently tease him as he tries to distract us from refocusing. At this point in therapy Liam is better able to notice these distractions and

to respond to my leading him back to where we were. I return to being curious about the episode with Taylor, and Liam quickly follows me into this affective/reflective dialogue.]

K: Okay, so we're building up a picture, which is starting to make a lot of sense to me. You're trying to do a job for the adults and (with a sad tone to my voice) you're failing in it. Who asked you to distract Tay?

L: No one.

K: So you took it on yourself? It wasn't because someone asked you to do it?

L: Well, no, but I just . . .

K: You could see things were wobbling?

L: I could see Jenny (turns to Jenny), you looked at me as if it was . . . I think anyway this is what the sense was, to get Taylor away.

J: I thought you took Tay.

L: (laughs, a bit embarrassed) I think I did as well.

J: I thought you got a DVD and took her with you.

L: I could see, yer. I actually told you after. I said I'll go upstairs. I was going to take her out so they could talk to you again.

J: Oh, I remember you telling me that you were taking her to watch a DVD. Then you just went.

L: That's why, to keep her out of the way.

[At this point Liam is on the verge of experiencing shame; presumably he has a sense of not being good enough—he chose to take care of Taylor but then wasn't able to. This developing sense of shame makes sense as we later discover how this episode has evoked past experience for Liam. For now he tries to deflect the shame by blaming someone else. He suggests that Jenny had asked him to take Taylor away. Jenny's accepting and curious attitude allows Liam to stay regulated and explore further.]

K: What would have happened if you hadn't done that?

L: (looks toward Kim) Something would have happened and Jenny would be telling her to go away.

K: So you were worried that Tay—What I'm hearing from you is that you were worried that Taylor was interfering?

L: Yes, or was going to.

K: The potential was there. Why would that have been so bad?

L: Because they needed some time to talk.

K: So you could see a situation brewing that you thought wouldn't be good.

L: Yer.

K: And who did you think was most going to be harmed in this situation, if it went the way you thought?

L: I don't know really.

K: Who was going to suffer?

L: (very definitely) Taylor.

K: So you were trying to protect Taylor, so she didn't experience the rejection?

L: No, not rejection.

K: It wouldn't be nice for her, would it?

L: No.

K: If they had said, "Go away, Tay, we're trying to talk."

L: Yer, not rejection, that's a bit of a strong word but um . . .

K: What would be a better word?

L: Told her to go away.

K: Maybe you thought Taylor might get upset? So it sounds to me like you were trying to look after Taylor? [*Editor's note: Throughout this section the reader is observing Kim co-create a new meaning with Liam, which is an element of the exploration phase and leads into the integration phase.*]

L: Yer, I would have thought so, in a sense, (with sadness) but in the end she did get upset.

K: (quietly and softly) And you got upset.

L: Yep.

K: Because for all your good intentions you weren't able to protect Tay, were you?

L: (sad) No.

K: Maybe that's what made you feel sad.

L: Yer.

[Together we are building up a more detailed picture of what happened on that day, and Liam is able to follow me into experiencing the sadness he felt when he could not protect Taylor. I again nonverbally attune to the sadness, talking quietly and softly, stilling my movements and maintaining eye contact to convey my feelings of compassion. This is an important moment for Liam, as he stays with the sadness, without any distraction. By maintaining the intersubjective relationship and using PACE we have helped Liam to stay regulated despite the sadness and feelings of shame that are evoked. Liam is able to use his relationship with us to stay reflective, further deepening the creation of meaning we are making.

Liam has done really well staying with this. This allows him to re-experience the emotions underlying his anger; emotions that were triggered for him on that day. I return to using curiosity to deepen this, now linking it to past experience.]

[*Editor's note: This is a fine example of the affective/reflective dialogue and how it leads to integration and healing by enhancing the reflective function.*]

K: Are there other times when you have tried to protect Tay, and it hasn't worked?

L: (long pause and looking thoughtful) No, I don't think so. No. Can you? (to Jenny)

J: You do feel responsible for Tay, I think.

L: Well yer, presumably.

J: That you need to keep an eye on her and make sure she's okay.

K: Where does that come from, do you think? Where does that need to look after Tay come from? [*Editor's note: The reader will now see how Kim works with Liam to uncover how the past still lives on in the present. The fact that Liam can engage in this deep exploration is a function of the strong relationship and alliance that Kim has built with this family.*]

L: (turns back to look at Kim and with sadness) I think, um, from when I was at home; when I was with my mum.

K: What happened if you didn't look after Tay, at home?

L: Don't know because I pretty much always been there.

K: Always looked after her?

L: I would have thought so, yer.

K: What might have happened if you hadn't?

L: Anything, I don't know.

K: (with empathy) You are looking quite sad. [*Editor's note: Here the reader is observing Kim reflecting Liam's internal affective state back to him so that they can reflect on this and what it may mean, thereby beginning to co-create new meaning and a more integrated autobiographical narrative.*]

L: Maybe, I don't know.

[Liam remains very engaged in this exploration and is able to let Jenny help him with this. This allows him to reflect upon his early experience at home with his birth family. Liam is reluctant to acknowledge the depth of sadness he is experiencing. This is difficult for him. Often at this stage in a session he would be drawing on major distractions to avoid staying with the experience. On this occasion, however, he is able to stay with it. I can therefore use empathy and attunement to deepen his affective experience as I continue the affective/reflective dialogue.]

K: I think you are feeling sad now, because I think we are tapping into something quite deep here, which is about the pressure that has been on you for years to look after Taylor. The pressure that came from living with Mum and Dad, and maybe them not doing a good enough job looking after her themselves, and perhaps having to do more looking after Taylor than you should have done when you were little. (Liam looks very sad and thoughtful) I wonder. This is what I am thinking. I am thinking of this eleven-year-old boy who is trying to look after his sister, doing a favor for his mum because he knows it is important. Trying to make a situation good, and Tay wasn't letting you do it. So you were feeling a sense of I can't do this, it's not working. And I wonder if that triggered for you a deeper memory of when you were three and it didn't work and you couldn't look after Taylor well, and that's why you got so upset. I know you won't know that because it won't have been in your head at the time, but that's the sense I am making of what we are talking about. [*Editor's note: In this comment by Kim we see the reflective element of the affective/reflective dialogue. By engaging Liam on a more reflective level she is able to help regulate his affect and continue to keep him engaged in this very deep and difficult exploration.*]

(Liam is close to tears; he hides his face behind his legs. We stay with him. Jenny hugs Liam quietly and I remain leaning forward. Between us we nonverbally help Liam to stay regulated, while I continue to facilitate Liam's deepening understanding.)

K: Sometimes we have reactions to things in the past that we don't even realize that it's there in the background. That's why your emotional reaction was so much stronger and bigger than it would normally be. (I pause to gauge Liam's reaction; he is looking thoughtful.) Quite a lot to take on; is it making sense? [*Editor's note: Kim's remarks are also helping Liam revise his autobiographical narrative, which is an important element of the integration and healing phases.*]

L: (tentative) I think so.

K: It's sort of making sense?

[I now lean back, away from Liam. This allows him to take a break from the intensity of emotion that he is experiencing. Liam has done really well staying with this affective experience, and allowing Jenny to help him with this.

I continue to be curious, as I feel we can go a little further in co-constructing meaning for Liam. Jenny is able to follow my lead and she helps Liam to explore his experience even further. He remembers some very difficult experience which highlights the reasons why he is so protective of Taylor now.]

J: Do you remember telling me how Mum used to send Taylor outside when you were out with your friend, Daniel, was it? When you were out on your bikes?

L: (turning to look at Jenny) Yes, I had to look after her.

J: Yes, you had to look after Tay as well and that's a really big ask, isn't it?

L: Yes, and she went over the road, over to the corner shop and I wasn't there to look after her.

K: So, she was at risk? And she might have been hurt.

L: (Liam's voice takes on a very young tone) Mmm, and that was when I got in trouble for it.

K: Tell me about that. [*Editor's note: The reader will observe how Kim deepens the experience with Liam by accepting what he says and asking him to say more. This will expand the affective/reflective dialogue and deepen the affective elements of his memory as he recounts the events of the past.*]

L: (thoughtful) No, I can't remember fully.

K: (gently) Tell me what you can remember.

L: Well, as I was playing with my mate, Mum came out and asked me to look after Taylor, asked me and Daniel to look after Taylor, but me and Daniel were so busy playing that we completely forgot that Taylor was there. So she went out on to the road, and over the road to the corner shop.

K: And she wasn't allowed to cross the road because she was so little?

L: Well, yer, but Mum, I think asked, after we had played and I came in, asked where Taylor was and I said I don't know. I didn't see her go anywhere.

K: Then she was really mad with you?

L: I should have thought so, but that's as far as I can remember.

[Liam has remembered a lot here and this has evoked some strong affect. He has become that very little boy again who was given too much responsibility. The baby tone to his voice illustrates how much he is reliving this experience. The shakiness in his voice reveals the intensity of this. Liam remains engaged. Comfortable in the support Jenny and I offer, Liam remains regulated despite the difficult content we are exploring.] [*Editor's note: It is very important for the therapist to be able to accept, tolerate, and be comfortable with strong emotions. If we, as therapists, cannot tolerate strong emotions, how can the child? Another important point to make here is that while Liam is experiencing very powerful emotions, he is not dysregulated. Dysregulation involves dissociation and an inability to be cognitively present; often dysregulation involves re-experiencing (flashbacks) rather than remembering. Kim's work here is an outstanding illustration of the therapist's use of self in maintaining the pace of treatment, keeping the affective and intersubjective experience at an intensive level, while avoiding dysregulation.*]

[I now move again to deepen the affective experience further, using empathy.]
[Editor's note: By sharing the emotion (empathy) the client will be less alone and be better able to experience and express a deeper level of affect.]

K: Do you know what I am thinking? You must have been one scared boy when you realized that you had forgotten to keep an eye on Taylor. I'm thinking you were so scared by that, that maybe you keep a really close eye on her now. You've forgotten that you don't need to do that all the time. You now have a mum and dad who can do that, and you are still doing it, aren't you? Because what might have happened? Taylor might have been hurt, she might have died. What if a car had come along at that time, and you would have felt that it was all your fault, because your mum gave you a responsibility she had no right to give you at that age. No wonder you felt sad and angry when Taylor wouldn't do as you wanted her to do, because it mattered. Sometimes it doesn't matter, but it mattered because you were trying to keep Tay safe, and you've been trying to keep Tay safe for eleven years. *[Editor's note: Here the reader observes the therapist co-creating a new meaning within the child's autobiographical narrative that connects past and present in a new and healthier manner.]*

L: Eleven?

J: Eight.

K: Eight years. That was me making a big mistake there. You're eleven; she's not. (laughs, then says to Jenny) He's so quick picking me up when I get it wrong. *[Editor's note: This is a clear and simple example of interactive repair.]*

J: I know. (we all laugh)

K: From the time that Mum started to get you to keep an eye on her. When was that?

L: I was about three. Tay was coming into toddler.

K: Yes, she was starting to get mobile, wasn't she? Eight years you've been looking after Taylor, trying to protect her in a way that a big brother shouldn't have to look after his sister. No wonder you felt really sad and angry that she wouldn't do what she was told. (to Jenny) You know, Liam is such a brave lad, isn't he? He has worked so hard all these years to try and get it right for Taylor.

J: I know he is a pretty special big brother. Whether she ever realizes how special you are is another thing.

K: And of course at three and at four you wouldn't be able to do a good enough job, would you? And that's really hurting you. It's really making you sad that you couldn't do a good enough job to look after her because you were too little.

[While we are talking Liam is leaning strongly into Jenny, drawing support from the physical contact. She can feel his body shaking with the intensity of his experience. With this important support Liam is again able to stay with me, and a mistake on my part gives him a natural break, allowing him to remain regulated. I quickly repair any threatened rupture to our relationship caused by my mistake and the laughter allows us all a brief respite from the intensity of this affective/ reflective dialogue. I then return to empathy and acceptance as I normalize Liam's current experience with Taylor based on our exploration of his past experience. Liam is now able to shift perspective, demonstrating his developing reflective functioning. He thinks about his birth parents and what they didn't do for him. He is able to acknowledge that they did not look after him properly.]

L: They should have looked after me properly, and that meant they lost me because I am here instead. [*Editor's note: Liam is able to integrate the new meaning into his autobiographical narrative, which represents healing.*]

K: Yes, they lost you; in fact they were a bit careless losing you like that—their precious, special little boy. Why couldn't they have done better? Such a special brother, but so hard for you, to keep her safe; so much responsibility for a little boy. So hard it makes you feel so sad. I just want you to turn to Jenny and tell her how sad you feel.

L: Oh no, not another one of these. (looks at Jenny and says quickly) I'm really sad at the moment, but I'll get over it.

J: I know you are and you don't have to get over it.

L: No, but you know what I mean. I'll sort it out. (looks at Jenny and in a baby voice) With a bit of help. [*Editor's note: This is a good example of the reflective function. Liam is able to maintain a mental representation of himself and Jenny, and clarify the miscommunication.*]

(Jenny hugs Liam, and he allows her to cuddle him for a moment) [*Editor's note: In this next section the reader will again see Kim manage the PACEing of treatment by allowing the emotional intensity to decrease and the subject to be changed. It is clear that Liam has had enough and it is very important that the therapist allow for such breaks so that the client experiences the ability to influence the course and pace of treatment. By supporting this sense of control, the therapist will allow the client to engage in deeper exploration because the client will "know" that the client is able to stop and the experience of exploring deeply disturbing emotions and memories never becomes overwhelming or dysregulating.*]

L: Yer, I've had enough of feeling a bit sad today.

J: Well done. That was really very difficult for you and you did it. (Liam reaches up and hugs Jenny)

L: (to Jenny) Can I have a deal with homework now?

(we all laugh)

K: Oh, he doesn't miss a trick.

J: (laughs) It doesn't work, boy.

L: It was worth a go though.

J: I thought you might think so.

[This has been difficult for Liam. He has allowed himself to think that maybe his mum and dad did not do a good enough job. I think this triggered some shame and some fears that maybe this is his fault after all, that he is not special enough, not good enough to be taken care of. I move too quickly at this point. Instead of regulating his feelings of shame, I try to deepen his affective experience by asking him to talk directly to Jenny. Liam moves away from Jenny, and becomes very fidgety, evidently anxious. My request that Liam talk directly to Jenny triggers his fear of being exposed to Jenny. I think that he fears rejection from her, that she will see that he is not special, not good enough. He is able to follow my direction a little way, but needs to reassure her that he will be all right. He emphasizes this nonverbally by reaching up and hugging her, a clear gesture that he can take care of her. Jenny gently counters this. She holds him tight and kisses his head as she quietly conveys that he can trust her to take care of him. Liam then tells me that he has had enough. Some playfulness allows us to co-regulate the shame that Liam is experiencing, as his vulnerability and need to rely on Jenny is revealed. I judge that Liam has had enough for this session and so leave further exploration for another time. After a bit of banter between the three of us and some summing up, I draw the session to a close.]

K: So I'll see you next time and I want you to carry on noticing when you are either experiencing something sad, or emotional or when you are distracting yourself from this. [*Editor's note: Finding ways to carry over the session's work into the home is an important element of treatment. It also underscores the vital importance of caregiver participation in treatment since what occurs at home in their interaction is a major component of treatment. Carers are the keystone for treatment and good outcomes.*]

L: (looks at Jenny) We can do that, can't we?

J: Yes, we can.

L: I'm sure we will be able to notice everything with our little beady eyes.

K: The next step is to let Jenny help with this because you still feel: I'll do this by myself, because you said to her, didn't you, I know I am feeling sad, but I'll sort it.

L: With a bit of help.

K: With a bit of help, yer, a little bit of help.

L: I would like some help though. Not lots.

J: We get halfway there, don't we, because we talk a lot about stuff? And you tell me things that you remember about stuff, so it's out there, isn't it? The information is out there; we just have to tackle the bits behind that and we're beginning to do that a bit.

L: (nods) Mmm.

J: And I'm incredibly proud of you because I know how hard that is for you to do.

K: And it would be so much easier not to do it. That's why I think you are a courageous lad.

L: (whispers) Thank you.

J: And you know the little brown-eyed beauty that really annoys you sometimes. (Jenny points to herself) I'm the one that deals with her, right. She's your sister to love and to keep a beady eye on, but it's my job to deal with her.

[*Editor's note: What we've seen in this transcript is a fine illustration of how a strong alliance is necessary for a secure base in treatment and how maintaining that alliance leads to deeper exploration, integration, and then healing. As the exploration proved positive, Liam was able to go deeper and this illustrates the iterative and cyclic quality of the phases of Dyadic Developmental Psychotherapy. Kim, as a seasoned and skillful Dyadic Developmental Psychotherapist, is able to use a variety of components of Dyadic Developmental Psychotherapy in creative ways to maintain concordant intersubjectivity and facilitate healing.*]

[I remind Liam that he might continue to notice how he is feeling, and he beautifully looks to Jenny for support with this. This session has been an important step for Liam in letting Jenny support him with difficult affective experience. Jenny also nicely lets Liam know that he can trust her to look after Taylor as well, thus rounding the session off with the theme that we have been exploring.]

REFLECTION

This session represents an important point on Liam's journey through therapy. He is leaving behind most of the distractions that have been so important to him earlier on. He is beginning to allow me to help him explore his affective experience, both of the present and his past. This means we can deepen our affective-reflective dialogue. Liam now trusts me and Jenny to use PACE and PLACE to help him remain regulated with the affect and understand this at a deeper level. Persistent PACE allows Liam to go back to his experience, to stay with it—to reflect on it. While previously he would move away from it through his major distractions, this has lessened over time. Playfulness has been an important part of this process. Jenny and Liam have a naturally playful relationship which helps Liam to get much-needed breaks from the intensity of this work. At times I keep the playful quite small and in the background because Liam moves so quickly into silly as a distraction, but the playful is an important element in bringing a rhythm to the work. [*Editor's note: It is useful to consider "defenses" as adaptive strategies to be accepted and explored in a nonjudgmental way. This has been demonstrated in this transcript. Describing behaviors as "resistance" or in other negative ways can increase the client's shame because so much of our understanding of the other is communicated nonverbally; even if we don't use the pejorative descriptive word, the therapist's demeanor will communicate it.*]

In this session Liam is taking an important step forward in learning that his memories are safe to explore. True safety comes from being able to integrate the memories which exist within him; once integrated Liam will remain safe even when something activates one of these memories. Liam learns through our reflective exploration that events in the present are often connected to events in the past. As we regulate his shame and fear about not being able to protect Taylor he is able to experience sadness for the little boy who should not have been asked to keep her safe. Through this co-construction of meaning, alongside co-regulation of affect, Liam is developing a coherent narrative, an understanding that integrates past, present and potential future.

While Liam does experience some safety with Jenny, he finds it hard to fully trust her. He fears what she might discover about him. He experiences shame and fear that she too might reject and abandon him, as he feels rejected and abandoned by his birth mother. He has far more to lose with Jenny than with me and therefore to reveal his experience to her feels dangerous. This demonstrates the importance of having the foster caregiver involved in the therapeutic work. If I worked with Liam alone, he would not experience the deepening safety with his foster mum. It would be much harder to help him modify his core beliefs about "mums."

Liam is making progress with Jenny. He now readily looks to her for help with reflection; he wonders does she know why he might be reacting as he is. In this session we also see him beginning to show her how he is feeling, and he is able to let her contain some of his sadness and shame. He cuddles into her and allows her to gently stay with him. When I direct him to share his experience more directly with her, however, this is too much. He quickly tells her how he feels but has to reassure her that he can manage this, he will sort it. Liam is sure that Jenny will like the clever Liam, the caregiver Liam, the entertainer Liam—these are aspects of himself that have worked well in the past. They have been an important part of his self-belief that he can be liked and he fears having to give them up. He is less sure that Jenny will like the sad Liam, the angry Liam, the Liam who needs her. I help Liam to experience Jenny loving all of him. He can be all of these things. He does not need to give anything up but can be open and honest about all of himself. Through this exploration his internal working model will be modified. This will allow Liam to develop true dependence and so open up his route to a well-balanced independence.

Liam's acknowledgment of needing a bit of help from Jenny is a brave and important step for him. During the remaining few months of therapy this will be our focus; the work between sessions becomes more important than the sessions themselves as Liam learns to express what he is feeling openly and to let Jenny help him manage this. Liam is calm, settled, and stable as he and Jenny talk things through and he becomes more comfortable letting her take care of him.

While Liam was going on his own particular journey with me, I also had a journey. He taught me much about Dyadic Developmental Psychotherapy. Most importantly, Liam taught me that I needed to get on with it. My previous therapy training had taught me to be receptive; now I had to learn to be directive as well—receive, direct, receive as I learned to follow-lead-follow. Liam always offered themes to explore, but was skilled in distracting us from the deeper exploration of these. I learned not to let go of these until we got to the core of them; to become the terrier, as Liam nicknamed it; not letting go but taking us deeper into Liam's experience. By using PACE I could accept Liam's current experience, contain his affective responses, and gently lead him into a deeper experience within which he both understood more fully and experienced more intensely. Liam could only do this through his developing trust in both myself and Jenny. I learned to use my knowledge to gently challenge Liam's own view of experience. As he told me that he did not experience things, did not feel sadness or pain, I expressed surprise. How did you manage to do that when other children would not be able to? Where did you learn this? What was it like when you were a baby and could not do this? PACE helped me to challenge without confronting. I was able to think aloud, to explain my reasons and so lead Liam into reflection of his affective experience. Through my experience of Liam, of what it may have been like as a very small child, I was helping Liam to experience his own sadness for his smaller self.

Liam also taught me to override my own early attachment experience; for different reasons I was very similar to Liam in trusting intellect over emotion—my inclination was to follow his distractions, to avoid the intensity of affective experience for fear it would overwhelm us both. I learned to stay with the affect and to trust that this would be helpful for Liam. We both needed to experience sadness getting smaller as it was explored, held and contained. It was safe to open the boxes and let the feelings out. Jenny's trust in me and love for Liam supported this exploration. Liam in turn learned to trust in this love and to discover its true unconditionality.

Jenny's gentle support of Liam was always a backdrop to our work. I learned to help Liam to connect to this source of support, to trust in it. As he experienced an emotional response to our reflections I helped to contain Liam's fear and shame while he took some risks in exposing this to Jenny. He experienced her support and discovered that she was not overwhelmed by him, that she continued to love all that Liam was, is and could be. [*Editor's note: This last paragraph underscores the importance of the carers in treatment. A treatment that relies so extensively on the intersubjective sharing of experience, the reflective function, sensitivity, commitment, and insightfulness necessarily requires caregivers, who are the keystone for good treatment outcomes. In many regards, the best predictor of treatment outcome is the carer's/parent's capacity.*]

REFLECTION BY JENNY AND LIAM

While writing this chapter I showed a draft to Jenny and Liam and asked them for their reflections on the therapy. Liam is now a teenager, tall and athletic; he is embracing life and his future. His sense of humor and caring nature are still very evident, as is his continuing ability to use his relationship with Jenny and Tom as a secure base. He is proud of his achievements, particularly his involvement with the "Children in Care Council." This is a group of children and young people, all experienced with the care system, who are supported to advocate on behalf of children living in care, ensuring these children have a local voice.

Liam and Jenny found revisiting the work quite emotional. For Liam it was a chance to reflect on what has changed. In the final report Liam and I reviewed the therapy as being composed of several levels. We gave the levels our own names to reflect the work we did together, and linked these to the analogies we had used to help us with our exploration. This framework helped Liam make sense of our work, becoming part of an autobiographical narrative that included our experience together in treatment. This framework was in evidence as he and Jenny reflected with me after reading the chapter. I will end with a transcript of some of our discussion.

> *K:* I am wondering what the therapy was like for you. How did it feel from your perspective?

> *L:* After a session I didn't really feel any different. I didn't notice a difference but everyone else did. You don't feel different but everyone else notices the little changes in your behavior and how you act. Stuff like that. (looks to Jenny) Is that true?

J: It appeared to be that way. Looking back, I suppose you do the sessions and Kim goes home and we go back to normal. We have tea, we get back into the routine of things. I must admit reading it back again I was quite surprised at how big a lump in my throat there was. Thinking back to how you were.

L: I didn't notice any difference. I don't notice it; I bet other people might.

K: You didn't notice yourself changing?

L: No.

K: What about your relationship with Jenny?

L: I don't know really. I don't think I felt it changing in any way. I just naturally started trusting her more as I lived here. I don't know really; that's a tricky one.

K: It is tricky, isn't it, because you don't know how it would have been if we hadn't done the work.

L: I don't know what I would have been like if I hadn't had the sessions. I suppose we'll never know really. I'm secure now.

[Jenny talks to Liam about how things were before the therapy started, and why she asked me to work with them.]

J: Reading the chapter I remembered how we began to open the boxes. It had already begun to happen, hadn't it, before the therapy? That was part of the reason that I asked Kim if she would help me. Help me to make sense of it and give me an idea of how to support you with all the things that you were feeling. It's quite a responsibility to try and help someone with these kinds of problems, because however much I want to put myself in your position I can't do that. You experienced things that have never happened to me. I can love you and protect you and care for you but I can't help you deal with those things on a level that I actually understand what you went through. I found all your sessions really useful, and although you dismissed them sometimes when we were together afterward, you would keep chatting to me. I could be washing up and you'd be chatting to me about it and I began to feel you feeling safer with me. [*Editor's note: This comment by Jenny illustrates the role of the therapist: to be a guide and supporter for the parent as well as for the child.*]

K: (to Liam) I'm thinking you're a wee bit anxious just now? Is it quite tough sitting and talking about this?

L: Yer, a little bit. (laughs) But I can deal with it, with a little bit of help. (more seriously) It brings back memories.

K: It does, and it was tough, wasn't it?

L: Emotionally that session was pretty difficult. That was one of the biggest sessions that I'd done; one of the big pinnacle sessions, at all the levels. I think the hardest level we did was past meets present, really.

K: Yes, you had to think about lots of things.

L: From being at home and that. (looks to Jenny) I think learning dependence wasn't that hard, was it? I don't think it was.

J: I felt that was quite a big one.

L: I am still quite independent. Anyway, after learning dependence, now I'm a teenager, I have to learn to be more independent.

J: (smiling) It really isn't black and white, is it?

K: And that was a large part of this session, wasn't it—learning to rely on Jenny. I think you found it difficult as we started the session.

L: I can't really remember how I was feeling at the start of the session. Because the feelings I had then weren't so important that I can remember them. I remember more to the end of the session when I had the major feelings, not nice things. I can remember the more major ones near the end.

K: Can you remember how you felt when you knew it was a session day, and that I'd be coming around?

L: Just, oh I'm going to see Kim. No anxiety or anything. It was just, when you got here and we started chatting about stuff, then I would start to get a bit jumpy—that's when I started.

K: So you'd be quite cool about me coming round?

L: Yer, it's just another chat, and I knew it's for a good cause really.

K: But then when we kind of started getting into it?

L: When we started getting into the big thing, then I'd get anxious. That was with all of them, unless it was just a catch-up, then I wouldn't be that worried. I might be just a little bit jumpy but not that bad really.

K: In the early sessions you would use a lot of distraction, wouldn't you?

L: Yer, when I first started I would use a lot of distractions, I know that. I'd use all my defenses then. And then, I just might as well get on with it really. I started to trust you more, and I started to form more of a relationship with Jenny.

K: After a session like this one, would it leave you feeling tired?

L: I don't know. (Jenny nods) Jenny's saying yes but I don't know.

J: Yes and you were very cuddly, which always quite surprised me. Always leaning in, and keeping very close.

K: What would you say therapy is like?

L: Just like a chat, really. But a bit more, it's a bit like a chat but it's deeper than a chat. If you have your carer with you, as long as you've got an all right relationship to start with, you'll build on that. Or if you don't have a good relationship to start, you will start to form one.

K: So do you think it was important having Jenny in?

L: Well, I felt a bit more safe with Jenny, because I knew I might not have had a really, really good relationship with Jenny back then, but I had a good enough one to know she would be there should anything go wrong. I didn't know what was going to happen.

K: Jenny, do you want to talk a little bit about what it felt like from your point of view?

J: The first day I met Liam his foster carer left me with a comment: he'll give you no trouble. She ruffled his hair and shoved him in through the gate and that was it. I mean, there right on the pathway was this little clown. A little entertainer and (to Liam) living with you I began to realize how much trouble you were in. I couldn't get close to you, at the beginning. You know that's not surprising, is it really? I mean, things happen and you get put somewhere and that must be the most horrendously scary thing. Although I felt we were moving in the right direction I still felt that you were very vulnerable and I wanted to try and help with that. I tried lots of things, you know, tried and tested things and you did respond to lots of those things. Loving you was the biggest thing and caring about you—actions speak louder than words; the things I did for you. I began to feel very concerned about you: when anything emotional happened, suddenly this little jack-in-the-box creature came out and entertained everyone. I could see it all going on. I just needed some help to deal with it. As soon as Kim started working with you and I'm watching her, I can begin to see how I can help you. Sometimes we adapt things, don't we? We adapt things and we go about it maybe a different way but with Kim, she gives us the tools to work things out.

L: Yer, like making friends; (to Kim) you gave me the tools for that.

(Liam and Jenny talk about the friends he has made recently)

K: So, Jenny, what was it like actually being in the session?

J: Really helpful. I found it really valuable. It was the three-way sharing of things that I found so valuable. In a way Kim's guidance in sessions made me think about things in a different way. I was at a bit of a loss as to how to help you deal with things. What really impressed me was how you described things. You described Kim as a terrier, the boxes with the key in, the blade in the pool. It was that and it was the way that helped me to understand a little bit more about how scary all this was. I mean, it's a pretty scary thought, isn't it: this pond with a blade going around the middle of it. I sat and thought, my goodness, it really feels like this. This is how he's describing it. And the onion, the layers. I could see the layers. When we were in sessions I could see all the distractions, all the head down, the no eye contact, all those things made me appreciate more how hard it was for you. You know I just sat here and you were the one that was doing the work, and it was hard work, and I admire you very much for tackling it. I think you've been really courageous.

K: You were very courageous. You stuck with it. There were times you could have run away from it.

L: What would have been the point of that, though? It's easier to say it than do it, but what's the point of running away from a problem that will always be with you? You might as well face it head on and sort it.

K: And that's what you did right from day one. No matter how much you distracted you never ran away. And your distractions were a way of saying just slow down a bit to me. I can't do it too fast. And I had to trust you on that and go with you at your pace.

L: That's what you've got to do with anyone, no matter how slow. Some people can deal with it fast, some people can deal with it slow. You've got to figure that out and look for the distractions to know when to slow down.

K: Yes, that's absolutely right. You would make a good psychologist!

(Liam laughs and tells me about his plans for the future. He then picks up the thread again.)

L: I've still got the entertainer, because that was one of the things I first remember being scared about, losing all the stuff I was good at.

K: You were worried about that. You were really worried that you were going to change in ways you wouldn't like.

L: That I was going to lose some of my good bits.

K: And how do you feel about that now?

L: Don't know what I was worried about, because you don't really feel any different. You don't notice it. It's the little things from people who really know you. How they notice little things about you changing. How your behaviors benefited.

K: Thinking about this session particularly, what you were remembering. That was hard, wasn't it?

L: That was a hard session from what I can remember. I had a couple of them. I really did not like that session much, I don't think. Trying to remember it and sort it out. I was really scared of people seeing me cry. I still don't like it but who does like people seeing you cry. But it's not so much of a big deal anymore.

[We move on to talk about some of the changes Liam would like me to make to the chapter. He wants me to include his involvement with the Children in Care

Council, in the hope that this will encourage others to join. I then ask him if he is happy for the chapter to go forward to publication.]

L: Yes, more than happy. You know one of the reasons I joined the council? I wanted to make a difference. I want this chapter for the same reason. I want it to help another person.

Chapter Nine

Erika's Shame: Middle Treatment

Arthur Becker-Weidman, PhD

This is the transcript of a session with a single therapeutic foster parent and her child, Erika, whom she will be adopting. I'd been seeing this family weekly for nearly six months when this session occurred. Erika had been removed from her birth family because of severe abuse and neglect when she was about six and placed in a series of foster homes before being adopted at age nine years. That adoption was disrupted when Erika was thirteen. She was abused by her adopted mother. Erika was in several residential treatment centers before her placement with this therapeutic foster parent, where she'd been for about six months before we began treatment. Erika is nearly seventeen in this session.

In the earlier part of the session Erika was talking about having had her cell phone taken away. Her mom had taken the cell phone away because Erika had taken some naked pictures of herself and, in a conversation with a former boyfriend, sent them to the boyfriend. (In the discussion it becomes evident that Erika was coerced into sending the pictures and her inability to defend herself from peer pressure is a major source of Erika's shame.) Erika felt very ashamed of what she'd done. The cell phone had been a contentious issue in the past. Mom had let Erika have a very closely monitored cell phone and because Erika had been quite responsible in using it, her mom let her use the phone without closely monitoring it, and then this event occurred. While Erika did not want to tell me about this or talk about it, in the previous session she'd "promised" to tell me next week (the session you are about to read) and that was her dilemma. This is one indicator of our clearly having a strong alliance and being largely in the exploration and integration phases; Erika knew I want to help her and her mom and so she wanted to tell me, yet her shame made this very difficult. The conflict was intra-psychic and not interpersonal. This transcript is from the middle of the session.

Art: It's up to you. This whole list . . . it's all things that you came up with. . . . (referring to Erika's list of "problems" and topics she wants to discuss in therapy)

Mom: I think there's probably a way that you could say what happened without going into graphic specifics . . . don't you think?

Erika: (tearfully) How though?

Art: (hands Erika a tissue box, as Mom puts her arm around Erika's shoulder) Here's a tissue . . . so what are your tears about?

Erika: Because it's really embarrassing and I'm still really ashamed about it.

Art: Do you think your mom, your mom looks down on you because of that? [I am trying to understand what she is ashamed of and whether there is a relational dimension to this.]

Erika: It's something I'm not proud of, something I'm . . . I wish I never did.

[At this moment my guess is that maybe she doesn't want to talk about it because she's worried about what her mom thinks and that her mom may be upset with her. I say, "Oh, maybe you're worried your mom will look down on you," and no, that's not it. I got that one wrong, but that's okay. The reader will see that even if I get it wrong that doesn't stop her because we have an alliance and she knows that I really am trying to help her and her mom and so she helps me help her.]

Art: Do you know how your mom feels about it?

Erika: Uh uh.

Art: You don't *know* . . .

Mom: I think you do. We talked about it earlier!

Erika: I don't know . . .

Mom: You don't know?

Erika: (raised voice) We've never talked about how you *felt* about it!

Art: You want to know how she feels about it? [Here I move the interaction to be between Erika and her mom. This allows them to deepen the experience and allows me to facilitate their developing relationship.]

Erika: Sure.

Mom: In what respect? I mean, we've talked a lot about it. What don't you know?

Erika: How you feel about it . . .

Mom: How I feel about *you* because of it?

Erika: NO! How you feel about *it* in general.

Mom: Well, I think you know you got yourself in a position that was very uncomfortable: you basically didn't know how to, you know, stand up for yourself really and made a mistake, but that's, you know, but I don't think that's a bad thing. It's just a learning experience, right?

Art: Do you want to know how your mom feels about you about it?

Erika: No, I already know. She doesn't look down on me. It's just one of those mistakes (Mom nods her head) that people look like back and they are ashamed of it and I don't want to talk about it with anyone.

Art: You don't have to . . . [In this interaction the reader will observe my accepting that Erika does not want to say, and the follow element of follow-lead-follow. I want to let Erika know that whether she discusses this event or not is entirely up to her. This keeps any conflict she feels on an intra-psychic level and avoids an argument.]

Erika: But I made a promise and I can't break a promise. [Here we see Erika struggling with, on the one hand, feeling ashamed of what she did and not wanting to discuss it and, on the other hand, her wish to keep her promise to me from the previous session. The strength and depth of our alliance leads her to value our relationship and to not want to jeopardize it.]

Art: What's so ashamed about it? If your mom . . . [This illustrates the lead part of follow-lead-follow.]

Erika: Because it was seriously bad!

Art: What made it, what makes it so bad? [Curiosity]

Erika: It's the worst thing I've ever done and I still hate myself for it.

Art: You hate yourself for it? [Acceptance and curiosity—I don't dispute her feelings about herself in regard to this event; I accept her feelings. However, I am curious about the depth of her feelings.]

Erika: Yes!

Art: That's pretty serious. . . . How come you hate yourself . . . because your mom doesn't hate you for it, right? [I try to make a connection between her feelings about herself and what I think may be her concern, that her mom may now feel negatively toward her.]

Erika: (impatiently) It's not *about* my mom. It's about what *I* did! It's not *to* my mom, it's not *toward* my mom. It was something I did that I hate myself for . . . [Clearly, my "theory" was wrong, and Erika corrects me. This is a lovely example of how being both curious and open allows the therapist to guess at what may be deeper while doing so in a way that is tentative so that the child can correct you. The important element in this intersubjective experience with

Erika is not whether I am right or wrong. The important element is that I am deeply interested in her experience and want to share that with her. This affective dimension of our intersubjective experience is communicated to Erika by my tone of voice, posture, facial expression, and cadence.]

Art: Right . . .

Erika: Because it was the stupidest, most worst thing that I have ever done.

[Erika is clearly invested enough that she wants me to "get it." Furthermore, she has moved away from feeling that she is a bad kid to saying that she did something bad; she has moved from feeling shame to feeling guilt.]

Art: I understand you do, but your grandma doesn't, I would guess, if she knows, and your mom doesn't . . . [Erika sees her grandmother (foster mother's mother) every day and the grandmother often watches Erika after school while the mom is working.]

Erika: (emphatically, waving hand) It's not about who I'm . . . it's about *me.* I don't care that they . . . it's not . . . I *hate* myself, I don't hate them.

Art: So why do you feel so badly about yourself?

Erika: Because I made a stupid mistake. (Mom nods) I made, I didn't . . .

Art: Yeah?

Erika: . . . know what to do. I hurt myself. . . . I'm so ashamed of it. (said with downcast eyes and in a whisper)

Art: Tell me, tell me more. What makes it so awful for you?

Erika: Because . . .

Art: Yeah?

Erika: Peer pressure especially is hard to get out of . . .

Art: Mmhm. That's true. And what makes this so hard and hurtful for you?

Erika: Because if you knew what I did, you'd understand, but I don't want to tell you . . . that's the thing.

Art: Mmm.

Erika: The only reason why Miss Betty knew is that (gestures angrily toward her mother) she went and ran around before even coming to me. [Miss Betty is Erika's caseworker.]

Mom: Honey, do you want to know *why* I did that, though?

Erika: I *know* why you did it.

Mom: Why?

Erika: Because you didn't want to talk to me about it *alone.*

Mom: Well . . . I was afraid you might really lose it and I thought it would be better for you and it would help you keep yourself together a little more if, you know . . . besides, I'm required to tell Miss Betty anyway. [I now want to move the discussion back to the immediate experience we are having with associated affect.]

Art: I'd like you to help me understand and I . . . there are other things you've done and you felt bad about . . .

Erika: But this is the worst . . .

Art: Right, I want to understand what makes it *the worst*, because . . .

Erika: Oh, I don't know how to put it, okay? Just give me some time to think about it, how to put it. . . .

Art: Okay, think about it and I'm thinking there've been times you, there've been times in the past when you've said things to your mom, and you've actually *hit* your mom. . . .

Erika: This is the most thing, I'm most ashamed of.

Art: So what makes this . . . ?

Erika: Because it hurts my future, it hurts the way I look at myself.

Art: How's it hurt your future and the way you see yourself? [By continuing to accept Erika's statements and view, she is better able to communicate what is difficult for her and I come to understand her better. Together we are beginning to co-create a new meaning for this event.]

Erika: Because . . .

Art: Yeah?

Erika: Because it just does.

Art: But . . . I mean how?

Erika: You don't understand. . . .

Mom: I don't understand how it would hurt your future *either*, sweetie.

Erika: Because—if I don't look at myself as someone who can get through things, then how I am I going to get through future things?

Mom: Well, because . . . don't we learn by making mistakes? And growing and . . . [Here the mom is trying to make Erika feel better, but what Erika needs, first, is to feel understood.]

Erika: (with exasperation) I don't *know*, Mom.

Art: Or are you kind of worried that you might do it again? [In this reflective part of our affective/reflective dialogue, I am trying to understand Erika so that she feels understood. I am guessing that her underlying fear is that she cannot trust herself.]

Mom: Mmhm?

Art: Is that it?

Erika: (with frustration) No, okay, I don't know!!

Art: You don't know.

Mom: Oh, okay . . . (nodding head)

Erika: Just like I didn't know this was going to happen. (raises arm wrapped in bandage) I didn't, I don't know. I didn't know I was going to fall out of a tree today. Sometimes you just don't know.

Art: That *would* be pretty upsetting if you did something you feel ashamed of and you're not confident you wouldn't do it again (Mom nods in agreement). . . . That would be really upsetting. Is that part of it? You're just not convinced that if you were put in a similar situation, you might not do something equally embarrassing? [Now I think I understand her fear and what makes this so very hard for her. Erika is afraid that she could do the same thing again. Now I feel real empathy for her . . . her worry is a big one.]

Erika: (eyes lowered, looking at the floor, barely audible) Yes.

Art: Is that what you mean? It is.

Erika: (nods slightly)

Art: It is.

[What the reader has observed is that when I finally "get it," and have empathy for Erika, she calms down; she feels understood and accepted. Erika is not alone with her feelings; now somebody (me) understands and can share those feelings with her. Now I *get* her and she knows that I *get* her. This is a good example of how powerful relationships are and how powerful is concordant intersubjectivity. Now all three elements of intersubjectivity (share affect, attention, and congruent intention) are in sync.]

Art: Okay, so you've learned that some . . . someone, another peer could put you in a position that later you'd really regret. You're not sure you'd be able to stop it or say "No." Is that what you mean?

Erika: (nods) Yes, and it scares me. [Now Erika is much more coherent and better able to reflect on the event and what it means. My understanding of her experience and sharing that experience with her enables Erika to become more reflective and to move toward integration and healing.]

Art: Okay. That must be so scary for you.

Erika: Yes, that's it.

Erika: (to her mom) Ouch, stop that!

[Mom has put her arm around Erika and Erika acts as if that hurts her arm, which she'd just sprained earlier that day. While this may seem like a "diversion," I take it to mean that Erika needs a bit of a break in the intensity of our work, so I decide to focus on this for a bit before returning to the subject of the her embarrassment. This is an example of how the therapist tries to manage the PACE of treatment and keep the ebb and flow of the dialogue and affect within therapeutic bounds.]

Art: You don't like your mom putting her arm around you?

Erika: If you had fallen out of a tree and hurt your wrist, you'd be the same way.

Art: I'm just saying I assumed you liked what she was doing, so you'd want to encourage her. You'd want to do things to encourage her that help her. (laughs) [Being playful.]

Erika: Oh, I do, I do.

Art: You want to do things to encourage her and have her do more of that and not be as, not be as . . .

Erika: I'm not trying to be *difficult*, it's just a bad day and . . .

Art: I didn't say "being difficult." I wasn't going to say "difficult." I was saying "Help your mom not be as, um, formal" . . . was that the right word? Would that sound right? [I am being a bit more playful here with both Mom and Erika.]

Erika: Formal?!

Art: I notice you two sitting next to each other. I think this is one of the first times I've seen your mom put her arm around you. . . . .

Erika: Really?

Art: Yeah, yeah.

Erika: She does it all the time, at home. [Now that Erika has reflected on her mom's support of her, I think we can return to the subject of her fear.]

Art: Okay, I'm just saying. . . . But it seems to me if you're really worried that, if you were put in a similar situation, you'd do the same thing again and you'd feel awful about it, this is something serious that we ought to work on so that, so that the next time we have a conversation you can say, "What I did I regret, and now I feel bad about it and I wished I didn't so . . . but I know I would just never do that again." You need to feel confident that you'd never do that again. Would you, would you like that?

Erika: (nods and looks at me) Yes!

Art: Yeah. So, so at some point to get there, we're going to have to talk about it. Whenever you're ready.

[Now that Erika has said that she wants to work on this issue, I can leave it to her to decide on the timing. It is up to her now. I don't want to push her; I know this is very difficult for her. I also am confident that we will get to it at *some* point. I really want her to feel I want to help her, I want to be there for her family and help them, but this is leading, not pushing so I'm going to keep encouraging her, leading her, but I'm not going to push her to do something she really doesn't want to do. Especially for children who have experienced their world as being one over which they have almost no control, creating experiences where they legitimately have some authentic sense of control over what happens is important. It's therapeutic.]

Art: It's up to you, at this point.

Erika: I don't know.

Art: Well, and you know, you did promise last time and . . .

Erika: A boy, over the phone, with pictures and I hate myself for it.

Art: Mmm. The pictures were of . . . ?

Erika: Me.

Art: Of you. Oh. And so, oh, you sent pictures over the phone?

Erika: And picture messages of me half-naked.

Art: Ah.

Erika: Now you see why I'm afraid to talk about it? (kicks off her sandal)

Art: I can see why you're embarrassed. I'm not sure why you'd be afraid?

Erika: Because . . . it's not something I want to talk about.

Art: Huh. So who was the boy?

Erika: My ex-boyfriend.

Art: So, when you lived with Amelia? [Amelia was Erika's first adoptive parent, the one who disrupted the adoption.]

Erika: (nods)

Art: Ohhh.

Erika: She actually let me *date* him. And now I think to myself "*Why* would my mother let me date him?"

Art: You were ten years old with her?

Erika: No, I was thirteen.

Art: Thirteen?

Erika: Thirteen, yeah.

Art: Mmmh.

Erika: I was dating him all the way up to the day before I left her house.

Art: So you stayed in touch with him?

Erika: Well no, I got in touch with him through MySpace and then we started to talk . . .

Art: Oh.

Erika: And then, made a mistake.

Art: Are you still on MySpace?

Erika: I'm still on MySpace but I blocked him.

Art: Oh.

Erika: And my MySpace profile is set private and I changed all my information on there.

Art: So only . . . is it like Facebook, only friends can see?

Erika: (nodding) Yeah.

Art: Is that how it's set up? Not friends of friends . . . oh, I see.

Erika: (nodding) Yeah.

Art: Has your mom looked at your Facebook page?

Mom: Not recently, but I do, yeah.

Erika: I haven't really even changed anything much.

Mom: Yeah, she only used it like once.

Art: (to Mom) Do you have a Facebook page? Is that how you see it or . . .

Erika: Yeah.

Art: Oh, okay, so you're friends of each other.

Erika: Yeah.

Art: Oh, okay, that's great.

Erika: (to her mom) I really have to go on and get Grandpa.

Mom: (whispers, patting daughter's shoulder) Okay. All right.

Art: So. . . .

Erika: (pointing to mom and smiling) Her *grandfather* is on Facebook.

Art: Oh, is he? Okay, that's cool.

Erika: An *eighty-three-year-old* man is on Facebook!

Art: Ah.

Erika: It's funny. (Mom and Erika laugh)

Art: It's a good way to stay in touch with people. So . . . so . . . so you sent (Erika's smile abruptly disappears) him half-naked pictures of you. . . .

Erika: (barely audible) Yes.

Art: So how did that happen? I mean, it didn't start out like that, did it?

Erika: We were talking and then he just randomly said that he liked me still and still wanted to be with me and all this other stuff and I thought "Oh, okay, whatever. . . ."

Art: Mmhmm.

Erika: And then he sent me a message saying "You know what, please send me some pictures of you." I started off by sending normal pictures. . . .

Art: Mmhmm.

Erika: . . . just thinking he wanted to see what I looked like now . . .

Art: Mmhmm.

Erika: And then he said, "No—*you*: half-naked or naked" and I just like, "I can't do that, sorry."

Art: Mmhmm.

Erika: (foot swinging up and down) And he's like, "If you don't face your fears now, how are you going to face them in life?" And that's when I kind of, well, didn't do it to the full extent that he wanted.

Art: So what was it about what he said, in the, that piece that he said that made sense to you?

Erika: Because people do always say to face your fears and . . .

Art: Uh huh.

Erika: I was, like, he might be right—I don't know.

Art: Mmhmm.

Erika: So now I feel so foolish, that was so stupid to think that!

Mom: Honey, you made a mistake . . . we all make mistakes; maybe you can learn from this to listen to that little voice in your head that knows what's best for you?

Erika: Yeah, I should have listened to myself and not him.

Art: Wow, Erika, do you see what you just said? That's wonderful!

Erika: Huh, what?

Art: You said that you want to have more confidence in yourself and that your judgment is good! You do know what is right for you. [Here we are co-creating a new meaning and a deeper understanding for Erika of herself.]

Erika: (big smile) Yeah, I guess I do.

Mom: Yes, sweetie, you do. (Mom pulls Erika closer to her and hugs her)

[From here the session winds down and we end this part. When I meet with the mom alone to discuss the session, the mom is feeling much better about Erika and Erika's ability to make good decisions. Mom now sees that what she wants to do is help Erika listen to that "voice in the back of her head," which sounds very much like this mom's voice.]

Chapter Ten

The Case of the Murdered Swimming Towel!

Geraldine Casswell, B.Sc. Hons.,
M.Sc. ClinPsy, M. Psychotherapy

Danielle had been adopted at the age of eight with her sister Sarah, age six, by a couple unable to have children themselves. The placement had been challenging for everyone and Danielle had some Dyadic Developmental Psychotherapy sessions two years into the adoption, at age ten, and following this there were increasingly settled periods. It was during this more settled time that the parents were contacted and asked to consider having another child, a boy who shared the same birth mother as Danielle and Sarah. After an extensive period of assessment and consideration Danielle's brother, then aged two, arrived. This coincided with the time Danielle moved up to high school.

When Danielle (at age ten) had previously seen me, she had been reluctant to come at first, but quickly recognized that this was special time with her mum and dad. Consequently she would immediately position herself between Mum and Dad on the sofa. Her guard had lessened within the first three sessions and she would start volunteering things that had been difficult in the preceding period. She appeared relieved when the misdemeanours could be spoken about and reconciliation made with her parents. This first period of work (ten sessions over a nine-month period) had explored why it was tough for Danielle to trust her adopted mum and dad. We had focused particularly on enabling the family to find ways of talking about Danielle's behavior that didn't induce shame and to help them find ways of reparation following incidents. This had strengthened Mum and Dad in their feelings of competency and helped Danielle see she wasn't such a bad individual as she had been brought up to believe.

Danielle's adoptive parents were very committed to caring for their children but, like many adoptive parents, had been astonished to discover the depth of disturbing emotions that their children had produced in them. They had already pursued some courses run for adoptive parents and had some understanding of the attachment needs of the children. They were very receptive to explanations about why these children were both hurting inside and able to hurt others. In our first course of work together we had interspersed sessions with Danielle with sessions just for them. They also made good use of email to reflect on how things had been, which gave me helpful insights as to how they were managing to make sense of the interactions. I felt we had a head start because they were by nature sensitive and insightful people. The biggest problem I concluded later was how Danielle's deep distrust of her birth mother, born from episodes of extreme neglect, was reenacted frequently with her adoptive mum. Over time this had made her adoptive mum feel very inadequate and we looked specifically in our first course of work at keeping Mum and Dad united so that Danielle did not split them apart and spoil the security and safety she so much needed.

The parents sought help again two years later, shortly following the placement of Jordan. They felt they were "back to square one" with Danielle. She was now argumentative and oppositional with everyone in the home, but of great concern was her attitude to her brother and they felt they could not leave her alone with him unsupervised. Danielle had been seen to nip and bite Jordan and had taken toys from him and watched him cry with no effort made to help or comfort him. She had pulled back emotionally from her parents and resisted their approaches for fun or affection.

I met with Danielle and her parents for a reintroduction. Danielle had matured into a young adolescent, approaching thirteen, and was well practiced into how to look cool and disinterested! However, at the first session she was receptive to the working alliance being built again and agreed to coming back for some more sessions.

This transcript is taken from the second session. Only Mum and Danielle could make it as Dad was unable to get time off work. Before the session Mum had sent me an email giving me an account of the week. She had felt particularly overwhelmed with a busy and demanding week and had seen deterioration in Danielle's mood and behavior. It had erupted in a massive argument over a swimming towel that had been left in a kit bag to go moldy. Danielle looked rather disinterested in being at the clinic and I was unsure whether our reconnection and alliance from week 1 would hold. I anticipated that we would need to reconnect and build our alliance and then hoped we could explore the incident of the swimming towel. I was pretty sure that this was an incident that masked a bigger issue of managing the arrival of her brother. Depending on how easily Danielle engaged I would move us to explore this topic. We went into my room and Mum sat herself down on the sofa and Danielle sat alongside her but with a noticeable gap.

Geraldine (G): I'm glad to see you back again. We only got to catch up a bit last week, and we talked about your new school, your new dance classes and your new brother—seems like it has been a really busy time?

Danielle (D): (shrugs)

Mum (M): It's been a busy week and a tough week.

G: Okay. Anyone going to help me know what's been busy and what's been tough?

D: She can! (pointing to Mum)

G: Do you think Mum will be able to remember everything? Can I ask you to chip in if she gets it muddled? [*Editor's note: Here we see Geraldine engaging Danielle in a nonpressured and playful way by asking her to think about her mum.*]

D: (shrugs)

G: We're developing a new language here! What about one shrug for yes and two for no . . . I suppose we could do three shrugs for I don't know! [*Editor's note: This is an example of the playful part of PACE, necessary here to develop and maintain the alliance. In addition, Geraldine is accepting Danielle's way of communicating.*]

D: (shrugs)

G: Great—I take it that's a yes!

D: (smiles slightly) [*Editor's note: Danielle's response indicates that she experienced Geraldine's intervention in a positive and enjoyable manner.*]

G: Well, Mum, could you let me know what has been busy this week?

M: It's been really busy because I have had to take Jordan to a number of appointments. I've had Sarah off school with a sickness bug and then I went down with it at the weekend myself.

G: Sounds like it all piled up last week—was there anyone around to give you a hand? [*Editor's note: Geraldine senses that Mum needs some support and provides Mum with empathy, which serves to maintain the alliance with her.*]

M: No! Michael (husband) was late back from work three nights and Danielle just complained I'd forgotten her cookery ingredients! She doesn't seem to understand that there is more than just her living in this house!

D: (looks away from her mother with a disdainful look)

[Within the first few moments I was aware that Mum felt overwhelmed with the events of the previous week, of Danielle distancing herself from Mum and my previous alliance with Mum and Danielle being put under some strain. I felt

I needed to affirm Mum's feelings, but also to connect back with Danielle and maintain the alliance before she saw the session becoming a support group for Mum. I felt pulled in two directions, but reckoned this must be what Mum felt so decided to empathize with what it felt like for Mum in the hope she would feel reconnected to me, and then together we could think about what it was like for Danielle to have such an overwhelmed mum.] [*Editor's note: This is a good illustration of the principle that whatever we wish the mum to do with the child we have to do with the mum.*]

G: It sounds like everything piled up so high last week and to make matters worse you didn't have Michael's support and extra pair of hands. To top it all, you get ill as well! [*Editor's note: Here Geraldine is beginning follow-lead-follow.*]

M: Absolutely. I didn't have any energy left to do the usual things like find cooking ingredients—but anyway, Danielle should be doing that herself by now.

G: It's difficult when you are the mum and everyone gets used to you being the organizer, the shopper, the cleaner, the taxi driver, etc.! [*Editor's note: This observation by Geraldine illustrates the acceptance part of PACE.*]

M: Too true!

G: (to Danielle) Sounds like your mum was pretty stressed last week—is it easy to spot when she is stressed? [*Editor's note: Here we see Geraldine gently helping Danielle develop greater insightfulness (the reflective function) regarding her mum.*]

D: Yeah! She shouts a lot.

M: Well, I do admit to that.

G: Well, at least it's easy to spot! Is it easy to spot when you get stressed, Danielle?

D: (shrugs) [*Editor's note: Geraldine now asks Danielle to reflect on herself. This is difficult, but their previous playful exchange gives Danielle a way to do so in their "secret" language.*]

G: I'll ask Mum the same question and see how good she is at noticing you. Mum, how do you know when Danielle is stressed? [*Editor's note: This intervention represents the Dyadic Developmental Psychotherapy component of insightfulness and the reflective function.*]

M: Well, sometimes she gets very quiet and takes herself off to her room, but sometimes she complains a lot and says she's bored.

G: That's interesting—sounds like sometimes she wants to be on her own, but sometimes she wants you to notice. Have I got that right?

D: (shrugs)

G: It seems like I did! Danielle, I'm kind of guessing—so put me right if I am wrong, that when Mum has so much going on she doesn't have as much time to think about what you need, or to spend time with you?

D: (nods)

G: Thanks—how does that make you feel?

D: (slightly tearful, but doesn't say anything)

M: (seeing the tears) I'm sorry, I hate it when it gets like this. (puts out a hand and Danielle accepts it)

G: It seems like you both hate it when it gets like this. [*Editor's note: Co-creation of meaning and the reflective dimension of the affective/reflective dialogue are illustrated in this exchange.*]

[We continued the discussion for a few more minutes about having too much to do and noticing how everyone in the family manifested that stress. It would seem that the secure base has been re-created, from our previous treatment, and that we are now moving into the exploration phase. This helped to regulate the feelings in the room and as a result I felt I had begun to establish a connection with Danielle and Mum. Mum's initial feelings of being overwhelmed were subsiding as she could now connect with Danielle's distress. I wanted to facilitate a dialogue between them both so that they could explore the other issue that Mum had given me prior warning about—the moldy swimming towel—and also provide a bridge into the much bigger issue concerning the arrival of the new brother.]

G: It might be helpful if we let Mum know how you feel when she is so busy. Do you think you could tell her? [*Editor's note: This intervention illustrates the lead part of follow-lead-follow.*]

D: (shakes her head but rather half-heartedly)

G: I'd like to help you do that as it can be tough finding words to say how we feel. Would you mind if I did that—like we used to do when we met before?

D: (shrugs—but doesn't resist)

G: Okay. [*Editor's note: Geraldine now begins to "talk for" the child, which is an effective means of co-regulating the child's affect.*] Let's see if I can help. Danielle, could you look at Mum? (I moved my chair near to Danielle, who is still holding hands with her mum; I lightly placed my hand on Danielle's arm.) [*Editor's note: This exchange shows the therapeutic and creative use of touch by Geraldine to regulate Danielle.*] "Mum—I hate it when you are so busy 'cos it seems like you have got no time for me and you expect me to do everything by myself. That makes me think you don't want me around and all you have got time for is Jordan." (Danielle was still looking at her mum and not resisting my hand on her arm so I decided to press on.) "It used to be good till he came and now you don't help me when I need you. . . . It makes me feel you don't like me as much as Jordan." (turning to Danielle) Is that how it feels?

D: (looking tearful) Yes.

G: (to Mum) Can you let Danielle know how you love to have time with her? [This intervention illustrates the co-creation of meaning.]

M: Danielle, I really love it when we have time together. Last week was tough for me, but I see it was tough for you too. I think we both need to start all over! (Mum leans forward and hugs Danielle, who accepts this and returns the hug.)

G: You two did well together just then. Is there anything else we could talk about from last week that might have been tough?

[Although we hadn't been in the session long it felt like the bridge was in place again between Mum and Danielle. I also felt Danielle was letting me take a lead in developing the alliance and thought we might be able to explore some of the issues Mum had alerted me to.]

M: (smiles conspiratorially at Danielle) Well, there was a story about a towel!

G: Ooh. I love stories. Who can tell me this one? [*Editor's note: Here we see the follow part of follow-lead-follow.*]

M: (looks at Danielle) Why don't you start this time?

D: (looking more confident) I forgot to get my swimming towel out of my bag.

G: So are we talking overnight?

D: (sheepishly) No, it was about two weeks 'cos it was the holidays.

[Knowing this story already, I knew it had caused a massive row, but thought we could use this as a playful example of when we forget to do things. I was also hoping to use this as an incident that had induced shame, but that could be managed by Danielle if she was given help. This would then serve as a base to move on to deeper shame-based states around the arrival of her brother.]

G: Oh my goodness, and are we talking smelly, wet towels? [*Editor's note: By being playful, Geraldine is able to co-regulate the affect in the session.*]

D: Yes . . . and Mum was annoyed 'cos it got mold on and we had to throw it away!

G: No! You mean the towel was dead—it had been murdered! [*Editor's note: In this instance, being playful leads to the co-creation of a new meaning, one that is less shaming and that both parent and child can relate to.*]

D: (laughing) It was an old towel.

G: Did you give it a burial?

D: We just put it in the bin . . . but Mum got annoyed with me 'cos she said it was my job to remember.

G: Now I get it—it was a tough week for your Mum, for you, and for the dead towel. [*Editor's note: The playful and empathy part of PACE is illustrated in this comment by Geraldine.*]

D: (smiles and looks at Mum, who smiles back)

G: Is it easy to spot Mum getting annoyed? [*Editor's note: Here we see Geraldine helping Danielle develop her insightfulness and reflective function.*]

D: Yes! She tells me off! And she doesn't let me watch TV!

G: Wow—let's see if I get this right. You forget to take your wet towel out and when you find it, Mum gets very annoyed with you and stops you having some fun?

D: (nods)

G: Guess you think "that's not fair—it's only an old towel—I didn't mean to do it—why do you always have a go at me . . . and (raising in pitch) you don't help me much, it's your job to do these things, it's your job to sort my things out, it's your job to get my cookery things—it's not fair!" [*Editor's note: This is another example of "talking for" the child and expressing her inner life. By reflecting for the child, both parent and child will come to a better understanding of the child's inner life and can co-create a new meaning. In addition, by deepening the emotional experience for both child and parent, we see the affective element of the affective/reflective component of Dyadic Developmental Psychotherapy.*]

D: (nods)

G: It's hard when you have a lot of big unfair feelings inside. Phew! I wonder if Mum knows how unfair you think things are nowadays. [*Editor's note: This intervention illustrates the reflective part of the affective/reflective dialogue.*]

D: (looks over at Mum)

M: I know it has been tough recently—especially since Jordan came to live with us—I don't feel like I have any time and it has been much harder than I thought.

[I was aware that Mum had now mentioned perhaps the hardest topic—the arrival of Jordan. I didn't know whether Danielle was going to be able to manage this topic in just our second session. I was not entirely sure if Mum had enough in her emotional reservoir to reach out to Danielle and I didn't know if we had enough time left to open up and explore this potentially big area. I needed a little reflective space so decided to test the waters.]

G: Mum—can you tell me what has surprised you, what you have found hard about Jordan coming into your family? Do you think Danielle is grown up enough to hear this?

M: (looks at Danielle, who looks back at her with big eyes as if to say "tell me more") Yes, I think Danielle could tell you herself what we have all found hard. For instance, we had to wait a long time for him to come—we didn't know if he was really going to arrive. The girls, and us, wanted him to, but when he came he took a long time to settle—he didn't sleep well, he didn't eat well, and he seemed miserable. We didn't think it would be like that.

G: Did everyone find it hard?

M: Yes—perhaps it was easier for Sarah as she just switches off and goes out to play whenever Jordan gets whingy. Wouldn't you agree, Danielle?

D: (nods)

G: How have you found it, Danielle?

D: He cries a lot and when Mum tries to help him he wants Dad.

G: Sounds like it is hard to know what he wants. Can you tell what he wants?

D: If I play with him he just cries so I don't play with him now.

G: That's hard for you—sounds like he makes you feel like you're not a good big sister?

D: (nods)

G: (to Mum) Seems you were right, Mum, it has been hard for all of you. What do you do, Mum, when he cries and doesn't know how to let you help him?

M: Well, I usually distract him, I might sing a song, or carry him into the garden to show him something. It's getting better, but I do spend a lot of time with him. I can't leave him with any of the others. (looks to Danielle, who starts to avoid eye contact)

G: Seems like I missed something there!

D: Don't tell her! (puts her hand over Mum's mouth)

G: Is this like finding the dead towel? [*Editor's note: The co-creation of a new meaning reduces shame and allows the child to engage in further exploration. This also illustrates the co-regulation of affect.*]

D: (looks at Geraldine as if she is crazy)

G: What I mean is—is it like Mum is reminding you of something when you felt bad inside and you really don't want her to tell me in case I think you are bad too?

D: (nods)

G: I have an idea—what about I have a guess at how Jordan makes you feel, I don't think I need to know everything of what you might have done, or said. What we could work on is helping you and your mum talk about what you both find hard and seeing if you can give each other some ideas when Jordan is making a big fuss—what do you say?

D: (shrugs)

[I still wasn't confident that Danielle would allow me to explore some of the unkind moments she had had with Jordan—that the shame would be high and her defenses working too well!]

[*Editor's note: We see here that Geraldine is deep into the exploration phase. When in this phase, the therapist has to carefully balance deepening the experience while ensuring that there is no dysregulation. By furthering the exploration Geraldine is helping Danielle move into the integration and healing phases of treatment.*]

[I wanted to keep my connection with her, explore the experience of her shame and accompanying thoughts and help them find a way of communicating again. I thought if I removed the necessity of having a forensic trawl through the specific acts and deeds it might make it more possible to progress.]

G: You and Mum have given me a pretty good picture already of how hard it has been for you *all* since Jordan arrived. This little chap sounded really confused about his new family and he is taking a while to get to know you all and trust you. Tell me what Jordan is like.

D: (somewhat angrily) He's a pest; he just cries all the time.

G: How loud does he cry—can you show me?

D: (screams loudly)

G: Now that's loud—does that give you a headache? [*Editor's note: This comment by Geraldine illustrates the acceptance part of PACE while moving into curiosity.*]

D: Yeah.

G: Does that make you feel a bit annoyed?

D: Yeah.

G: Does that make you feel really annoyed . . . like "for goodness sake, Jordan, will you shut up!"

D: Yeah.

G: What do you do when he gets like that?

D: (looks at her mum) Don't tell her!

G: Sorry! Did you think I was being nosy? [*Editor's note: This intervention by Geraldine illustrates interactive repair. Geraldine explains her intention to co-regulate Danielle's affect and reduce shame. Geraldine's sharing of her inner*] *experience is part of creating concordant intersubjectivity.*] Or that I was going to tell you off? I was thinking if you lived with that amount of noise I'd be looking to see where the volume switch was! Does it make you feel—"Oh Jordan, I wish you'd shut up and be quiet or just go away!"

D: (small nod)

G: I guess there might be other thoughts as well like—before you came here we were getting on okay and you just messed it up.

D: (looks over at Mum to check out)

G: (addressing Mum) You know I think this has been really hard for Danielle. Can I help you to tell Mum just how hard it has been?

D: (nods)

G: (sitting next to Danielle) [*Editor's note: By "talking for" Danielle, Geraldine deepens the experience by focusing on the affective part of the affective/ reflective dialogue. Talking for a child can be a very powerful way of helping the child come to understand and know the child's internal emotional life. By putting Danielle's inner life into words, Geraldine is helping develop Danielle's reflective abilities.*] Mum, you know I wanted Jordan to come and live with us because he has the same birth mum as me, but since he came it has been much harder than I thought. It seems like he just screams all the time and it does my head in! He doesn't seem to want to play with me and that makes me feel he doesn't like me. (big breath) And to make matters worse, he takes up all your time and you don't have time for me. Sometimes I just wish he would go away. Have I got that about right? (to Danielle)

D: (nods)

G: Is there anything you would like to add?

D: (shakes her head)

G: Could you try and ask Mum if she could help you when you feel like that— something like "Mum, can you help me when Jordan screams?"

D: (quietly) Can you help me when Jordan screams? [*Editor's note: This intervention illustrates the lead part of the follow-lead-follow component.*]

G: Well done! Can you say that again a bit louder and look at Mum 'cos I want to make sure she hears you?

D: (normal voice) Can you help me when Jordan screams?

M: Of course. I know it's hard; it's hard for me too. We can try and work out a plan.

G: Mum, I'm guessing that when Danielle finds it extra hard she might want to do something to shut him up, only it makes it worse—like shouting back or pushing him or slapping him. Only I reckon that probably makes Jordan even more mad.

M: That's right. Sometimes Danielle has nipped Jordan and he really cries loud then.

D: (glares at Mum and pulls away from her) I said don't tell her!

G: You know I think this is a dead towel moment! [*Editor's note: In this instance, Geraldine is co-creating a new meaning for the family.*] Danielle is worried that she has done something bad and if we could only leave it alone we could forget it is there. Trouble is, when we leave things they get a bit moldy and smelly! (to Danielle) Has Mum just let something out of the bag?

D: (nods)

G: Thanks. I think I get it. [*Editor's note: In this comment by Geraldine we can observe the empathy part of PACE.*] You were worried that if Mum told me you had been nipping Jordan I would think you had been messing up big time with your brother. Let's see if we can sort this one out just like you and your Mum sorted out the wet towel. Okay?

[At this point Danielle gives me no nonverbal signals, but neither does she refuse. I can see she has felt betrayed by her mum telling me so aim to give her a respite moment while I prepare Mum.]

G: (to Mum) I'm guessing Danielle is feeling pretty mad at you right now as she thinks you have let her down by telling me about nipping Jordan. I'm wondering if it is so hard for Danielle when Jordan wants lots of help because she didn't get help when she was two. She had to do things all on her own— and that's tough—in fact, it shouldn't happen to children. They deserve to be looked after, even if they mess up, or break things or cry; they deserve to be loved. I'm thinking that just like you look after Jordan and even when he is crying you pick him up and cuddle him and take him into the garden, that is what you would have done for Danielle if she was living with you aged two? [*Editor's note: This intervention is complex and illustrates the reflective element of the affective/reflective dialogue and the co-creation of new meaning component. This illustrates how multiple components of Dyadic Developmental Psychotherapy can be put together in creative ways to deepen work in the exploration phase and create integration. This interchange facilitates the child developing a more coherent autobiographical narrative, which is an outcome of the integration phase.*]

M: Absolutely. I think Danielle missed out on so much. Sometimes she still wants to do things by herself—I wish I had been able to look after her when she was little.

G: Could you tell that to Danielle?

M: Danielle, I wish you had been with me when you were little. I would have loved to have been your Mum and hold you and cuddle you and play with you. (reaches her hand out to Danielle, who accepts it)

D: (is slightly tearful)

[I was aware of Danielle reducing her defenses and that she had felt touched by Mum's declaration. I wanted to help her find words for this moment and to deepen the experience of trust.]

G: Danielle, can I help you find some words to tell Mum how you feel or would you like to try?

D: You can.

G: [*Editor's note: Another example of "talking for" follows.*] Thanks—let's see . . . Mum, I felt mad when you told Geraldine that I had nipped Jordan because it's like you are telling everyone I am a bad kid. It doesn't feel fair that if Jordan is a bad kid he doesn't get told off. I wish I could have lived with you when I was little so that you and Dad could have taken care of me.

G: (checks out Danielle) Okay so far?

D: (nods)

G: Could you tell Mum yourself that you wished she had been your mum when you were little? If you look at her and say, "Mum, I wished you had cared for me when I was small like Jordan."

D: I wish you had looked after me. [*Editor's note: This is a clear expression of the integration phase.*]

G: Well done. Do you feel ready to say "I'm sorry for nipping Jordan—can you help me Mum when I get mad with him?"

D: (hesitates, Mum squeezes her hand) Sorry, can you help me? [*Editor's note: This illustrates the verbal/nonverbal dialogue. It also represents the affective element of the affective/reflective component of Dyadic Developmental Psychotherapy.*]

M: I really want to. I know it's hard for you; it's hard for me too.

(Danielle is tearful and Mum reaches over and hugs her; Mum then becomes tearful.)

G: Great to see you two hug. Feels like you found each other again. Feels also like you are both sad. Things have been hard but you would like it to get better. Is that right? [*Editor's note: This comment by Geraldine is an example of reflection.*]

M: Definitely.

D: (nods)

G: Well, I think you have made a great start, but I'm guessing it might take a bit of practice. Mum, I think Danielle really did mean that sorry and that she wants you to help her, but I also think that when Jordan gets tricky at home it might make her feel like a bad kid again, so while she is getting used to having a mum and dad who care for her it might be a good idea to give extra help—like, for instance, she could help you with Jordan while you are there so you can show her what caring mums do. If Jordan needs help only grown-ups can do, you might like to give Danielle a special treat for herself, while you are busy.

M: Well, she likes playing with the rabbit, but I can't normally let her do that when Jordan is around, so I suppose if I was looking after him she could feed the rabbit and even clean out his cage!

D: Yes.

G: Excellent. Mum takes care of Jordan and you take care of the rabbit—what's the rabbit's name?

D: Flopsy.

G: I look forward to hearing how you and Flopsy get on next time we meet.

[Our time was running out but I thought we had reached a place when we had begun to explore Danielle's feeling of insecurity that had reawoken since the arrival of Jordan. There seemed to be more we would need to develop in future sessions but this experience had facilitated a dialogue between mother and daughter which could be built on.]

Chapter Eleven

Integration in Dyadic Developmental Psychotherapy: Amran's Story

Karen Sik, MClinPsy

This chapter is primarily about the later phase of Dyadic Developmental Psychotherapy in the treatment of a traumatized child: Amran, aged five, who had experienced physical and emotional abuse and neglect. In this later phase of treatment known as the integration phase (Becker-Weidman, 2010b), the primary task is to help the child develop a coherent autobiographical narrative, such that the child is able to integrate the past and present of his experiences into a meaningful whole and ultimately a more balanced and healthier view of himself.

It is the early caregiving relationship that provides the primary context within which children learn about themselves, their emotions, and their relationships with others. When children are raised within a loving and stable caregiving environment, their internal working model, or the lens through which they view the world is often a safe, predictable, and meaningful one. This results in their capacity to relate well with others and develop a coherent sense of self. Children who experience early chronic trauma within a caregiving relationship often do not view the world as safe and predictable. With an erratic and hostile, rejecting, or abusive caregiving history, they do not have the ability to respond in a coherent and organized manner in challenging situations. This often is a reflection of their internal state, which is one of disorganization and fragmentation. Dyadic Developmental Psychotherapy seeks to repair the negative internal working model of these children by using experiential methods that have several overlapping themes and dimensions that include modeling the attachment cycle, regulating and containing emotions, reducing shame and finally integrating experiences (Becker-Weidman, 2010b; Becker-Weidman and Shell, 2005). With the case of Amran, the last phase of treatment is illustrated here through using a transcript of a session where, together with the therapist, his birth mother and godmother were present to help him develop a more balanced affective experience of his birth family and early childhood experiences.

AMRAN

Amran was referred to child protection services in March 2009 for being abused by his birth father's girlfriend and her brother. There were multiple bruises and abrasions, both old and new on his face, body, and limbs. These included pinch marks on his arms and fingers, bruises under his eyes, thighs, neck, chin and abdomen, with tenderness and swelling around his elbows, cane marks, and abrasions over the base of his spine. His height and weight were in the third percentile and multiple dental cavities were found. After a stay of one week in a hospital, he was discharged into the care of a foster caregiver. The child protection officer then referred Amran to the psychologist with concerns about Amran's "bizarre" behaviors (e.g., head banging, yelling out of the blue) and the foster mother's distress in caring for him.

Amran's parents divorced when he was a few months old. His birth mother, who had a drug history, did not have a home then and the custody was awarded to his birth father. As his father had trouble with childcare, Amran went into his mother's care. His birth mother's friends, cousins, and eventually his godparents helped to care for Amran. However, at age four, his father took him for an outing and never returned him. His birth mother and godparents did not know of his whereabouts for more than a year until they were contacted by child protection services.

Amran was registered in a school kindergarten when he was in his father's care. However, he had very poor attendance and the teacher had observed him to be a quiet boy who hardly spoke up. His performance in his work was very poor. He was notably slower than the rest of his peers in terms of written and communicative abilities.

When he was first seen in May 2009, his foster mother was at her wits' end about how to manage Amran's behaviors. He had been in her care for a month. He was described to be on his best behavior during the first two weeks of care. However, "everything changed in the third and fourth weeks." She candidly shared that she was exhausted and traumatized by his "scary behaviors." These included his screaming and hitting behaviors, head banging and scratching his arms. He was demanding and would shout at her for causing him to be in pain and then demanded why she did not save him from the abuse. On some occasions, he would ask her to hit him. Sometimes, he engaged in "baby talk" and would curl up and suck at his thumb. Once in the doctor's waiting room, he insisted that she had given birth to him. He also had a very short attention span and was described as "hyperactive."

The Vineland Adaptive Behavior Scales–II, completed by his foster mother, revealed that he was functioning at age two in the communication domain, age three in the daily living skills domain and age two in the socialization domain. The Child Behavior Checklist (Ackenbach) showed significant scores on the thought problems, attention problems, rule-breaking behaviors, and aggressive behavior scales.

PREVIOUS SESSIONS

The first session was with Mdm Sunita alone and was spent gathering information about Amran's behaviors and also about Mdm Sunita's own emotional functioning and state of mind with regard to caring for Amran. Although visibly tired, Mdm Sunita was assessed to be open and honest in her concerns about her ability to help Amran with his behaviors. The effects of abuse, attachment disruptions, and trauma sustained in the early years of a child were explained to her and Mdm Sunita started to share more about his "trauma behaviors." She began to demonstrate some good insights into Amran's behaviors and showed commitment in working with the therapist in helping Amran.

During the time that Amran was seen, he was residing with his foster mother. Seven sessions comprised of working with his foster mother and Amran in creating a secure and safe environment for him. During these sessions, the use of PACE and PLACE (see Becker-Weidman and Shell, 2005/2008) helped the therapist and Mdm Sunita establish a safe and healing place for Amran, both in the therapeutic sessions and in foster care. The need for interactive repair was also emphasized to Mdm Sunita to help lessen the shame and fear that many children like Amran have about themselves and the world. In each session, Mdm Sunita was first seen separately to address the previous week's events and to provide her with support and then both she and Amran would be seen together to address any misattunement that arose in the relationship. The use of PACE principles helped facilitate the co-creation of meaning and shared emotions that are essential in the repair and deepening of the interaction between Mdm Sunita and Amran. Over time, Mdm Sunita reported a decrease in his behavioral dysregulation and described him as "just a normal boy who had many hurts in the past." It was evident that Mdm Sunita and Amran had developed a concordant intersubjectivity of shared experiences (i.e., shared emotion, attention and intention) over time.

Amran's birth mother was also interviewed separately to gather more history about Amran's early caregiving. Although her life was dotted with hardships and many obstacles (i.e., her own chronic caregiving history, victim of spousal violence and substance abuse history), she was open in sharing her personal history and maintained a coherent and cooperative stance. At the point of interview, she was residing with her daughter, Amran's birth sister, while her current husband was in Malaysia. Sharing that she was looking for a job and will likely experience further changes in her life, she and Amran's godmother agreed that his godmother will be the main caregiver for Amran in the near future.

Amran's godparents were also interviewed with the use of Adult Attachment Interview to assess their state of mind with regard to attachment and their insightfulness into Amran's behavioral and emotional functioning as well as their commitment to his care. Following the assessment, it was recommended that they be caregivers for Amran in the near future.

TRANSCRIPT

This is the ninth session. In this session, his birth mother and godmother are present with Amran and the therapist. It is Saturday and this is Amran's third time seeing his birth mother and godmother for visitation access. He is dressed up in his favorite shirt and pants and he was visibly excited, pacing up and down, waiting for them to arrive. When they enter the waiting room, he stops and smiles shyly, asking about the contents they have in their shopping bags. It is a toy figurine for him. I invite them all into the room. Present in the session is a Malay interpreter who is a child protection officer whom Amran knows well and feels comfortable with. While his birth mother and godmother could speak English conversationally, we planned for the autobiographical narrative to be said in the language that they had always used with Amran.

> *Karen Sik:* (gesturing to the long sofa) Why don't you all sit there? (Mom sits down with Godma while Amran stands at the table looking at the figurine.) Amran, why don't you sit between your mom and godma?
>
> *Godma:* (picking up the cue) Yes, Amran, come here and sit with us.
>
> *Amran:* OK. (sits between them and smiles but appears hesitant to get too close)
>
> [From my previous sessions with Amran and his foster mother, I knew that he was someone who enjoyed physical affection and it was especially important that Amran felt comfortable and safe in this session. I had also discussed this

previously with his mother and godmother and they did not express any discomfort at the thought.]

[*Editor's note: In the previous section we see Karen working to maintain the alliance and create a secure base and safe setting within which exploration and integration can begin to occur.*]

Karen: (playfully) OK, I want the both of you (gesturing to Mom and Godma) to let's pretend that Amran is the burger in the hamburger so let's wrap him up tightly! (Mom and Godma oblige and wrap their arms around him, and they all burst into laughter, smiling.) Why don't you help Amran to take off his shoes and while we all talk, you can leave your arms around him. [*Editor's note: This intervention illustrates PACE. Karen playfully engages Amran while coaching the mom and godma, thereby engaging the family in positive intersubjectivity.*]

Godma: (offers Amran a packet of biscuits) Here, let me open this for you. It's your favorite, isn't it?

Amran: (nods and nibbles on the biscuits)

Karen: How does Godma know that those are your favourite biscuits? [*Editor's note: Here we observe the reflective element of the affective/reflective dialogue.*]

Amran: Because she take care of me. (he looks at her and smiles)

Karen: When did she take care of you?

Amran: (softly) When I very small baby.

Karen: (turning to Godma) What was Amran like when he was a baby?

[I decided to take this opportunity for us to start talking about the past and how it led to the present to help Amran co-create a new meaning that will lead to a more coherent and less shame-based autobiographical narrative. In the previous session with his birth mother and godma, we discussed his early childhood and what were some of the things they had remembered about him. Although his birth mother had shared openly about her inability to care for him due to her own circumstances and her ambivalent feelings toward Amran after his birth, we all agreed we wanted Amran to have a real but pleasant account of his early childhood. They understood Amran's feelings of confusion, hurt, and abandonment following the recent abuses. Hence, during the session, I helped them to put a narrative together where they decided which parts of his childhood they wanted him to know about and which parts they felt were not necessary to know about at this point in time. We had a shared goal of helping Amran create a new narrative, by weaving in memories of his childhood he had blocked out or could not recall, to help with his healing. I explained that the purpose of our session with Amran was to create a new meaning where he was a wanted and loved child who could not control the circumstances that led to the abuse. I had felt that his birth mother and his godmother were in a comfortable place with me and this gave me the confidence to have them share this narrative with him, with my guidance. At this point in the session, his birth mother and godmother pick up my cue that an important part of the session is about to start.]

Godma: (looking at me) He was a cute baby . . .

Karen: Could you tell him more? Maybe this time, you could show him how you cradled him as a baby. It's OK for Amran to be stretched out and perhaps, Mom, you could hold his legs and feet. And you can talk to him in Malay if you'd like.

[They all smile with Amran giggling. He has his head on his godmother's lap and he is holding the toy figurine. While he appears to be in a relaxed state and stretched out on the sofa, I cannot help but feel that he is a little anxious as he did not make eye contact with anyone in the room. His godmother attempts to take away the figurine but I gesture to her to let him have it. I think that he has stayed focused in session despite the toy and it may be a good temporary distracter for his restlessness.]

Karen: Amran, did Godma used to hold you like that?

Amran: (smiles and nods his head)

Karen: (turning to godmother) What else do you remember?

Godma: (in Malay) When your mother gave birth to you, I was at the hospital too. You were very very small and you had the cutest feet and hands and you cried a lot. You were the cutest baby in the hospital! Your mother and I loved you lots and lots and lots.

Mom: (in Malay) Amran, I wanted to care for you very very much. I remember I took you home from the hospital but I was poor and did not have much money. I was also looking for a job and a home I could call my own so I couldn't be with you a lot.

Amran: (fiddling with his toy) How come?

[At this point in time, his mother is at a loss for words and looks to me. I sense Amran's curiosity to know much more about his past and his mother's attempts to explain her story to him. However, I do not want the conversation to be about Mom's story and I appreciate that she paused to think about this. I want to steer the conversation to what Amran needed as a baby.]

[*Editor's note: This is a very clear illustration of Karen's use of self. In this example Karen could have begun further exploration of the mother-child early history, since Amran was curious about that. However, keeping the focus on Amran's story and what it was like for him, as the reader will observe in just a moment, is very effective and leads to some deep exploration and integration, which is necessary for healing to occur.*]

Karen: Amran, what do you think babies need?

Amran: Milk.

Karen: That's right. Babies need milk and they need a lot of love. They need to be carried when they cry and they cry all the time because they don't have the words to say what they want. (looking at mother) And what do mothers do?

Mom: (in Malay) A mother should pick you up when you cry and get you milk and take care of you when you poo poo and wee wee because you cannot do all that yourself. You were just a baby. I wanted to care for you but I couldn't. I needed to go to Malaysia to find work so I left you with my friends. But Amran, I wanted to give you more because you deserved more. So that's why, when you were one year old, I asked Godma to help me care for you.

Godma: (in Malay) And taking care of you made me so happy every day. I remember singing to you every night to help you sleep and thinking how perfect you are, all of you from your curly hair to your little toes. I remember your favorite food was Nestum and as you grew older, you liked chicken nuggets and boy you could eat lots of rice!

Karen: Amran, do you still like nuggets and rice?

Amran: Yes! But I don't eat Nestum.

[I start to make a connection with his past and present even though it is about something small such as food. I sense his delight in discovering this new information about his past.]

Godma: (smiling) That's because it is baby food so that babies can grow big and strong.

Karen: (turning to his mother and godmother) What else do you remember?

Godma: (in Malay) I and Godpa took care of you every day. Godpa worked every day and was always looking forward to play with you every day. We cared for you every day and your mommy would try to visit you every weekend.

Mom: (in Malay) I always thought of you even though I was in Malaysia and each time I saw you, I couldn't wait to carry you. You were happy and that made me happy too.

[I am glad that his mother is making an attempt to let him know he was always loved. This is especially important as she is going to now be part of his life and in some way I sense her attempts to make amends with Amran as well.]

Mom: One time, I took you to Malaysia with Godmother and we had a fun time there. Your Godpa drove us there. . . .

Amran: (stops fiddling with his toy) It was a green car.

Mom: (in surprise) You remembered that? [turns to Godma] He remembers that!

Godma: (looks to me in surprise) It was an old car and with cracked paint but it moved.

Karen: (nodding) What else do you remember, Amran?

Amran: Papa didn't go with us. How come? How come I stayed with him?

[This is the first time in all our sessions that Amran had asked about his birth father. The questions he had previously were more about his father's girlfriend and the neighbor who had hurt him. I am reminded at how children, when traumatized, are often not ready to talk about the past in the initial stages as they are often in a state of high alert and psychological danger. Amran's foster mother had created a safe and secure environment for him without which this conversation would not be taking place. Amran's question created a perfect opportunity to talk about his birth father and how he had landed in his care. His mother looks at me, as if to ask if it was okay to now talk about her and her husband.]

Karen: Amran, that's a really good question and is something that your mother wants to talk about today.

Mom: (in Malay) Amran, your papa and I don't talk to each other anymore. We separated when you were just a baby because we always quarreled with each other. One day Papa came and said that he wanted to bring you out.

Godma: (in Malay) Your mommy wasn't home and I thought he was only going to bring you out to play and then bring you back to me but he took you and then we didn't know where you went.

Mom: (in Malay) We couldn't find you and we were very upset and very worried.

Godma: (in Malay) I tried to look for you and got upset and was very, very sad.

Amran: (quietly and staying very still) Me too.

[At this point, I sense Mom's and Godma's attempts to convey their sadness about the abuse and Amran's response tells me that he is ready to experience a deeper emotion with regard to the hurt he had sustained and the loneliness he had felt.]

Karen: Amran, you must have been very scared. You were in a safe place and very loved. But then your father came and took you away. (pause) [*Editor's note: This intervention illustrates the co-creation of meaning and the affective/ reflective dialogue. It is also a good example of how the various components of Dyadic Developmental Psychotherapy are usually used in tandem with other components.*] All children need big people to care for them and be there to help them because all children are too little to do a lot of things themselves. They need help to do things right like bathing and putting your clothes and shoes on. All children need someone they can play with and feel safe with. They need to go to school. The job of big people is to help them do this. (pause) But instead the big people in your father's house hurt you and they hurt you badly. Instead of helping you do the right thing, they hurt you. (pause)

[At this point, I stop to summarize our dialogue to help Amran to make the connections in his past. The pauses were deliberate to allow time for him to think more deeply about his needs not being met rather than his perception that he was a bad child not deserving of love. At this time, Amran is nodding quietly to what I say. The toy is left on the sofa and Amran starts to put his arms around his godmother who starts to stroke his head. I feel that we are in a deep state of attunement and intersubjective sharing of affect.] [*Editor's note: What Karen is describing here is the reflective element of the affective/reflective dialogue and an intervention that serves to enhance both Amran's and the caregivers' reflective function and insightfulness.*]

Amran: (in Malay) They beat me many many times.

Mom: (in Malay) When I heard that, I was very, very angry, Amran. I thought, how can they do this to my son? They are supposed to care for him and they hurt him. I was very, very angry and I wish I knew because I would have taken you away from them!

Amran: (in Malay, softly) Me too. I waited for you very long.

Godma: (in Malay) I and Godpa also waited for you very very long; we thought about you every day. We were sad and angry when we heard you were hurt. We are going to make sure that this will not happen again. We are not going to let anyone hurt you again.

Amran: (nods and buries his head in Godma's arms)

[I am pleased at the way the session is going at this point. Mom and Godma are accepting of and responding to Amran's affect and Amran is turning to his godmother for comfort. This is very important.]

Karen: Poor Amran. When you were born, your mother couldn't take care of you so you were moved around until your godma came to care for you. But your father took you away and the big people in the house hurt you. Your mother and godma did not know where you were so you had nobody there to care for you and keep you safe. No wonder you were angry. You were very angry because you needed a lot of love and care but nobody was there to give it to you. I wonder what would have happened if your father did not take you away and you stayed with your godma . . .

[I am now linking the past to the present to help him understand his behaviors during his stay with his father and the initial weeks with his foster mother—that it wasn't that he was unlovable but that bad things had happened to him and hence his behaviors.]

Amran: (in Malay) Amran would be happier and safe.

Karen: . . . and not so angry?

Amran: (nods)

Karen: Yes, because you needed care and no one was there to make sure you got your favorite foods, and no one took you to school or helped you sleep better and taught you things. So yes, I can see why you were angry, but now you are not angry? [*Editor's note: Karen demonstrates empathy. Karen normalizes Amran's behaviors by connecting those behaviors with the past hurts he experienced. In this way, Karen is helping Amran develop a more coherent autobiographical narrative.*]

Amran: I'm not angry now because I have Godma and Mom.

Godma: (picks him up and kisses him) I love you, Amran.

Amran: (smiling) I love you too.

Mom: I love you very very much. You will stay with Godma, OK? Mommy will come visit you every weekend and take you out!

Amran: OK!

Karen: Amran, is there anything that you would like to say to Godma and Mom?

Amran: That I am happy they found me!

Karen: OK, before we leave, let's give Amran another big hamburger hug!! [*Editor's note: This illustrates the importance of touch as a powerful way to communicate acceptance, love, and unconditional positive regard. These are important for the child to experience so that the child's self-concept can become more positive.*]

ENDING TREATMENT

Following this session, there was a dialogue conducted with Amran's birth mom, his godparents, and separately with his foster mother. A review of the past sessions, events, and experiences were discussed with them, helping them to form a narrative of all that had happened. This reflection also helped everyone recognize the gains that Amran had experienced as a result of their efforts and care of him. Compared to the Child Behavior Checklist administered in May 2009, the scores on the CBCL in Oct 2009 showed that there were no significant behavioral concerns. All scores were in the normal range. Thereafter, Amran's child protection officer arranged for joint sessions between Amran's foster mother and his godparents where his care routine was discussed, along with everything that would help his gradual integration back to his godparents' care.

[*Editor's note: This case is a lovely illustration of how in a relatively brief period of time, and with committed, sensitive, insightful, and reflective caregivers, significant progress can occur. The caregivers, with Karen's help, were able to create a deeply safe enough secure base so that the painful exploration necessary for Amran to become more integrated and heal, could occur. Central to his healing was the development of a more positive, non-shame–based, coherent autobiographical narrative. This narrative was co-created through the intersubjective sharing of experience within and outside of the treatment sessions skillfully guided by Karen.*]

Chapter Twelve

Endings

Sian Phillips, PhD, C.Psych.

Students often ask, "When do you know that you are done with therapy?" For Zach I had an inkling that he was well on his way about two months prior to our last session. His mother had come in to speak to me and was overwhelmed with a family crisis. She had spent many days in the hospital with her brother, relieving her elderly parents of caring for their son. Family routines had had to be altered. She was up early and home late and when home was preoccupied, worried, and short-tempered. She was irritated by Zach's recent return to acting out in school. My first reaction was also to be worried. I feared that the building trust that Zach had been forming was going to crumble. Historically, when there was increased stress, he would be moved to another home. I was worried that he would be catapulted back to all of his core fears of not belonging, being a no-good throwaway kid.

Zach was twelve when he was adopted by Donna and Cliff. He was apprehended from his mother and stepfather's care at the age of three. His first three years were characterized by neglect, significant physical abuse, and contempt. Zach's stepfather favored his biological son and disliked Zach. When he was apprehended, Zach was badly malnourished since he was often left hungry (while his brother was fed). The boys were frequently left alone and Zach took on the role of taking care of his younger brother. Zach's stepfather physically abused Zach regularly and at one time tried to hang him. Both brothers were apprehended following the family's attempt to move away from a jurisdiction where authorities were concerned about the boys' safety. They were placed in a foster home. Zach was considered to be hyperactive and unruly and this placement broke down. He moved to Donna and Cliff's home and was there for a period of two years. They fell in love with him and tried to adopt him, but he was placed with relatives with whom he had no previous relationship.

This home was characterized by physical abuse, tension, and frequent arguments. He was not allowed to stay in contact with Cliff and Donna despite their many frequent attempts to see and talk to him. He continued to be seen as hyperactive and difficult and was placed on Ritalin in an attempt to lessen his difficulties. After three years he was apprehended when a neighbor reported an incident of domestic violence while Zach was present.

Zach was then sent to live with a family in a different province who had adopted his younger brother and sister with the hope that they would adopt him also. Zach was required to learn a different language since English was not the family's first language. His name was also changed. He was enrolled in a non-English-speaking school. Not surprisingly, Zach's behavior was challenging. He was involved in many fights at school and was often suspended. At home, Zach was hyperactive and noncompliant. The parents struggled with discipline for all three children and were especially frustrated with Zach. Despite his difficulties, Zach was often in a position of caring for his younger siblings while these parents were at work, which unfortunately replicated the earlier dynamic of him caring for his siblings. The family felt unable to manage Zach's behavior and he was placed back into protective services. Donna and Cliff discovered that he was back in care and fought to have him placed with them for adoption. By the time he came to live with them, Zach had experienced eight caregivers in twelve years.

The family contacted me shortly after his adoption to ensure that Zach made the transition into their family in an optimal way. Donna and Cliff have other foster children who have been with them for a number of years. Donna was quite concerned that he had experienced so many changes and was not talking about his feelings. There were a few anger outbursts, but these had decreased over the first few months of living with them. They had taken him off Ritalin and found that there was little change in his behavior. The greatest concern was that he got support for the losses and difficulties that he had faced. In terms of his relationships, they noticed that he tended to maintain his distance from others and didn't know how to work well with others.

The themes that arose early in therapy for Zach were his need for self-reliance and anxious pleasing of others. He found it very difficult to understand that he didn't have to do anything for his parents to love him. He initially avoided his feelings and over the course of therapy began to process some of the trauma he had experienced and began to understand that it was not his fault. Rather than see himself as inferior and incapable, he began to experience different parts of himself such as strength and courage and intelligence. He struggled for a long time with the rejection from the family who had promised to adopt him, but eventually the yearning to prove that he could be "a good boy" and earn their acceptance faded and he was able to turn more fully to his new family. His sense of responsibility remained strong. The primary emotions that he was able to experience were sadness and anxiety, but over the course of therapy he was able to tolerate anger and shame, and expanded his repertoire of both positive and negative emotions.

His adoptive parents are very supportive and have fought long and hard to have Zach in their home. They both want what is best for all of their children and are skilled and loving parents. They too had their own hurt, loss, and trauma about losing Zach and knowing that the years were difficult for him. In the initial sessions, their own hurt and anger frequently overwhelmed them and interfered with their ability to be fully present for their son. To help them, it was necessary to have a separate session to help them process their own grief and anger at the events in Zach's life. In that session, we explored their own painful feelings and I was also much more directive about how I needed them to hold Zach emotionally in sessions. Fortunately, both Donna and Cliff were quite healthy psychologically and were able to understand what I was asking of them. They are also two individuals with enormous capacity for love and grace and were willing to go to the end of the world for their son. Consequently, following this session, our work deepened and we were able to relatively quickly help Zach integrate his story and heal. At the time of this last session, Zach had just turned fourteen years old and had been living with his family for almost two years.

As Zach entered the session, I was aware of my anxiety, my heart rate was faster and there was a not-so-silent wish in the back of my head: please let him be OK, please let him be OK. As had become usual we chatted about some of the activities he was involved in. I then jumped in and asked him how he was handling the stress at home.

Sian (Therapist, referred to in this transcript as T): Your mum has told me a lot about how stressful it is right now with your uncle being sick. I know it's going to be stressful for a while. Have you had any ideas about how you are going to handle it?

Zach: Haven't got to that yet.

T: (playfully) Well, good job you and your mum came here today then! I know you well enough, that when you get stressed, you get into more trouble at school. (starting with something concrete and reflecting upon what his mum had told me earlier about getting into trouble at school) [*Editor's note: This is a good example of both PACE and the reflective part of the affective/reflective dialogue. Sian's statement demonstrates quite nicely how various components of Dyadic Developmental Psychotherapy can be combined.*]

Z: Yeah. (grinning, somewhat resigned, but not going into shame)

T: So, what is going on at school that you are having trouble?

Z: Not concentrating or doing my work.

T: (gently) How come? [*Editor's note: This is an illustration of the curiosity part of PACE.*]

Z: Every day I am stressed and worried about what they are doing to him [uncle]. I don't know what's going to happen. He is fun to play with. The other thing I am going to miss is that he won't be at my birthday and he always starts the singing of "Happy Birthday."

T: That's on your mind a lot and you have figured out that when things are on your mind it's hard to pay attention. [In an earlier session, Zach had struggled with feeling that having difficulty with paying attention was reflective of there being something wrong with him. That session was a turning point where he began to believe that maybe his difficulty paying attention was a result of having worries and feelings that he wanted to avoid rather than being a "bad kid."]

Z: I know that it's hard for Mum too, not to be stressed out.

T: Mmmm. Do you worry it's because of you? (leading, since I know that has been a common fear)

Z: No, it's not because of me, Mum wouldn't say that, at least I don't think she would? (turns to Mum)

T: Sometimes mums when they are stressed get mad at things they don't usually. [I knew from chatting with Donna earlier that she had become very angry at a pair of shoes lying in the hallway that morning.] Kids sometimes start to worry that it's their fault.

Z: Yeah. I don't like to see parents hurt; I don't like to see Mum sad. I just want to make them happy.

T: I bet you do—that's what you have done so well in the past, figure out what adults need to make them happy. [*Editor's note: Sian's comment illustrates the use of insightfulness. Sian offers a suggestion or insight and, over time, the child and parent will develop deeper insight.*]

Z: That's what I do best!

T: You are right! (quieter) And there is no fixing this one, is there? Your uncle is going to be sick for a little longer.

T: (to Donna, talking about Zach) Your boy knows himself well: he wants to make people feel better, and he doesn't like to see people stressed. It's hard for him. There are so many stressful things in your family right now.

[Zach is still focused on pleasing his parents, but does not seem to be worrying about his security. My anxiety has reduced, but I want to challenge him on taking responsibility for the adults in his world and am still not convinced that he is not operating from fear and the underlying schema of being unworthy.]

Z: (big sigh) I don't know how to do it. They do a lot of things to make us happy; we have to do a whole bunch of things to make them happy.

T: That's what families do when there are stressful times. Everyone has to help each other and do things they might not normally do. The biggest thing for me is to make sure you are not feeling responsible for your mum's feelings. You might have to do extra dishes and extra chores for a while, but it's important not to take care of your mum's feelings; that's her job.

Z: Yeah.

T: Is that "yeah, you are right, Sian," or "yeah, you are right but I am going to try and do it anyways"? [Here I am combining being a bit playful with being reflective.]

Z: I am going to do it anyways! (grins)

T: OK! So your mum is going to have to tell you, "Not your job, Zach!"

Z: She is going to have to get it anyway. She does need more sleep.

T: And whose job is it?

Z: Mine!

T: No, no, no, no, no! [*Editor's note: Sian is able to directly challenge Zach because she has developed a delightfully solid alliance with him. This solid alliance has created a safe base in treatment. Zach clearly knows that Sian's intentions are to help him, so exploration, integration, and healing are clearly evident in what follows. This is also an example of the therapist's use of self in treatment.*]

[Part of my intent in this session was to explore Zach's experience of the stressful time in his family. The other intent was to help Donna reconnect and have empathy for her son and to support him by ensuring that he was not trying to take care of her emotionally. The dialogue drifted into how the family was able to have fun together during the recent March holiday, despite the stress. I wasn't upset with the change of direction because this dialogue was a lovely, reciprocal conversation about some of the activities they had done and how there were many family traditions and rituals to look forward to in the summertime. As they chatted, I was aware that Zach could be reflective about times that he was not part of the family and secure in the sense that he would be an integral part of the future with his family. I could also sense the ebbing of tension in Donna as she reconnected in this lovely way with her son.]

I still, however, wanted to address Zach's determination to help his parents and to ensure that he wasn't using pleasing as a way to mitigate bad things from happening. I turned to Donna to help her reassure her son that she was still able to manage.]

T: Such lovely things to look forward to this summer! But for the next little bit you guys have to get through some stressful times.

Z: Yepppp.

T: And whose job is it again to make sure Mum is sleeping or not stressed out?

Z: (mischievously) Mine.

T: No, no, no, no! It's not your job. (at this point I sit on Zach and we both fuss about our points of view briefly)

Z: I am going to work to make her happy!

T: You can work to do the things you have to do, like chores . . .

D: . . . and going to school and paying attention.

Z: I do do my chores and stuff for her.

T: That's not your job!

Z: I know that but I just can't stand it when she is unhappy.

D: Just go to school and pay attention.

T: (turn to Donna) Donna, can you just tell him that it's not his job to look after you? Say, "Son of mine, who I have been fighting for since you were four years old, I can take care of my feelings." [*Editor's note: In this interchange we observe Sian deepening the affective experience. It is largely through intersubjectivity that therapy progresses.*]

Z: (giggling, thinks it's funny)

D: (gets serious, reaches for his hand) Zach, it's not your job to look after my feelings.

Z: (still giggling; I take his hat off, playfully direct him to look at his mum's eyes while she talks to him)

D: (still serious) It is not your job to look after me; it's your job to be a kid.

T: Donna, can you add, "I am going to be stressed for a little bit, but it's not about you. It's not that I don't love you, but it's still not your job to make sure I am happy." (turns to Zach, who is still a little anxious) Would you look at your mum when she is saying this to you? [*Editor's note: Zach may be anxious, but he does not appear to be dysregulated. Dysregulation implies being dissociated or unable to be coherent and in the moment. Experiencing strong emotions is not the same as being dysregulated. This interchange illustrates the therapist co-regulating affect.*]

D: I am really stressed, you know that, but it's not your job to fix that and it's not because of you. I love you. (holding and stroking his hand)

Z: (quieter) I do too.

D: (jokes) Good, we both love you! (everyone giggles)

(Donna and Zach continue to hold hands, and make rocking movements with hands)

T: (very quietly) You love her too.

D: He shows it to me too, that's all I care.

Z: Every time I say to my mum, "I love you, Mum," she says show it to me!

D: Talk is cheap. Show it to me is what I say to the kids. There is some people
. . .

Z: I will do and I have done it.

D: Yes, you have, and that's what I try to do to you too.

Z: You don't have to show it because I know you do.

D: I show it to you.

T: How does she show you that she loves you?

Z: With all the things she's done, going on trips, doing all this stuff, buying us the best clothes money can buy, going swimming.

D: What I think of about showing you that I love you is being at home, having suppers together, making sure that everyone is tucked in every night and you are caring about everyone and where they are at all times, nobody is left out. [Donna does a lovely job of moving the focus to the relationship, which reflects how far she has come in understanding how the relationship takes priority.] [*Editor's note: This also illustrates the "pre-session" work that Sian must have done with Donna getting her ready for treatment. It underscores the importance of working with the caregiver until that person is able to be reasonably supportive, insightful, committed, sensitive, and reflective.*]

Z: Yep.

D: That's what it means to me, not what you get bought. (still holding hands)

T: I think what your mum is saying is that you are in her heart all the time.

Z: Me too! All the time, even when I wasn't living with her she was in my heart and so was Dad.

T: Yes, those were such rough times.

Z: (quietly, but emphatically) I bet I could say that they are the best parents in the world.

T: Go ahead, say it!

Z: Donna and Cliff are the best parents in the world. (looking at me)

[I direct Zach to say it again, this time looking at his mum's eyes. This allows for a deepening of the intimacy. This is evident in his next comment where he refers to them in the first person rather than by name.]

Z: (turns and looks at his mum) You and Dad are the best parents in the world. [*Editor's note: The effects of Sian's deepening the emotional experience can be seen in the way Zach moves from talking about "Donna and Cliff" to "you and Dad."*]

D: (gently) Thank you.

Z: To me and anybody else who is with you [meaning the other foster children].

D: I do love you, Zach, and I am so glad that you are fitting in and realize that you are part of a big family and with [names all the children, including her own grown-up children]. Everyone has a place, everyone does. (both holding each other's eyes beautifully—Zach is fully present in the experience) It's just going to take some time to get everything straightened around, that's all. We managed until now—just another week and then we will get things back to normal; then we will be able to do more things as a family. (pulls Zach toward her and he melts into her arms)

T: (watches them hug quietly for a moment, then says quietly) That's a great hug! I am so glad that you are able to love each other. (Zach just allows himself to be held and I am quiet, not wanting to interrupt this lovely moment.) It's been such a long wait, hasn't it, to find this love. Finally, finally, this boy has the best mum and dad in the world! [*Editor's note: This illustrates how the affective/ reflective dialogue can deepen the intersubjective experience.*]

D: (breaks the tension) Oh God, look at Sian! [I have tears in my eyes, in part due to how moving their interaction is and in part because I am so relieved that their relationship is still so strong.] [*Editor's note: This is a beautiful example of how the therapist practicing Dyadic Developmental Psychotherapy must be emotionally engaged with the family. Sian's use of self by sharing the experience, by entering into the intersubjectivity of the moment, is therapeutic. It is therapeutic because the focus remains on the client.*]

Z: She looks like she's crying. (doesn't break the hug)

T: Yes, I love it that you have found each other after so long. (quietly) I am so glad that you know how much your mum loves you and holds you in her heart and how you have let that love in so that you can start to know that you are a loveable kid. You didn't always know that.

(still hugging)

Z: You know I still have it; it's up on the cupboard. I got this thing in the mail one day, it was last year I think, I got a certificate and uh! It says, I showed commitment and love to try new things.

T: Mm mmm, you are such a brave kid that way, even when you are scared.

D: We are proud of him for that—that's what the certificate was for.

T: Mmmmm. Donna, you have always said that, even when he was a little guy, he was always trying stuff; that was the guy you knew.

Z: I would try anything when I was little and I still do.

T: Yeah.

D: You were afraid when you first came back, do you remember? You had all these fears. You were afraid to go upstairs when everyone was downstairs, afraid all the time.

T: I think he might have been so scared to make a mistake when he first came back to your house. [*Editor's note: Sian is moving to co-create a new meaning that will allow for further exploration and integration.*]

Z: I am not going to make any mistakes. (an element of playing)

T: (playfully pushes his leg) Oh, you will too! Everyone makes mistakes! I think what you have learned is, so what! You don't have to go anywhere! Donna and Cliff still love you no matter what. [*Editor's note: PACE—by being playful Sian lightens the tone while keeping Zach engaged in this very hard and important exploration.*]

Z: True. I love myself.

T: You do! (slaps knees) Say it again!

Z: I love myself!

T: Yipeeeee!

Z: For what I am made of . . .

D: That's right!

[I was now sure that the stress in the family had not interfered with the relationship between Donna and Zach, but in fact was contributing to the sense that this was family; everyone helped each other when someone was hurt, sick, or overwhelmed. Zach had not returned to the old, fearful place of experiencing stress and anticipating rejection. Donna had done a wonderful job of reconnecting with her son, finding empathy for how he responds to stress and celebrating his place in the family.]

We had one more check-in session, which confirmed that Zach and his parents had accomplished their goals. They had their son back and he had found parents with whom he truly felt safe and wanted.

Our last session perhaps reflects less of the actual Dyadic Developmental Psychotherapy process in real time, but the culmination of our work over a number of months. It is the last session with Zach and his parents—a time to celebrate the work that he had done and acknowledge that he no longer

needed therapy to help him belong in his family. I felt very emotional anticipating this session. It was important to me to really mark the work Zach and
his family had undertaken. Even if at some point in the future they needed to
come back to address issues that were present, the family would not ever be
in the same place or stage of being a family. What came to me in the middle
of the night was that I needed to give Zach back his story as he had told it to
me over the months of knowing him.

We started the last session by reflecting about how much everybody had
learned over the past eight months. As we chatted about how each family
member had seen the role of therapy, Zach's parents rattled off a long list of
how their son was managing better. Zach grinned and nodded his agreement
as they talked about better concentration, doing better in school, worrying
less, getting along better with his brothers and sisters, and trying new things
without a second thought.

As we neared the end of the session, I presented Zach with a photograph
book and the story I had written for him. He was thrilled and taken aback
that I would have written something for him that was nine pages long! The
following story reflects the themes in Zach's life that we had identified, explored, and integrated over the course of therapy. The story also highlights
some key moments in therapy, where Zach was able to experience himself
differently and integrate some very painful beliefs and feelings of shame.
His now-coherent narrative was born from all those aspects of Dyadic Developmental Psychotherapy: playfulness, acceptance, curiosity, empathy,
intersubjectivity, affective-reflective dialogue, times when I followed, times
when I led. He could tell his story because he first developed a sense of safety
with his parents and with me his therapist. Each week, he was able to experience and explore his story on a deeper level and finally to be able to truly
see himself as the exceptional boy that he is—a consequence of integration
and healing. [*Editor's note: This is a wonderful description of how exploration leads to integration and healing. Significant healing has occurred and
the story to follow frames this process for the family in a beautiful manner.
It further illustrates therapist use of self. By allowing herself (Sian) to enter
into intersubjective experiences with this family, she is able to help them develop a coherent narrative, new meanings, and heal. The story that follows
co-creates a new meaning and helps Zach develop a more coherent autobiographical narrative.*]

ZACH'S STORY (MAY 10, 2010)

Once upon a time there was a beautiful baby named Zach. He came into the
world full of hope and energy to learn what life had to offer. He had big, curious

eyes and a heart built for love. Unfortunately, Zach had parents who, although they wanted to be good parents, had no idea how to care for babies. When Zach cried, they didn't know how to make him feel better. When he was hungry, they forgot to feed him. When he cried louder to try to make them understand, his father would get angry and yell and sometimes be rough with him. Because he had been born with curiosity and willingness to learn, Zach learned that he couldn't rely on his parents at all and began to figure his world out all by himself. He learned that he couldn't approach his mum and dad with his feelings or excitement about life; he had to keep it to himself. He learned that he couldn't ask questions about what he didn't understand; he had to figure it out himself. He learned what he had to do to keep the peace as best he could so he didn't get yelled at or hit as much. What a smart kid he was. Although he tried really hard, he couldn't help wondering if there was something wrong with him and maybe that was why his mum and dad were so mad at him all the time and why they would hurt him with their words and with their fists. This feeling became a kernel of doubt inside him: maybe he was a bad kid.

Zach made up his mind to work harder at being a good kid. He was helpful, polite, didn't complain. He looked after his younger brother, Mathew, even though his parents seemed to be better at loving Mathew than him. This took so much energy trying to figure out how to get his parents to love him that he was often tired. Now tired in little kids doesn't look like tired in adults. When little kids are tired and stressed they can't seem to stop moving. Their brains and bodies move along at top speed. Soon, people were calling him hyper. Zach didn't know what that meant, but he didn't think it was a good thing. He tucked it away with all the other hurts and fears inside him and tried not to think about it.

One day, a lady he didn't know took him and his younger brother to a strange house. Zach was scared, but again he didn't let anyone know in case it got him into trouble. He just watched and wondered what was going to happen. He learned that this home was a home for kids whose parents didn't know how to care for them. Someone had realized that Zach and Mathew were being hurt badly and whisked them away to this emergency house.

Zach was really scared. Even though his mum and dad were not very helpful and often mean to him, they were the only mum and dad he knew. Now he had two new adults that were looking after him and telling him that he was safe. He didn't believe them for a second. His experience with adults in his four years was not a good one. He concentrated on looking after his brother and trying to keep out of trouble.

The trouble was that trouble seemed to keep happening to him. He always seemed to be making mistakes or not following the rules. He wasn't used to rules. Because he had always looked after himself, he was the one who decided what he was going to do, when he was going to do it and how. Now, there was someone else telling him when and how to do things. Zach was confused. These two new adults often had irritation in their voice and looked tired. Zach decided it must be because he was a bad kid that he didn't know how to fit into this family.

Because this was an emergency home, he and Mathew were not able to stay there long. Just as he was beginning to like a house where he wasn't being yelled at or hit and was fed when he was hungry and given drinks when he was thirsty, they moved him. This time it was even scarier. He had to get to know two different adults. That feeling that he must be a bad kid kept following him because in this new house, the adults wanted him to sit still and he couldn't. They wanted him to eat properly, but he couldn't. They wanted him to settle at bedtime, but he had too much energy. He tried, he tried so hard, but when he looked at the adult eyes, they didn't seem to understand how hard he was trying or how hard it was for him. Their eyes seemed to reinforce for Zach that there was something wrong with him and that nobody would ever love him. Again he tucked the very difficult feeling away deep inside him.

The adults in this home didn't really know how to parent a boy who had had so much hurt and so much practice at doing things for himself. They asked two other adults if they would try to parent Zach. Zach moved again! He was beginning to think that he would have been better to stay with his first mum and dad—at least he knew what to expect!

Zach was placed (whatever that meant, other than he didn't really have a home) with two people called Donna and Cliff. They lived on a farm with animals and lots of fields around them. Very soon after he moved there, the family was taking a trip to the big city and took him with them. Don't forget that Zach was born with a great deal of curiosity and wonderment for his world so this was exciting. The first time on a bus. The first time in a big city. His big eyes took in all the people and all the cars and city sights. There was something else that Zach took in that day, but he didn't let himself think about it very much. He noticed that these two new people in his life had a different kind of eyes. They were softer somehow and interested somehow and playful somehow. Zach had a very funny experience; he both wanted to look into these eyes and run away from them at the same time.

As he spent a few more days and weeks with them he noticed other things too. Donna and Cliff would let him run and run and run and didn't seem to be irritated with his need to move all the time. In fact they would encourage him to climb and try new things all the time. There was something else too. He noticed that these adults seemed to want to spend time with him. They laughed at the things he said and did and that gave him a funny, weird feeling inside. Sometimes he would say things just to see if they would laugh, hoping to feel that funny tummy feeling again. Donna and Cliff wouldn't get angry at him when he didn't know how to do something; they would just patiently teach him how. Because he was a quick learner, he learned so many new things quickly. One very special thing happened every day. Zach would sit on Donna and go to sleep on her chest. He loved this time best of all. He could hear the steady beat of her heart and feel her strong arms around him and he for the first time in his life began to think that he might be able to trust an adult to take care of him. He began to think maybe he wasn't such a bad kid after all. However, when he was away from Donna's eyes it was hard to hold on to this thought that he may not be a bad kid and he would go back to feeling that hard yucky feeling at the pit of his stomach.

Zach slowly slowly began to believe these parents' eyes. They seemed to say to him that he was loveable, special, smart, and funny. They never yelled at him or seemed irritated by him. He was always fed good food and grew bigger muscles and longer legs that helped him run faster and climb bigger trees. These parents seemed to talk about him like he was their own boy and they would introduce him to everyone they met as their son. Wow! What a special feeling that was to Zach who had never felt this belonging before. He even felt safe enough to start calling them Mum and Dad.

One day, Zach overheard Donna and Cliff talking about wanting to adopt him. His heart skipped a beat. He didn't really know the word adoption, but it seemed really important because Donna and Cliff had very serious looks on their faces and Donna had tears in her eyes. He was very afraid that he might have to move to a new house and held his breath. As he listened he got the idea that adoption meant becoming part of this family forever. Was it possible? Oh, Zach really hoped it was.

Donna and Cliff had to talk to a number of social workers and someone called a judge to see if he could become their son. It was a very stressful time and Zach's energy was especially high because he was so scared and hopeful at the same time. Donna and Cliff seemed to be different too. Zach tried hard not to think about it and put all of his energy into playing.

One day, he looked at Donna and Cliff and got a sudden feeling of fear. Because he was so used to doing things by himself he didn't show his fear on the outside. He just waited to see what was going to happen. Donna and Cliff sat him down. Donna was crying. Cliff looked so sad. Zach disappeared inside himself. He knew what was coming couldn't be good and he needed to protect himself. He made himself go numb inside so he couldn't be hurt. He had had lots of practice with that when his first dad used to hurt him.

Donna and Cliff told him that the judge wouldn't let him stay with them because he thought it would be better for him to live with his aunt and uncle. All Zach heard was that he would have to move again. He grew even more numb inside. All those old feelings that he hadn't felt in a while came rushing back. He wasn't good enough, he was a bad kid, he was just a throwaway kid!

The next few days were really hard. Everyone was so sad. The day came where Zach had to move. Donna drove him on her motorcycle far away to his new house. Zach felt desperate inside. He really didn't want to leave Donna and Cliff. He didn't know his aunt and uncle and didn't really want to find the energy to get to know another set of adults who were supposed to take care of him. Donna had packed lots of pictures of them doing things together and told him to look at them whenever he felt like he missed them. She promised that they would call often and come and visit him whenever they could. Zach could feel anger behind her words and worried that she was angry with him. He tried not to think of anything.

When he arrived at his aunt and uncle's house he made sure that nobody knew what he really felt on the inside. He was polite and answered their questions and went with them when they showed him his new room. Donna helped him unpack. Then the awful time came when she had to leave. Zach was sure this was happening to him because he was a bad kid. He tried to think of talking to her and seeing her on a visit to help himself feel better.

Zach had a really difficult time with his aunt and uncle. They used to fight a lot and this used to scare Zach. It reminded him of the times when his first mum and dad would fight. He felt lonely and unsure. His energy level was so high because he was so worried all the time about whether his aunt and uncle would be fighting and because he was missing Donna and Cliff. In grade 1 his teacher would always be complaining that he couldn't pay attention. Zach felt miserable. He remembered that Donna told him to look at his pictures or to call if he missed them. He knew that his aunt and uncle didn't want him to keep contact with Donna and Cliff. They had put his pictures high up on his dresser where he couldn't reach them. They wouldn't let him call to talk to them and hear their voices. Zach was tricky though. He was a good climber and a smart kid and figured out how to place his drawers and use his bed to get to the top of his dresser so he could look at his pictures without his aunt and uncle knowing. One glorious day Donna and Cliff showed up at his house to take him out. He knew his aunt and uncle were not happy, but he didn't care. He skipped out of the house right into their car. They had a lovely few hours together. When Zach was with Donna and Cliff he felt different again. It somehow felt like a little bit of hope that he wasn't just a throwaway kid. That afternoon he asked them if they would buy him a cell phone so he could call them. Who ever heard of a six-year-old kid with a cell phone? That was how smart Zach was though, always thinking of ways to stay connected to the two people who seemed to think so much of him.

After another two years, a strange man came to Zach's school and told him that he couldn't live with his aunt and uncle anymore. Another move! Zach was sick and tired of moving. But again, he stuffed his real feelings inside and went along with this man, wondering what next.

What next involved moving to another province to the family who had adopted his younger brother and sister. They thought that they might be able to adopt him too. Zach had to pack his bags again and travel with someone he didn't know to live with other people he didn't know. These were parents number 6. What were they going to be like as parents?

When he arrived he found that this family spoke French and would expect him to speak French too. They changed his name and enrolled him French school. Zach knew he could do hard, but this was so hard. So many changes and he seemed to be getting things wrong all the time. He was in so many fights at school. The boys would tease him and Zach would just explode. He didn't know it yet but he was angry! He was angry at all the decisions big people had made about him without asking him. He was angry that he missed Cliff and Donna. He was angry that his first mum and dad were not good enough to take care of him. He was angry that now he seemed to be back in the position of caring for his younger brother and sister like he did as a little kid. Who was there to care for him? Because Zach was so used to doing things by himself and had had nobody to help him with hard things, he didn't know how to identify his feelings or know how to express them. He just got angrier and angrier and felt more and more like he wanted to explode. More and more he had the feeling that there was something wrong with him. His new parents always seemed to be looking at him with a look that reinforced that. What he didn't know yet was that look reflected their own sense of not being able to parent him. It was their own shame. But for now Zach just took it in as it being his fault.

One day he found himself back in foster care. Another move. This time back to Ontario to yet another set of foster parents. What he didn't know was that he was almost done moving.

Donna and Cliff had never, never stopped fighting to get their son back. Yes, they had always thought of him as their son because love like that never stops burning. They found out that Zach was not going to be adopted by George and Leah and they were determined that they would adopt him. They talked to everyone and didn't stop fighting until Zach arrived in their home one day with his suitcase.

For Donna and Cliff, this was the day they had been fighting for. For Zach, he was scared and unsure whether he could ever feel like he belonged in this family. After so many moves, he reckoned it would just be a matter of time until he would be asked to move again. Donna recognized that some of Zach's spirit had died. She remembered a boy who was adventurous and would try new things. This twelve-year-old Zach seemed scared and afraid to try. He was angry and confused and didn't want to play with the other kids in the home very much. He was really good at taking care of himself and didn't much want anything from this new mum and dad.

Luckily Donna and Cliff knew kids and they could see that Zach's spirit had died and they were determined to help him find it again. They contacted someone called Sian who they knew worked with kids who had been hurt and asked her for help.

Zach, Donna, and Cliff met with Sian for eight months. At first they went every week and then not so often. Zach began to learn how hard his life really had been and how he had needed to learn how to look after himself because the adults around him didn't know how to parent him. He realized that he had lots of questions that he hadn't allowed himself to ask, like "why didn't his first dad want to know him?" and "why hadn't he been good enough for George and Leah?" He struggled for a long time with wanting to go back to George and Leah's house. Part of it was that he was worried about his brother and sister because George and Leah always seemed to be overwhelmed by the children and Zach felt it was his job to look after everyone. He had learned that lesson so well from when he was a little boy. Part of it was a feeling that if he had just been a better kid it would have worked out right. Then he began to realize that it wasn't his fault at all, but it was the adults' responsibility to look after kids.

Then he was angry. If they had lied to him about wanting to adopt him, what else had they lied about?

Zach also grew to realize how little practice he had asking for help. He began slowly to ask his parents for help. Initially he was terrified. When they would hold him in Sian's office he was stiff and the feelings were so big that he would make himself go numb inside. But gradually, gradually he began to feel his spirit waking up. He realized that he didn't have to do anything for Donna and Cliff to love him. One week something very important happened. Zach was struggling because he couldn't pay attention in school and thought that it was because there was something wrong with him. Then suddenly with everyone's help he realized that he wasn't a bad kid at all, but everyone had troubles paying attention when there was so much on their mind. Wow, you should have seen the relief on his face when he realized that he had been wrong. There was nothing wrong with him!

Sometimes in sessions, Donna or Cliff would hold him in their arms. Zach had memories of what it had been like when he was four and five years old to be held by strong arms and to have loving eyes look at him. He started to remember that he was special. He realized how fierce Donna and Cliff's love for him was and he didn't have to do anything to get it, just be him. Zach began to do better at school and to not be so worried all the time. He started to let their love in and feel more hopeful and alive again. He started to believe his mum, that another move would happen over her dead body. He wondered how he managed to keep his heart open after so many hard things and believed that his kind heart was a part of him that nobody could destroy because it was just part of just him. He was kind and courageous and smart and best of all had the ability to love back. He had never thought that was possible.

Zach believed that God had put him on this world for exactly his life. Donna and Cliff had wanted another son and he had needed parents like Donna and Cliff. Although all that hard life had been difficult and hurtful, perhaps it was what brought him here to this place where he belonged. Parents and brothers and sisters who loved him and parents and brothers and sisters he could love back. He belonged.

Zach wondered if he could manage all these hard things, imagine what he would be able to do with the rest of his life now that he had some help and a whole lot of love. Watch for him, because, for sure, he is a boy who will make a difference.

As it came time to end our session, I read just the last part of Zach's story to him and took a picture of him and his parents on the Therapy Couch to put in the book with his story. His dad with tears in his eyes looked at his son and said, "You sure have made a difference in my life." Zach thoughtfully, but resolutely, whispered, "I have made a difference in my own life."

What better way to end?

Chapter Thirteen

The Girl Who Becomes Aggressive

Arthur Becker-Weidman, PhD

In this chapter you will read three clips from sessions with a family I saw for approximately one year. These clips are from the middle of treatment and represent, primarily, the exploration and integration phases. Mary is eleven. She was adopted when she was about five years old. She is developmentally delayed, with an IQ of about 76. What brought the family into treatment was her aggression. Mary would hit her mother, punch her, hit her sister, and hit others. Mary would get physically aggressive at school with teachers and other students. In the first clip you will read about Mary hitting her mother in the session and how her mother responds in a re-regulating manner. The mother *very, very* effectively manages this, especially the way she makes sure the situation does not escalate. In the next two clips you will see a more integrated child. As Mary talks about herself you will observe her reflective abilities.

> (Mary is seated next to her mother on the couch, trying to hit, scratch, and kick her.)
>
> *Mom:* (softy, gently, and firmly) Mary, now stop it. That's enough. Come on now. . . .
>
> *Mary:* (squirming) No! No! No! No!
>
> *Mom:* (calmly, while looking at Mary) You need to calm down. I know you're angry.
>
> *Mary:* (standing up, she starts pulling away from her mother, who is holding Mary's wrists)
>
> *Mom:* Now, is this a time when you have me confused with Emily?

[The mom is referring to Mary's birth mother, Emily. Mary's confusing Mom with Emily, on an affective basis, was a recurrent theme during treatment. At times when something upset Mary, the affect associated with Emily's abuse of Mary would be triggered, without the associated episodic memory being triggered. Gradually Mary became better able to recognize this. This helped Mary re-create a narrative that could make sense of her behavior in a nonblaming, nonshaming, and nonjudgmental way. It also helped Mom understand her daughter. That understanding allowed Mom to not get as disturbed and upset by this kind of behavior. In this event, Mom asks Mary if she is confusing her, Mom, with Emily—not that she expects an answer but she's just trying to talk out loud and reflect on the experience and help her daughter learn how to do that as well.]

Mary: (standing and pulling her arms away from her mother, who is seated and holding on to Mary's wrists) No, no, let go!

Mom: (softly, while looking up into Mary's eyes with calm assurance) Come on. Come on.

Mary: Let go! Let go!

Mom: (gently and quietly) Sit down. I'll let go when you sit down and relax. (Mary pulls her arms away and drops down on seat next to mom, calming)

This segment highlights how important it is to co-regulate the child's affect and that this can be accomplished, in part, by remaining calm. The mom's calm helps regulate Mary. Another important point this illustrates is how important it is to focus on your primary objective (calming Mary, rather than mere compliance with the statement, "I'll let go when you relax"). Mary sits down and yanks her hands away and that could have turned into a really large battle if the mom had said, "No . . . I said I won't let go until you sit down and relax." But the mom recognized that was probably okay; Mary wasn't doing exactly what she asked her to do, but she was beginning to calm down. She, Mom, was safe. And so Mom lets go and Mary sits down and then begins to get herself organized. So it's a nice example of how to manage that kind of beginning dysregulation you sometimes see with children at home and in the office. It is also an example of the importance of shared intersubjectivity and attunement. Mom's attunement with Mary allowed her to know that the Mom was safe and could let go of Mary at that point.

In the next segment Mary is sitting calmly next to her mother. I comment on how quickly she was able to get herself back under control. Mom and I also reflect on some of the progress that the family has made in the last few months.

Art: You really have done well, Mary. Did you hear all the things your mom said are going better for you and the family?

Mary: (buries her head in the couch) No. [I am not sure at this moment what she may be feeling shame about.]

Art: I'm sorry, did I say something wrong? What makes it hard for you? [I begin by accepting responsibility that I may have said something that made Mary feel badly about herself and that I am sorry if that is what I did (interactive repair).]

Mary: It hurts!

Art: What hurts? [I am curious about what hurts her.]

Mary: My heart, when you tell me all these things that I've done good.

[We had just been talking about something positive that she'd done and she got upset, didn't want to talk about it, and what she said is "It hurts my heart when you talk about good things I've done." And so, that's curious. I don't understand that, it doesn't quite make sense to me, so that reflects my lack of empathy. I want to explore that with her to figure it out. Why would that be?]

Art: Hearing about the good things hurts your heart?

Mary: (subdued) Yes.

Art: Huh. And what about hearing these good things hurts your heart, or how does it hurt your heart?

Mary: Seeing the bad things I did before the good things.

Art: Oh, so when we talk, when I tell you all the good things you've done, it makes you think about all the other bad things you did do? [Now I get it and have empathy for her.]

Mary: (subdued) Yes.

Art: And that's what hurts you.

[Mary is exhibiting a good example of the reflective function. She is able to recognize that talking about positive things leads her to think about negative things she did and said that she now regrets. This allows us to have an affective/reflective dialogue, in contrast to the previous week in which she became behaviorally dysregulated. At this juncture I can either move along this path or stay with what Mary has said and talk about what that felt like for me to hear her say that. However, I wanted to better understand what about talking about good things would hurt her heart.]

Art: Oh, I see. Okay, now I get it. That makes sense. Okay. Do you worry, have you ever worried that your mom is angry about those other things you used to do? (Mary nods her head) You do. [Empathy part of PACE.]

Mom: (holding Mary) I'm really not. I'm not angry. I understand why it happened. I'm not angry a bit, honey. [While Mom is responding to the content of Mary's comment, she is missing the underlying insecurity Mary is experiencing and misses an opportunity to explore what Mary is feeling and accepting Mary's experience.]

Art: I can see why you feel bad about them, all those things you used to do, but you're not doing them now, are you?

Mary: (subdued) No.

Art: No, you're getting stronger. . . .

Mom: She sure is.

Art: And you know, it's okay to feel, to feel bad, to regret, to feel bad about the things you wished you didn't do. And then you could just tell your mom that. You could tell your mom. Like, for instance, if you were sorry about all those things you could even say to her, "I'm sorry about the times I hit you or were mean to you or said mean things to you." You could tell her that . . . [In this comment I am trying to acknowledge that Mary does have good reasons for feeling badly, that feeling badly is OK. I am also suggesting an interactive repair strategy.]

Mary: (shakes her head no) [Now I am baffled about what to do . . . so I accept her no and explore that with curiosity. I also offer my thoughts on what may make her not want to tell her Mom that.]

Art: No? You'll feel better . . . no? Are you afraid if you said it, she'll be mad at you?

Mom: (softly) No, I wouldn't be.

Art: Oh. She said she wouldn't be. You know what? Your mom might even . . . you know what, Mary? Your mom might even like to hear those things.

Mom: (smiles and chuckles) I think I *would*.

Art: Could you tell her that, that you're kind of sorry about those things . . .

Mary: (lying in mom's lap, vigorously shakes her head no)

[So now Mary is clear that she does not want to say that. At this point, I think, if she can't say that, maybe I can say it for her.]

Art: Well, maybe I could tell Mom for you?

Mary: (shakes head vigorously no) Nope!

[So now Mary is clear that she does not even want me to talk for her. I could just talk about her with Mom, but I am concerned that this would ignore and discount her feelings, so instead I change the question from "who" to "when."]

Art: Who's going to tell her then?

Mary: (lying in mother's arms, murmurs) I'll tell her later.

Art: Oh, you'll tell her later? Oh, okay, you can tell her later . . . but when is later? When do you mean, "later"?

Mary: When we go shopping.

Art: Ah, when you go shopping. You're going shopping after you're done with here?

Mary: (nods) Yes, we are.

Art: Really. Where?

Mary: Macy's and Target.

Art: So that's when you're going to tell Mom those things that you're sorry about, the times you've hit Mom, the times you pinched and kicked her, the times you shoved and pushed Mom, and said those mean things to Mom. Is that what you're gonna do when you go shopping after here? [What I do here is describe what Mary may be telling her mom later. This is a bit of "talking for" her that may help her later in her chat with her mom. It does turn out, as Mom reports in the next session, that Mary had a rather long talk about all those specific incidents and events that Mary regretted and told her mom she was sorry. Mom reported that she was very touched by Mary and they had a wonderful week. We used that experience in later sessions to help Mary see the value of "interactive repair."]

Art: See, I bet she'd like to hear that. And I bet you would feel better, too, telling your mom that you feel bad about those things you did. And you're really, you know, you're hardly ever now doing those thing. A year ago, a year ago those were things that happened, I don't know . . . every day, more than once a day. . . .

Mom: (nods)

Art: And now, they hardly ever happen! Isn't that, isn't that true, Mary?

Mary: (sits up, takes a tissue, and blows her nose)

Art: Yeah, they hardly ever happen. Really, you're getting so much stronger in your heart!

(Mary nods as she wipes tears from her eyes and cheeks.)

Art: All the hurts and boo boos to your heart are healing and so now you can even think about Ann and it's not as bad as it used to be. . . .

Mary: (leaning over, examining wastepaper basket) [I am wondering what just happened that she is now distracted.]

Art: What's there? Oh, your ring. Oh, oh, don't want to lose your ring! Where'd you get that ring? [She'd dropped her ring when she was blowing her nose. I am thinking, also, that, perhaps, she needs a break from the intensity of the previous few minutes, and so decide to pursue a lighter topic for a bit to manage the PACEing of our session.]

Mary: At Clare's.

Art: At Clare's?

Art: You have to be careful. You don't want to blow your brains out in your ears. . . . [The playful part of PACE.]

Mom: (chuckles)

Mary: (snuggling up next to Mom) (joking) I've blown my brains out before. It don't hurt.

Mom: (laughing)

Art: You don't want to do that. It's hard to get them back in your ears then. Who got you the ring?

Mary: My daddy.

Art: Your daddy? Clare's is a nice place. They have all kinds of things.

Art: Did you get your earrings there, too?

Mary: Yes, I did and these, too. (she holds out her arm and shakes the bracelets)

Art: And the bangles? Is that what you call them? Bangles?

Mary: Yes.

Art: Yeah. So, how are things different this year compared to last year? [I'd like Mary to reflect on her growth over the last year. However, given her low IQ, she tends to be quite concrete.]

Mary: Well, my sister didn't go to camp. . . .

Art: Mmhm.

Mary: This summer we had a Fourth of July party. (looks at Mom)

Mom: And we'll have a Labor Day party.

Mary: Yeah, and we did have a Fourth of July party and I baked a cake. . . .

Art: Hmm.

Mary: It was chocolate . . . (looks at Mom) Or was it white?

Mom: (whispers) It was white.

Mary: And I put vanilla frosting on and I put blueberries for the stars and straw-berries for the stripes.

Art: Mmm. Very nice!

Mary: (leans over to her mom)

Mom: And we picked blueberries . . .

Mary: We picked blueberries this summer. I'm going to my Aunt Mary's this summer . . .

Art: You didn't go last summer?

Mary: No. We're going for a week.

Art: Is that, is that good?

Mary: Yeah.

Art: What do you like about Aunt Mary's?

Mary: Well, there's Steven and my cousin, and there's Jolene and there's Sub-way and there's a lot of things.

Art: Huh!

Mary: (sings) Subway!

Art: Now, here's a hard question. How do you think you're different this sum-mer compared to last summer?

Mary: Well, I'm older this summer. (giggles)

Art: I know. What else? How do you think you're either acting different or feel-ing different or being different when you compare the two? [I wanted to see if Mary could reflect about herself, and as the reader will notice, with some guid-ance, she is quite able to reflect on how she is different.]

Mary: I'm being a lot better.

Art: What does "better" mean? [It is important for the therapist to be curious and not assume that what the child means and what the therapist may mean by the words are the same. To press a "suit" means two very different things to a tailor and an attorney.]

Mary: Oh, I'm behaving better?

Art: What do you mean . . . ?

Mary: I'm acting good.

Art: So what is it you're doing or not doing?

Mary: I'm not hitting as much.

Art: Ah. So when's the last time you actually did hit? Do you know? Can you remember? [Having met with Mom before we all met, I know that it has been several weeks since Mary has hit her mom.]

Mary: (looks at her mom)

Art: Was it today? (Mom and daughter, looking at each other, both shake their heads.) Was it this weekend? (Mom and daughter, looking at each other, both shake their heads.) Was it the weekend before?

Mary: It was probably last week.

Art: So you think it was just like one week ago? [Now I am puzzled because Mary's answer does not fit with what her mom has told me, so I will want to explore this further.]

Mary: Uh-huh.

Art: (turning to Mom) Does that sound right to you?

Mary: It was like early in the week, a week ago Tuesday.

Mom: Maybe. Did you hit Casey? [Casey is her older sister, both adopted at the same time.]

Mary: (nods)

Mom: But you haven't hit me, though, for quite a few weeks.

Mary: But I hit Casey Tuesday. [Now it is clear, I was asking about when was the last time she'd hit her *mom*, but was not explicit and Mary responded to the general "When was the last time you hit" question.]

Art: Oh, but your mom, it's been . . .

Mary: A longer time . . .

Art: Wow, well, that's . . .

Mary: Six weeks!

Art: So last summer how, I mean about, how often do you think you were hitting your mom last summer?

Mary: Mm, once a week, once or twice a week.

Art: Twice a week? (to Mom) What do you think? More? Less?

Mom: Oh, a little more often, I think.

Mary: Every other day? [Mary is very well regulated here and is able to discuss her past behavior without any evident shame—quite a contrast from the previous session.]

Art: Every other day?

Mary: (to Mom, lying on her back on couch, next to Mom) Belly, rub my belly, Mommy. [Mom briefly rubs Mary's belly and then pulls Mary's shirt down and Mary sits up. We can look at this nonverbal exchange as Mary asking her Mom if Mom still loves her and Mom responding, "Yes, I do." The reader may wonder if Mary's moving around and fidgeting are "distractions" or represent Mary's having a hard time with the topic. My experience was that Mary was feeling very good and beginning to find the subject boring—the subject does not have the same heavy affective tone it has had in the past. She does not feel a dysregulating amount of shame. At this point Mary is relating and is engaged in what we are doing, so if she has to move around to stay focused that is fine. She does have sensory issues that were identified in the assessment, and while she is about eleven in this clip, her developmental age on the Vineland Adaptive Behavior Scales–II (Becker-Weidman, 2009) is closer to five years.]

Art: So that's a big change, Mary, going from every other day, which in six weeks would be. . . . It would be like, in six weeks it would be like twenty times, to zero in six weeks. That's a big change. So how'd you do that? How're you doing that? How is it that you're not hitting? (Mary rolls over to put her arms around Mom, who laughs.) [I am wanting to see if Mary can describe how *she* has made this very big change happen.]

Mary: Last summer I didn't have as much counseling . . .

Art: Yeah, anything else?

Mary: Last summer I thought someone loves me and now I know someone loves me.

Art: Wow! So that's a huge difference. So now you know somebody loves you?

Mary: Yes.

Art: Who? Who do you know loves you?

Mary: Her (puts her finger on Mom) and Daddy and my sister and my doggie and my fish.

Art: And you didn't feel that way last summer?

Mary: Nope . . . cause I didn't have a fish! [Here Mary becomes playful in a rather engaging way.]

Art: (laughs)

Mary: And I didn't have two kittens. The kittens got spayed and neutered, whatever that means.

Art: They can't have babies.

Mary: Yeah, I know.

Art: So last summer you didn't really feel that anybody loved you and now you do?

Mary: (nods, smiling and hugging her mom)

Art: What a big change! That's really big, and so that makes you feel, when you get angry . . . so what do you do instead of hitting when you get angry, like at your mom and your dad?

Mary: I try to get them to hug me before I get angry.

In this exchange we see the huge difference for Mary in thinking (cognition) that her family loves her and knowing (affective) that her family loves her. What seems to have made a big difference for Mary is that in the past she had *thought* people loved her, but now she *knows* people love her. This difference seems to have allowed her to become much more regulated emotionally and behaviorally. Another important point that Mary makes is that now when she starts to become upset she hugs her mom and that helps her feel better (co-regulation of affect). When the family began treatment, Mary was quite aggressive toward her mom. Mary is also taller, heavier, and stronger than her mom, who would back away whenever Mary became agitated out of fear that the agitation would escalate into physical violence, which is often what did occur. When it became clear to Mom that Mary's agitation was often fueled by a sense of insecurity and of feeling rejected, abandoned, and being unloved, then Mom would step in and hug her daughter when Mary became agitated or upset. This acted to calm Mary. Now they are at the point where Mary can recognize that she is becoming upset and that a hug will help her. This represents a significant advance in her reflective function and her capacity to self-regulate. This sequence captures the common sequence in parenting that first the parent does "it" for the child, then they do "it" together, and then the child can do "it" independently. "It" can be brushing teeth or learning to identify internal states and self-regulating.

Art: And what do you do, because everybody gets angry about things, I mean, things happen that are bothersome or irritating, so what do you do when something happens, when your mom says or does something you just don't like? What do you do instead of hit?

Mary: I don't slam doors. . . .

Art: Yeah, that's what you don't do, but what do you do instead?

Mary: I hug my mom or dad.

Art: Anything else?

Mary: I may go play in my room. . . .

Art: You play in your room?

Mary: Yeah, or go to sleep.

Art: Oh.

Mary: Sometimes I take a big long nap, right? (looks at her mom)

Mom: Sometimes.

Mary: One or two hours.

Art: Does that help you?

Mary: Yeah, it helps me forget about it and get over it.

Art: But what about when something just bothers you? Your mom says or does something and you're just irritated by her? What do you do now? Not a big thing but, you know, you say, "Let's do this." And you (to Mom) say, "No, you can't do that now."

Mary: I just let Mom know and then she hugs me and I know she loves me and that's it!

So, in this transcript the reader has observed how Mary has made some significant improvements in her capacity to self-regulate and how this is grounded in her mom's strong commitment to Mary, her insightfulness, and her ability to stay with the intersubjective experience with her daughter. This underscores the importance of parents as central to treatment outcome and the importance of working closely with parents by building an alliance with them.

Chapter Fourteen

Conclusion

Arthur Becker-Weidman, PhD

The reader should now have a good appreciation for the power and efficacy of Dyadic Developmental Psychotherapy as practiced by a diverse group of clinicians. The various chapters together illustrate how each therapist implements the various components of Dyadic Developmental Psychotherapy within the phases of treatment and how these phases cycle within each session. The transcripts clearly demonstrate that the phases of treatment occur in a repetitive and cyclic manner, each cycle deepening the intersubjective experience, strengthening and maintaining the alliance, and leading to further exploration, integration, and healing, even within the very first meeting with the therapist.

The reader should also now have a thorough appreciation for the importance of use of self in treatment. Each therapist uses the components of Dyadic Developmental Psychotherapy in a personally unique manner. The transcripts share in the common use of different components of treatment in a differential manner, depending on the phase of treatment. However, each transcript demonstrates how each therapist's unique style and personality is used creatively to help the family. Dyadic Developmental Psychotherapy is an approach to treatment that can be taught and used in a variety of circumstances, with many different types of families, and across cultures (U.S., Canadian, Finnish, UK, and Singaporean). At the core of the practice of Dyadic Developmental Psychotherapy is the healing power of affect and experience. The therapist uses self in an authentic and planned manner, focusing on creating concordant and therapeutic intersubjective experiences. This treatment requires a therapist with a highly developed reflective function, reasonably secure state of mind with respect to attachment, good insightfulness, flexibility, and a broad tolerance for strong affect—the very same traits that are necessary for effective attachment-facilitating parenting (Becker-Weidman, 2010b; Becker-Weidman and Shell, 2010).

These transcripts clearly illustrate the validity of the concept of phases of treatment. These phases are: developing the alliance, maintaining the alliance, exploration, integration, and healing. The transcripts demonstrate how an understanding of the phases of treatment deepens our insight into the therapeutic process and improves practice. An understanding of the phases of treatment helps the therapist in the differential application of the components of Dyadic Developmental Psychotherapy in different phases of treatment. These phases are grounded in attachment theory (Bowlby, 1988; Holmes, 1993; Holmes, 2001) and based on the clinical experience of a broad range of therapists practicing Dyadic Developmental Psychotherapy (Becker-Weidman, 2010b). These phases occur in a cyclic and iterative manner, much like the phases of the moon. Each element of the therapeutic process is present, but at different points in the process different elements are highlighted and take on greater salience. An understanding of the process of therapeutic phases will assist the therapist in the differential application of the components of Dyadic Developmental Psychotherapy, as these transcripts show clearly.

Table 14.1 presents the different components of Dyadic Developmental Psychotherapy and in which phases those components may be most salient. As the transcripts clearly demonstrate, each component may be used in each of the phases. But for pedagogic purposes, it is useful to consider which components are most relevant to a particular phase of treatment. This consideration can enable the therapist to be more planful about the therapeutic experience and to engage in the experience in a more reflective manner. The table is not meant to be prescriptive so much as an aid to thinking about the therapist's work with a family and a child.

I edited this casebook with the intention of providing interested readers and experienced practitioners of Dyadic Developmental Psychotherapy with a window into what actually occurs in sessions in different phases of treatment. My intention was to clearly illustrate the different components of treatment, the differential use of components in different phases of treatment, and how the phases concept helps illuminate the work and guide the therapist. By selecting experienced practitioners of Dyadic Developmental Psychotherapy from around the world, each of whom has a unique style, I hoped to illustrate how this evidence-based, effective, and empirically validated approach to treatment can be taught and used successfully across cultures. I believe I have been successful in this endeavor and I hope that readers have found this

Table 14.1. The Application of Components in Different Phases of Treatment

Component	Developing the Alliance	Maintaining the Alliance	Exploration	Integration	Healing
PACE	X	X	X	X	X
Follow-Lead-Follow	X	X	X		
Insightfulness					
Reflective Function			X	X	X
Commitment	X	X	X		
Therapist Use of Self	X	X	X		
Talking For & Talking About			X	X	
Co-Creation of Meaning			X	X	X
Co-Regulation of Affect	X	X	X		
Affective/Reflective Dialogue		X	X		
Interactive Repair	X	X	X		
Verbal/Nonverbal Dialogue	X	X	X	X	X
It's about connections, not compliance	X	X			
Intersubjectivity	X	X	X	X	X
Coherent Autobiographical Narrative			X	X	

book illuminating and valuable. This casebook, in conjunction with the book *Dyadic Developmental Psychotherapy: Essential Practices and Methods* (Becker-Weidman, 2010b), can serve as a detailed treatment manual for the practice of Dyadic Developmental Psychotherapy.

References

Ackenbach, T. M. (1991). *Manual for the Child Behavior Checklist/4-18 and 1991 Profile.* Burlington, VT: University of Vermont Department of Psychiatry.

Becker-Weidman, A. (2006a). "Treatment for Children with Trauma-Attachment Disorders: Dyadic Developmental Psychotherapy." *Child and Adolescent Social Work Journal* 23 (2), 147–71.

Becker-Weidman, A. (2006b). "Dyadic Developmental Psychotherapy: A Multi-year Follow-up." Pp. 43–60 in *New Developments in Child Abuse Research*, ed. Stanley M. Sturt, PhD. New York: Nova Science Publishers.

Becker-Weidman, A. (2005, 2008a). "Dyadic Developmental Psychotherapy: The Theory." Pp. 7–42 in *Creating Capacity for Attachment: Dyadic Developmental Psychotherapy in the Treatment of Trauma-Attachment Disorders*, ed. Arthur Becker-Weidman and Deborah Shell. Oklahoma City: Wood 'N' Barnes.

Becker-Weidman, A. (2005, 2008b). "The Logistics of Providing Dyadic Developmental Psychotherapy." Pp. 43–65 in *Creating Capacity for Attachment: Dyadic Developmental Psychotherapy in the Treatment of Trauma-Attachment Disorders*, ed. Arthur Becker-Weidman and Deborah Shell. Oklahoma City: Wood 'N' Barnes.

Becker-Weidman, A. (2007) *Assessing Children with Complex Trauma & Disorders of Attachment.* DVD set. Brookfield, VT: Resourceful Recordings.

Becker-Weidman, A. (2009). "Effects of Early Maltreatment on Development: A Descriptive Study Using the Vineland." *Child Welfare* 88 (2): 137–61.

Becker-Weidman, A. (2010a). *Assessing Caregiver Reflective Capacity, Commitment, Insightfulness, and Sensitivity.* DVD. Brookfield, VT: Resourceful Recordings.

Becker-Weidman, A. (2010b). *Dyadic Developmental Psychotherapy: Essential Practices and Methods.* Lanham, MD: Jason Aronson.

Becker-Weidman, A., and Hughes, D. (2008). "Dyadic Developmental Psychotherapy: An Evidence-Based Treatment for Children with Complex Trauma and Disorders of Attachment." *Child & Adolescent Social Work* 13: 329–37.

Becker-Weidman, A., and Shell, Deborah (eds.). (2005, 2008). *Creating Capacity for Attachment: Dyadic Developmental Psychotherapy in the Treatment of Trauma-Attachment Disorders.* Oklahoma City: Wood 'N' Barnes.

Becker-Weidman, A., and Shell, Deborah. (2010). *Attachment Parenting: Developing Connections and Healing Children.* New York: Jason Aronson.

Beutler, L., Malik, M., Alimohamed, S., and Harwood, T. (2004). "Therapist Variables." Pp. 227–306 in *Bergin and Garfield's Handbook of Psychotherapy and Behavior Change*, ed. M. Lambert. New York: Wiley.

Bowlby, J. (1988). *A Secure Base.* New York: Basic Books.

Bretherton, I., Ridgeway, D., and Cassidy, J. (1990). "Assessing Internal Working Models of the Attachment Relationship." In *Attachment in the Preschool Years*, ed. Greenbert, Cicchetti, and Cummings. Chicago: University of Chicago Press.

Cook, A., Blaustein, M., Spinazzola, J., and van der Kolk, B. (2003). *Complex Trauma in Children and Adolescents: White Paper from the National Child Traumatic Stress Network Complex Trauma Task Force.* Los Angeles: National Center for Child Traumatic Stress.

Cook, A., Spinazzola, J., Ford, J., Lanktree, C., Blaustein, M., Cloitre, M., et al. (2005). "Complex Trauma in Children and Adolescents." *Psychiatric Annals* 35: 390–98.

Craven, P., and Lee, R. (2006). "Therapeutic Interventions for Foster Children: A Systematic Research Synthesis." *Research on Social Work Practice* 16: 287–304.

Dozier, M., and Lindhiem, O. (2006). "This Is My Child: Differences Among Foster Parents in Commitment to Their Young Children." *Child Maltreatment* 11 (4): 338–45.

Dozier, M., Stovall, K. C., Albus, K. E., and Bates, B. (2001). "Attachment for Infants in Foster Care: The Role of Caregiver State of Mind." *Child Development* 70: 1467–77.

Elliott, R., Greenberg, L., and Lietaer, G. (2004). "Research on Experiential Psychotherapies." Pp. 493–539 in *Bergin and Garfield's Handbook of Psychotherapy and Behavior Change*, ed. M. Lambert. New York: Wiley.

Fonagy, P., Gergely, G., Jurist, E., and Target, M. (2002). *Affect Regulation, Mentalization, and the Development of the Self.* New York: Other Press.

Holmes, J. (1993). *John Bowlby & Attachment Theory.* New York: Routledge.

Holmes, J. (2001). *The Search for the Secure Base: Attachment and Psychotherapy.* New York: Routledge.

Hudson, J. Personal communication, April 16, 2010.

Hughes, D. (2004). "An Attachment-Based Treatment of Maltreated Children and Young People." *Attachment and Human Development* 6: 263–78.

Hughes, D. (2007). *Attachment-Focused Family Therapy.* New York: W. W. Norton.

Hughes, D. (In press). *Attachment-Focused Family Therapy: The Workbook.* New York: Norton.

Hughes, D., and Becker-Weidman, A. (2010). *Introduction to Dyadic Developmental Psychotherapy.* Three-DVD set. Brookfield, VT: Resourceful Recordings.

Lambert, M., and Ogles, B. (2004). "The Efficacy and Effectiveness of Psychotherapy." Pp. 139–94 in *Bergin and Garfield's Handbook of Psychotherapy and Behavior Change*, ed. M. Lambert. New York: Wiley.

Norcross, J. C. (2001). "Purposes, Processes and Products of the Task Force on Empirically Supported Therapy Relationships." *Psychotherapy* 38: 345–56.

Orlinsky, D., Ronnestad, M., and Willutzki, U. (2004). "Fifty Years of Psychotherapy Process-Outcome Research: Continuity and Change." Pp. 307–89 in *Bergin and Garfield's Handbook of Psychotherapy and Behavior Change*, ed. M. Lambert. New York: Wiley.

Psychology Wiki. (2010a). "Mirror Neuron." http://psychology.wikia.com/wiki/Mirror (accessed June 6, 2010).

Psychology Wiki. (2010b). "Attachment Story Completion Test." http://psychology.wikia.com/wiki/Attachment_story_completion_test accessed (accessed August 26, 2010).

Saunders, B., Berliner, L., and Hanson, R. (2004). *Child Physical and Sexual Abuse: Guidelines for Treatment.* http://academicdepartments.musc.edu/ncvc/resources_prof/OVC_guidelines04-26-04.pdf (accessed April 17, 2010).

Schore, A. N. (2009). "Right-Brain Affect Regulation: An Essential Mechanism of Development, Trauma, Dissociation, and Psychotherapy." Pp. 114–15 in *The Healing Power of Emotion: Affective Neuroscience, Development & Clinical Practice*, ed. D. Fosha, M. Siegel, and N. Solomon. New York: W. W. Norton.

Spottswood, R. (2005). *The Bean Seed.* Hartland, VT: Adoption Conversations.

Stern, D. (1985). *The Interpersonal World of the Infant.* New York: Basic Books.

Stone-Zander, R., and Zander B. (2000). *The Art of Possibility.* Boston: Harvard Business School Press.

Sunderland, M. (2003). *Teenie Weenie in a Too Big World.* Bicester, UK: Speechmark Publishing Ltd.

Trevarthen, C. (2001). "Intrinsic Motives for Companionship in Understanding: Their Origin, Development, and Significance for Infant Mental Health." *Infant Mental Health Journal*, 22: 95–131.

Tronick, E. Z. (1989). "Emotions and Emotional Communication in Infants." *American Psychologist*, 44 (2): 112–19.

Tronick, E. Z. (2005). "Why Is Connection with Others So Critical? The Formation of Dyadic States of Consciousness: Coherence Governed Selection and the Co-Creation of Meaning Out of Messy Meaning Making." Pp. 293–315 in *Emotional Development*, ed. J. Nadel and D. Muir. Oxford: Oxford University Press.

Tyrell, C., Dozier, M., Teague, G. B., and Fallot, R. (1999). "Effective Treatment Relationships for Persons with Serious Psychiatric Disorders: The Importance of Attachment States of Mind." *Journal of Consulting and Clinical Psychology* 67: 725–33.

Zander, R. S., and Zander, B. (2002). *The Art of Possibility.* New York: Penguin Press.

Index

abandonment, 148

abuse: emotional, 54, 55, 113; memories of, 190–91; physical, 184, 205; sexual, 83–84; substance, 65, 113; triggers around, 212

acceptance, 117; by caregiver, 148–49, 191; of child, 130, 133, 135, 136, 143, 161, 196–97; definition of, 16; of emotions, 93, 214; follow-lead-follow with, 92–93; in PACE, 118, 149, 172, 177; by therapist, 92, 130

accident-prone, 114

Ackenbach, 2, 185

activities, 80

ADHD. *See* attention deficit hyperactivity disorder

adoption, 32, 84; age at, 99; emotions about, 100; narrative of, 93, 95–96, 98, 103–4, 207; preparation for, 128; subsidy for, 65; talking about, 107, 108, 109, 110; visitations after, 124

Adult Attachment Interview, 186

affect: ability for, 144; arousal, 15; containing, 149, 163; co-regulation of, 86–87, 93, 130, 134, 148, 173, 174, 176, 177, 200, 211, 212, 220, *225*; deepening of, 200; heightened, 89; matching, 49, 134; in memory,

143; re-attunement, 92; reflective function, 141; regulation of, 11, 68, 81, 130, 136, 142; responding to, 191; "talking about," to reduce, 47, 72, 86; trigger for, 212

affective/reflective dialogue, 19–20, *225*; affective element of, 175, 178; alternation of, 129; deepening of, 147; for emotions, 137; expansion of, 143; integration from, 141; for intersubjectivity, 202; management of, 105, 119; for new meaning, 75; reflective function in, 106, 115, 142, 162–63, 173, 175, 179, 187, 191, 197, 213

affirmation, 16, 88

age: at adoption, 99; chronological, 11; expectations by, 128

aggression, 41, 212; property destruction, 84; sorrow as counterbalance for, 117. *See also* violence

agitation, 220

alcoholism, 113

alliance: building, 7, 44, 74, 81, 91, 92, 93, *225*; with caregiver, 171; conflict about, 90; with family, 90, 141; follow-lead-follow for, 22, 47, 67; as healing, 28; indication of, 157;

About the Contributors

Arthur Becker-Weidman (PhD) has achieved diplomate status in child psychology and forensic psychology from the American Board of Psychological Specialties. He is a registered clinician with the Association for the Treatment and Training in the Attachment of Children and is a certified therapist, consultant, and trainer in Dyadic Developmental Psychotherapy®©.

Dr. Becker-Weidman has been treating the families of adoptive and foster children for over three decades. As director of the Center for Family Development he consults with governments, departments of social services, residential treatment centers, mental health clinics, and professionals throughout the United States, Canada, Singapore, Finland, Australia, the Czech Republic, and Slovakia. Dr. Becker-Weidman's work has focused on the evaluation and treatment of adopted and foster children and their families, complex post-traumatic stress disorder, and alcohol-related neurological dysfunction.

Dr. Becker-Weidman is on the Board of Directors of the Association for the Treatment and Training in the Attachment of Children, serves as a vice-president for clinical issues, serves on the Research Committee and Training Committee, and chairs the Registration Committee. He is an adjunct clinical professor at the State University of New York at Buffalo. Dr. Becker-Weidman is president of the board of the Dyadic Developmental Psychotherapy Institute.

Dr. Becker-Weidman has published over a dozen papers in peer-reviewed professional journals. He is the coeditor of the book *Creating Capacity for Attachment* (2005, second printing 2008). He is coeditor of the book *Attachment Parenting* (2010). He is the author of *Dyadic Developmental Psychotherapy: Essential Practices and Methods* (2010), which is a treatment manual for the practice of Dyadic Developmental Psychotherapy. Dr. Becker-Weidman has several DVDs for parents and professionals, including *Principles of Attachment Parenting* (three-DVD set, 2006), *Assessing Children with Complex Trauma and Disorders of Attachment* (two-DVD set, 2007), *Assessing Caregiver Reflective Capacity, Commitment, Insightfulness, and Sensitivity* (two-DVD set, 2010), and *Introduction to Dyadic Developmental Psychotherapy* (four-DVD set, 2010). He is available to provide training and consultation to professionals and agencies.

Geraldine Casswell (B.Sc. Hons., M.Sc. ClinPsy., M. Psychotherapy) is head of clinical psychology in the NHS Child and Adolescent Mental Health Service in York, North Yorkshire, United Kingdom.

Craig W. Clark (MFT) is associate professor in the College of Professional Studies, Masters in Marriage and Family Counseling Program at John F. Kennedy University, in California, and maintains a private practice. He is a contributor to *Creating Capacity for Attachment* (2005/2008).

Kim S. Golding (B.Sc., M.Sc., D.ClinPsy) is a clinical psychologist in the United Kingdom. She is the author of *Nurturing Attachments*.

Mary-Jo Land (CPT) is a certified child psychotherapist and play therapist and a registered Dyadic Developmental Psychotherapist in private practice in southern Ontario, Canada. She is the president of the Association for Treatment and Training in the Attachment of Children and coauthor of *A Journey of Peace*, a psycho-social peace education program for children in Afghanistan.

Sian Phillips (PhD, C.Psych.) is a clinical psychologist in private practice and adjunct professor at Queens University, Kingston Ontario, Canada.

Karen Sik (MClinPsy) is senior psychologist of the Psychology Unit of the Ministry of Community Development, Youth, and Sports in Singapore. She supervises and trains other psychologists in evaluation and treatment.

Pirjo Tuovila (M.Soc.Sc., Lic.A.(Psych)) is a clinical psychologist in private practice in Tempere, Finland. She also provides consultation and training for therapists.

Breinigsville, PA USA
03 March 2011
256818BV00003B/32/P